THE WAGES OF SIN

Jean Turvey
THE WAGES OF SIN
A New Zealand prostitute's story

RANDOM
HOUSE
NEW ZEALAND LTD

For obvious reasons, some of the names of
people and places have been changed.

A RANDOM HOUSE BOOK

Published by
Random House New Zealand
18 Poland Road, Glenfield, Auckland, New Zealand

First published 1999

ISBN: 1 86941 368 7

Cover photograph: J.P Fruchet/Imagesource
Printed in Malaysia

CHAPTER 1

It all began with a phone call from my daughter, one afternoon in early December 1982. At that time I was working in a hairdressing salon in downtown Auckland. The management didn't encourage personal calls, but this one seemed to be urgent, so they let me take it. I made my apologies to the lady whose hair I was blow-waving and hurried to the phone.

'Mum, some men came to repossess the furniture,' said Emma casually. 'They said you had a letter from the collection agency.'

I suddenly felt sick. I hadn't read any letters from a collection agency, because all envelopes that looked remotely like accounts I fired straight into the rubbish bin, and had done for weeks. 'Did they take everything?' I asked, trying not to sound as panic-stricken as I felt.

'They didn't take anything because I wouldn't let them in,' she replied.

'What do you mean you wouldn't let them in? Those guys usually mean business.' I'd heard stories of them beating down people's doors to repossess their belongings.

'I said they were scaring me and I was going to call the police, and they went away. What's for dinner?'

I remember mumbling something about bubble and squeak — a cheap meal of fried potato mixed with cabbage — and making the excuse of not being allowed personal calls at work. Then I hung up and burst into tears. My boss was standing close to me, and got the gist of what was said. She was very sympathetic. 'Oh Angie! Is there anything I can do to help? You're due a pay rise of just over ten dollars a week. That should make life a bit easier, shouldn't it?' she beamed at me.

If I hadn't been so upset I would have laughed. My net pay was a hundred and ninety-five dollars a week; my out-goings were

5

three hundred and fifty a week. Ten dollars was but a drop in the bucket. I thanked her very much and went back to my blow-wave. Luckily my client wasn't a talker and preferred to sit quietly and relax. Had she wanted to chit chat, she would have had a howling mess on her hands. The lump in my throat was at bursting point. How did I get into this mess? I asked myself a hundred times, and how was I going to get out of it without losing everything I had?

On the way home, I stopped at our local fruit shop to buy half a cabbage for our dinner. Pay-day was two days away, and all I had was seventy-five cents to my name.

Only two months earlier I hadn't had a care in the world. I was living in my apartment, surrounded with beautiful furniture, and driving a new car. I really didn't need to work, but I enjoyed my job and workmates, and went along for the company. I had bought the apartment with a deposit from my half of the matrimonial property after a nasty divorce. It was far beyond my means, but with the help of a very generous, elderly 'gentleman friend', who lived in and paid the mortgage and anything else I set my heart on, life was a breeze.

Frank had answered an advertisement I'd put in the *New Zealand Herald* for a boarder, as I knew I would have a hard time coping with the mortgage repayments, and making the spare room pay for itself seemed an ideal way of solving the problem. He was a lovely Australian man in his late sixties, a widower of fifteen years and a director of a finance company in Auckland. He told me that he would rather board than take an apartment because he hated being alone and also couldn't cook for the life of him. A month or so after Frank moved in, I happened to mention that I had seen a nice microwave oven in the appliance department of Farmer's. When I came home from work, there on the kitchen bench was the very microwave I'd mentioned earlier, and Frank looking extremely pleased with himself.

'A gift,' he said. And that was the beginning of a stream of very generous gifts and sums of money he would not let me say no to. Then he offered to pay the mortgage. Once again I told him no, but he said 'Angels, until I moved in here, I was a lonely old man. Sure, I've got money to burn, but money can't buy what you and

Emma bring into my life. Please let me help you with the mortgage, I know damned well it's a struggle for you, and the money? Well, what's money after all?' So I agreed to let him pay the mortgage.

Then my old Vauxhall Viva failed its WOF and I was in for huge panelbeating expenses to get it back on the road. In a blink of an eye a new Honda Civic had arrived. 'For you,' he said, grinning from ear to ear. It was all a bit of an embarrassment at first, but as life became extremely comfortable, I started to take Frank for granted. The fact that he didn't ask for anything in return made it a lot easier, only three meals a day and our company. On two or three occasions I accompanied him to different functions organised by his firm. He never once asked me for sex.

But it was all short-lived. Frank's company in Australia had a major collapse, and he was obliged to return to his home in Sydney. He asked us to go with him, but we chose not to as Emma was doing well at college and I didn't want anything to disrupt that. Also I had no fondness for him and he'd actually begun to get on my nerves. I thought I could manage without him, and looked forward to his departure.

A week later I realised just how much he had had on hire purchase, and that I couldn't afford to keep up the lifestyle I had become accustomed to.

I arrived home to find my daughter in high spirits. She was prattling on about end-of-term exam results, and could she have some money for summer camp in February — it had to be in by the end of the week — and were we going to Nana's for Christmas? I was trying to explain to her about the lack of funds, when the phone rang and Emma rushed off to answer it. I hoped like anything it was one of her girlfriends and that they would talk for hours to give me time to think. 'It's for you, Mum,' she said, then whispered, 'a man!'

It was my lawyer. 'You are two months behind with the interest repayments for your mortgage, Mrs Blake. May we expect a cheque in the mail?'

'No,' I replied bluntly. 'Sorry, but I haven't got the money and I can't see me ever having it.' I was on the verge of crying again and unable to elaborate any further.

There was a brief silence. 'I would suggest you sell the property posthaste, Mrs Blake. Perhaps buy in a little less expensive area. Papatoetoe, say,' he said, in one of those voices that come straight from the ice-box. 'Meanwhile, phone my secretary first thing in the morning for an appointment, and we can come to some arrangement with the interest arrears.'

Papatoetoe? That will be the day, I thought. 'Yes, if you think it's for the best, Mr Clarke, I'll list the property tomorrow morning. Good-bye,' I said, and hung up.

Later that evening, while I was preparing dinner, something happened that would change my life forever. I reached into the plastic bag that contained the half cabbage I'd bought earlier, to find it neatly wrapped in the front few pages of the *New Zealand Truth*. Now, I was brought up in a household that held this publication in contempt. It was not allowed in our house. Time after time my mother used to say, 'This family does not have to stoop to reading gutter press!' Her opinion was that the *Truth* was only suitable reading for peasants and people of low breeding. So it was with trembling fingers that I unwrapped the unfortunate vegetable from the clutches of that disgusting tabloid, at the same time trying to avert my eyes in case they should spy a word lurking in the sordid columns that was only fit for a sailor to utter. And yes, just as mother had warned, the word SEX was written in huge black letters across the front page. I quickly looked to see if Emma was around, but I could hear her rummaging about in her bedroom. My eyes darted back to the *Truth*.

'SEX FOR SALE ON THE STREETS OF AUCKLAND', read the headline. I was hooked. All thoughts of my financial problems were temporarily forgotten. I could not help myself, I just had to read on. The article was about the massage parlour and sex industry in Auckland. It told of their popularity and, to my surprise, it said that they were open in the daytime. I had always imagined dirty old men in raincoats frequenting such places in the dead of night. But it seemed your average man in the street was popping in and out from seven in the morning onwards.

One paragraph I found really interesting. The prostitute who was being interviewed revealed that she earned on average a thousand dollars for a four-day week. I read the passage several times to make sure I'd got it right, then highlighted it with a fluorescent pink felt-tip. The article went on to say that not all massage parlours offered sex, or 'extras' as it was known, though most did and straight parlours were few and far between. The woman seemed to be extremely happy in her work and in the environment she worked in. She seemed not to have any fears of being beaten up by the men she entertained, or of contracting any sexually trans-mitted diseases. Indeed, she took more precautions than your average single woman indulging in regular one-night stands. The article gave me a tremendous feeling that all was not lost.

After Emma had gone to bed, I pondered my predicament. I liked my apartment in Remuera, Auckland's most prestigious suburb. I certainly didn't want to live in Papatoetoe. Yes, I should have been aware of what my gentleman friend was up to financially, but at the time it hadn't seemed to matter. And there was no way my ex-husband would or could help out; he was on the bones of his bum himself.

I read the *Truth* article again. A thousand dollars a week would have me back on my feet in no time. Then and there I decided to give the sex industry a go. Only if I couldn't handle it would I consider Papatoetoe.

In 1982, Karangahape Road was the red-light district of Auckland. Before work the next day, I took a walk up this notorious road to check out the places of ill-repute.

At eight o'clock in the morning it didn't look any different from any other street in Auckland, except that the buildings and shops were old and shabby; the footpaths were bustling with ordinary people on their way to work. In those days there were only about twenty parlours in the whole of Auckland, half of which were in Karangahape Road, so my choice was pretty limited. The parlours offered nude massages, some offering two-girl sessions, and charges were between twenty-five and thirty-five dollars an hour.

I eventually settled on an establishment called The House of Eve, because it didn't look as sleazy as the others. I stood outside and looked up a long staircase that disappeared into a fog of red light. The doorway was festooned with photographs of scantily clad ladies.

Back at work, I tried to phone The House of Eve in my lunch break, but just as someone answered a customer arrived at the desk and I had to hang up. I thought it best to wait until later that evening after Emma had gone to bed.

It was not very busy at the salon, and the day dragged on and on. At three-thirty I started to worry about Emma and what would happen if the repossession men returned. To keep them off my back, I decided to ask my dad for a loan until I was earning some real money. But I didn't want my family to know about my financial predicament. Mum would worry herself sick, and Dad would lecture me from here to kingdom come.

I phoned Dad as soon as Emma went to bed, and he said yes, he would be happy to lend me some money to get my car fixed and how much did I want? At ten-thirty I dialled the number of The House of Eve. The phone rang and rang. It was eventually answered by a lazy-voiced girl. 'The House of Eve, can I help you?'

'Oh yes,' I stammered nervously. After all, it isn't every day one phones a massage parlour for a job. 'Do you have any staff vacancies?'

'Have you worked before?' she asked.

'Hmm, no,' I replied, then hastily added, 'but I'm a quick learner.' I couldn't believe what I was saying. What was there to learn? Surely it was only a matter of lying there looking sexy and gorgeous.

'You'll have to see Tony. He's the boss,' she said.

'Okay, can I make an appointment to see Tony at, say, twelve-fifteen tomorrow?' I asked.

'No, he's never here in the daytime. He's here at the moment, though. Come in now. He'll be here until about midnight.'

I was aghast. She was asking me to walk up Karangahape Road at this time of night. It would be crawling with prostitutes and drunk men. What did she think I was? 'Look, how about tomorrow at six o'clock,' I pleaded.

'Okay, I'll tell Tony you will be here at six. See you then. Bye,' she said a bit too quickly, and hung up in my ear.

I spent most of the next day in a dream. Was I doing the right thing, I asked myself, and would I be able to handle being mauled by a lot of strange men? But then I thought, I have a child to feed and educate, and I don't have the means to do it — not even the means to feed her. I was about to lose our home and furniture, and was absolutely desperate. Then something I'll never be able to explain took over. An inner strength grew within me that blotted out any fears I had, replacing them with a feeling of immense determination not to fail. If it was going to take a life of prostitution to win through, I would do it and that was final!

The next question, of course, was should I tell Emma? Well, that took care of itself. I arrived home from work to find her sitting at the dining room table reading the article in the *Truth*. 'What's this, Mum?' she asked without taking her eyes away from the paper. 'Why have you highlighted these bits?' She was running her fingers along the line.

'Have you read it?' I asked, trying to sound matter of fact.

'Yes. It's about prostitutes and stuff. They make a lot of money, don't they? Hey! You should give it a go,' she added, killing herself with laughter.

'Emma, sit down. I've got something to talk to you about.'

Her laughter stopped abruptly. 'We're in the pooh, aren't we Mum?'

'Yes, Emm, we are. If I don't do something soon, those men will be back to take the furniture, and we'll lose the apartment and the car. My present wages just can't cope with the debts.' I picked up the *Truth* and waved it in front of her. 'This could be the answer. What do you think?'

Emma didn't hesitate. 'Give it a go, Mum. If you don't like it, and we do lose everything, we can always go back to the Waikato and live with Nana and Grandad.'

I clearly remember wondering if I would have been so under-standing at fourteen years old. I feel not. She accepted the situation without hesitation, which astounded me. But maybe time would tell, I thought, and promised myself that if she had even the smallest problem with my new profession, I would quit immediately.

The next thing was to decide what to wear to the interview with Tony. Something seductive and sexy, I thought, and settled on a pair of black satin spandex pants, high stilettos with diamante-studded heels I'd bought in a weak moment, and a skin-tight, low-cut top. I teased my hair into the fly-away Farrah Fawcett hairstyle that was all the rage in the late seventies and early eighties, applied my make-up with reckless abandon, and looked in the full-length mirror. A real tart looked back at me. 'Perfect,' I whispered under my breath.

Emma looked me up and down once or twice. 'You look like Golden Dream Barbie,' she said.

I drove to Karangahape Road to find it was late-night shopping. Parking was impossible and the only space available was more than half a kilometre from The House of Eve; so I was obliged to walk, looking like a tart, all the way there. People stared rudely at me, some making filthy comments just loud enough for me to hear. One man stopped and asked how much I charged, then laughed loudly when I brushed passed him. 'Is she a prostitute, Mum?' said a little girl to her mother, and two teenagers sniggered into their hands while passing me.

Arriving at the entrance, I hesitated a second, then started up the stairs. The carpet was red and well worn, threadbare in some places; red and gold flocked wallpaper lined the walls. As I approached the top, loud rock music hit my ears. I eventually came to a black door with a striped two-way mirror alongside. The window slid back and a blonde woman of about twenty-four smiled at me from the other side.

'Hi. Can I help you?' she asked sleepily.

I don't know why, but I spoke in a whisper. 'My name is Angela Blake, I have an appointment with Tony at six o'clock.'

'What was that?' she said, cupping her right ear with her hand. I repeated myself, and she said, 'Sorry, he's not here.'

'But I have an appointment,' I said indignantly. 'I made it only last night.'

She slid her tongue across her front teeth, as if wiping away some imaginary lipstick. 'Sorry. He'll be in later. Come in around ten-thirty, he should be here then.' She smiled at me through the smoky red haze. Behind her stood a girl who looked no older then fifteen, wearing a short black halter-neck dress. A large, dark tattoo adorned her shoulder and disappeared down the low neckline. She puffed at a cigarette with nicotine-stained fingers, and appeared to be drunk.

This is definitely not for me, I thought, so I thanked the receptionist and left. Someone wolf-whistled as I stepped into the street. Stumbling back to the car, my eyes stinging with tears and too much mascara, I promised myself never to go through that again.

On the way home the petrol light on the dash board started to flicker on and off. I pulled into a dairy and bought another *Truth* with some five-cent pieces dragged up from under the front seat. Surely not all establishments were like The House of Eve, I thought to myself. And, still sitting in my car, I turned to the adult entertainment pages.

A large advertisement immediately caught my eye: 'The Harem, clean modern facilities, luxurious decor and elegant sophisticated ladies.' That sounded just what I was looking for. I started the car and drove towards home.

CHAPTER 2

As soon as I reached home, I telephoned to see if they had any staff vacancies. The receptionist was well spoken and very helpful. 'At the moment we are fully staffed, but after Christmas we will be needing a lady. Have you worked before?' she said.

'No I haven't. Does it matter?' I asked.

'Oh no, experience isn't necessary,' she replied. 'We will train you. How old are you, Angela?'

This was a tricky one. I was under the impression that men preferred young women, and I was two months off forty, but was lucky enough not to look it. 'Thirty-five,' I lied, then hastily added, 'but I look years younger.'

'That's okay,' she said. 'Mature ladies are very much in demand — most parlours have one or two working. Now, when would it be convenient for you to come in for an interview?'

'I have a full time job at the moment, so how about twelve-fifteen tomorrow lunch time,' I said.

'Yes, twelve-fifteen will be fine. See you then.'

Emma was interested to know what had happened at The House of Eve. I didn't go into too many details. 'This other place sounds a lot nicer,' I said.

For the interview, I tied my hair back and wore a burgundy suit with a pink blouse, and grey shoes and handbag. I was not going to make the same mistake as last time. I didn't feel as nervous as I had done before going to The House of Eve. I looked good and I felt good.

It took only a few minutes to walk to The Harem from the salon. The building looked old and a bit dilapidated from the outside, but once through the big double doors at the bottom, it changed to a warm and businesslike interior. The stair carpet was brown and pretty new by the look of it, though perhaps a little grubby with the many feet that must have trodden its thick pile. The walls were of a beige toning, but clean and crisp looking. I walked up two flights, then came to a sign that simply said 'The Harem'. Not a flashing light or picture of a near-naked woman to be seen. I walked in through the large door and looked around.

Presently, a woman of about twenty-eight appeared from a room to the left of the entrance. 'Hi,' she said, 'you must be Angela. My name is Trish. I'm the person you spoke to on the phone yesterday. Come into the office and we'll have a chat, then I'll show you around.' She made a cup of coffee for us both, and I explained why I needed the work.

'That's why most of us start,' she said, 'and believe me, it won't take long before you're back on your feet.' That was exactly what I wanted to hear.

Trish told me that The Harem had only been in business for a couple of months. 'The last people to have these premises ran a "gentleman's club". They had gambling evenings and a few ladies working the rooms. Of course, it wasn't long before they got busted by the vice squad and closed down. Then Mel took over. We don't pay a wage like other parlours, but we do pay a small percentage of each massage you do; so the more massages you do, the more money you get from us. Mel thinks it fairer than the request system.'

'What's a request system?' I asked.

'Some of the parlour bosses count up how many times a girl is requested by clients, and at the end of the month, the ones with the least requests are fired automatically, and new ones are hired. They think it keeps everyone on their toes, but in fact it only creates a lot of bad feeling among the staff and encourages dirty hustling.' She could see by my face that I didn't know what she was talking about. 'You know, muscling in on other girls' clients.'

I didn't know, but I nodded and said, 'Oh! Right.'

'Mandy, our top lady, will teach you how to massage on the night you start. Any tips you receive in the room are yours. You do not discuss it with anyone outside the working rooms in this establishment, is that understood?'

I didn't understand, but if that was the rule, I'd go along with it. 'Yes, I understand,' I said.

'Management supplies tea, coffee, milk, sugar, oil, powder and tissues. You will only need to bring your joes.'

'Joes?' I looked at her blankly.

'You know, protection.' She pulled a face at me and motioned with her fingers. 'Protection,' she repeated.

The penny dropped. 'Oh! you mean condoms,' I said, a bit louder than I meant to.

'SHHH!' She rushed over, closed the office door and whispered, 'You must not refer to anything relating to "extras" outside the working rooms. You must understand that. You don't know who's listening.' She wrote something on a piece of paper and handed it to me. 'Put this in your handbag and read it later.'

I couldn't help thinking how peculiar it all was. Strange rules that didn't make much sense, and words one wasn't allowed to utter in certain parts of the premises. Trish was proving to be a bit neurotic. I stuffed the note into my jacket pocket and finished my coffee.

In the blink of an eye, Trish's frown disappeared. She smiled at me and said, 'Come on, I'll show you around the place.'

The Harem was certainly luxurious; the décor was the latest in fashionable colours and there was long shagpile carpet throughout. The lounge was large and expensively furnished with huge leather couches and glass coffee tables, and at the far end stood a long bar complete with tall bar stools. Behind it a door led into an ultra modern kitchen with dishwasher, waste-disposal and every other gadget you could think of.

From there we went back across the lounge and into a sauna, where, through the steam, I could see a couple of men relaxing on the wooden slatted forms. An enormous spa-pool bubbled away in another room. Next to it was a small, dimly lit lounge for watching videos. Another large room contained two snooker tables. A girl in her early twenties was vacuuming the floor. Then there were two what they called de luxe rooms with ensuites tiled in black marble. A proper massage table sat in the middle of each room. These tables looked out of place somehow. Along a small corridor were two 'cushion rooms'. These were much smaller than the de luxe rooms and were decorated with wall hangings. Each cushion room had a mattress on the floor, which was festooned with many colourful cushions and Persian-style blankets. These rooms had a definite Middle Eastern look about them.

Across the corridor were two showers. 'The girls are responsible for the cleaning. It's usually done after the night shift is finished, but if it's a really late night, the day girls have to do it,' said Trish.

We went back to the office and Trish pulled out a large sheet of paper from a manila folder. It was divided into columns and headed with the days of the week. 'Do you want to start on days or nights?' she said.

I thought for a minute. Days would be more convenient, but I figured the men visiting at night would be more likely to be tipsy and would not notice if I didn't get things right to start with. 'Umm . . . nights please,' I said.

'Right, you can start on the twenty-ninth of December. The night shifts are from seven o'clock in the evening to about two in the morning. If it's busy we work to three or four. Okay?'

I nodded, and we walked to the door. 'We'll see you on the twenty-ninth then,' said Trish. 'Good-bye.'

I walked out into the bright sunshine, practically danced back to work and gave notice to quit at Christmas. My boss was genuinely sorry to lose me and asked what I was going to do. 'We're going back to the Waikato,' I lied, for the second time in two days.

Later that evening, while on my own, I read the note Trish had scribbled on the piece of paper. She had written 'Durex', followed by a word so hurriedly written it was unreadable. Everyone knows what Durex are, so the second word didn't seem important. As long as I had some condoms to take with me, and they were Durex, I'd be okay, I thought.

In my lunch hour the next day I started my quest to buy some 'joes'. I have to confess that at the age of thirty-nine I had only ever seen one condom, and that was floating down the Waikato River one Sunday afternoon. Well, girls didn't have to look at them when I was young. You left that sort of thing to the guys. I guess that's why so many girls got pregnant in those days. Any sexual activity usually took place in the dark, so the only contact one had with a condom was the sound of the packet being opened, the few seconds it took for a pair of fumbling hands to put it on, and the slamming of the car door after the thing had been discarded. The thought of actually purchasing a packet of condoms was a bit scary.

Of course, all this took place prior to the AIDS epidemic. So to save children and gentle folk from themselves, condoms, vaginal lubricants and the like were all kept under the counter in chemist and barber shops. One had to personally front up and ask for them, which was a bit of an ordeal even for a man; and, of course, women didn't do that kind of thing, not decent ones.

In one hour I ended up with a whole heap of useless junk and make-up I'd never wear from a lot of different pharmacies. I had been on a kind of pharmacy crawl, trudging from one to another, and hadn't met one assistant I could comfortably ask, 'I'd like a packet of Durex condoms please.'

I went back to work a nervous wreck. Then I had a brainwave. The pharmacy in the Downtown Shopping Centre was self-service, like a supermarket. Surely they would have condoms on display.

The following lunch time I boldly walked into the Downtown Pharmacy and made my way up and down the aisles, checking each product carefully. The second time around I realised that condoms were not on display. The dispensing counter was at the back of the shop and was perched on a sort of platform, so shorter customers had to stand on tiptoes to speak to the chemist. He looked about fifty, with a kind, grandfatherly face. Well, it was now or never. I fronted up to the counter, and standing on tiptoes whispered, 'Twelve Durex condoms please.'

He bent forward and, looking down at me, whispered back, 'Pardon?'

I cleared my throat and said, 'Twelve Durex condoms please.'

He nodded, then yelled to the young lass on the check-out at the other end of the shop, 'Twelve Durex for this lady, Shirl.'

I nearly died of embarrassment as the whole shop came to a standstill. There was a sharp intake of breath from an elderly lady clutching a box of corn pads, and every eye in the place watched as I tried to walk nonchalantly down the centre aisle to Shirl, who was standing behind her check-out waving the packet of condoms in the air to catch my attention, and for all the world to see.

'Gossamer okay?' she asked.

I nodded, not knowing what she was talking about and wishing she would put the damn things in a paper bag or something. Back at home, in the privacy of my bedroom, I opened up one of the tiny foil packets to inspect the offending purchase in detail. Not a lot to them, I thought, just a long tube of rubber with a kind of bubble on the end. What a lot of fuss about nothing. How could a small, insignificant piece of rubber cause so much embarrassment?

The next most important thing to do was to keep Mr Clarke and all the other creditors off my back. I popped into the nearest real estate office to home and, so no one would buy it, I listed my apartment for a hundred thousand dollars — fifteen thousand dollars more than it was worth. It would keep Mr Clarke happy and, I hoped, give me time to prove that I could manage the repayments.

It sounded simple, but when the agent came to look the place over he said politely, 'Mrs Blake, this is indeed a very attractive and well-positioned apartment, but I don't think you will get a hundred thousand for it. You have to be realistic, you might get eighty-five, but a hundred thousand? It wouldn't be worth our while listing it at that price. How about you think about it, and get back to me if you change your mind.'

I promised to do that and set out to track down the agent who originally sold me the property. I'd found him to be extremely helpful with the mortgage finance by introducing me to Mr Clarke. It was not easy for a single woman to raise a mortgage in those days, and it came down to the old 'it's not what you know, but who you know' rule. Because Bill, the real estate agent, knew Mr Clarke, I got the finance required, but at a phenomenal rate of twenty-five percent interest.

I eventually found Bill working in a real estate office in Epsom. I explained my predicament, but left out the massage parlour bits.

'That's not a problem,' he said. 'You tell old "Clarkie" you've listed the property with me, and I'll back your story up. But if you find you can't manage, give me a call and I'm sure we'll get the best price for you. The property market is starting to boom, so you could come out of it quite nicely.'

I thanked Bill, then phoned Clarkie's receptionist and made an appointment to see him at nine o'clock on Monday morning to make arrangements for the interest arrears.

Next on the list was Smith, Brown and Maple about the furniture. I telephoned them, and the accounts lady was wonderful. As long as I made some sort of regular payments, I could take over the hire purchase arrangements of my elderly gentleman friend, and they would call off the repossession agents. I took a cheque into the shop straight after work and left feeling very relieved. It was a similar story with the other creditors; as long as I made an effort to arrange some kind of regular payments, they were all willing to hang back with any action they'd previously threatened. The money Dad had lent me to 'fix the car' soon dwindled away, and the only thing left to worry about was Christmas presents.

Emma solved that one. 'Tell everyone you're saving. You know what Nana and Grandad are like, they're always telling us to save our money. They'd be chuffed to think you actually are. We could make our prezzies, you know, chocolates and stuff. I'll do it!'

At nine o'clock on Monday morning, I was ushered into Mr Clarke's office. 'Sit down, Mrs Blake,' he said in that ice-box voice. He shuffled through some papers, then looked over the top of his reading glasses at me. 'I see here that you are eighteen hundred dollars in arrears.'

'Yes, Mr Clarke,' I said, surprised that it wasn't more.

'Have you listed the property as instructed?'

'Yes, Mr. Clarke, with Bill Elliot, the agent who sold it to me.'

Clarkie's face squeezed itself into a thin smile. 'Good old Bill, eh! I'm having lunch with him on Friday, so I dare say he'll tell me about it.' His smile faded and he went on, 'Now, on the sale of the unit, all funds owing will be repaid to us, plus twenty-five percent interest on the arrears. The amount will depend on how quickly it sells. With whatever funds are over at the end of the day, we can organise for the deposit on a unit in a less affluent area for you.'

'Thank you, Mr Clarke,' I said.

We spent the next two weeks making Christmas presents in our spare time. The salon was very busy, and I did as much overtime as possible and also did the odd perm and colour at home, so Christmas wasn't as lean as I'd imagined it would be. Before I left the salon for the last time, the staff gave me a set of pretty black underwear, there was a twenty-five dollar bonus in my pay packet, and someone else had been employed to take my place. As I walked out the door a feeling of apprehension swept over me. It was too late to go back now; I'd burned all my bridges.

At home, Emma was waiting with all our bags packed, and after filling the car with petrol, we started on our way to the Waikato for Christmas. The traffic was thick with holiday-makers, and progress was slow. We sang carols as we drove along. Emma told me a joke which was a touch risqué, and we shrieked with laughter. I realised that I was enjoying myself and hadn't felt so happy for a long time.

CHAPTER 3

The twenty-ninth of December dawned very quickly. I didn't get much in the way of sleep the night before, and awoke that morning with the nervous, sick feeling one gets before visiting the dentist. Emma made me some toast for breakfast, but I couldn't eat a thing. Nine cups of black coffee sufficed that day. I tried to busy myself with the chores that needed doing around the apartment, but wasn't able to concentrate long enough to do any of them properly. The day dragged on interminably. My mind was going round and round with the same old questions. Was I doing the right thing? Do the means justify the end? Was I hurting rather than helping the situation? The answer was the same as ever, it was the only way to an acceptable lifestyle for us.

About three o'clock that afternoon the phone rang. It was Mandy from The Harem. 'Can you come in right away? Two girls haven't turned up for their shift, and we're really busy.' I told her I'd be there in as long as it took me to have a shower, put my face on and do my hair.

It took twice as long as it should have done to get ready. My nervousness completely took over. The Farrah Fawcett hairdo just wouldn't 'sweep up'. My mascara wand refused to do as it was told and stuck me in the eye. Then I couldn't find my shoes and I felt sick. Eventually I found them. I said good-bye to Emma, who gave me a comforting hug, and drove to The Harem massage parlour.

I climbed the two flights of stairs and stood outside the main door. I pulled my top down to show a little more cleavage, smoothed out some imaginary wrinkles in the spandex pants, took a deep breath and went in. There were three gentlemen sitting in the lounge.

Two were reading magazines, and one roly-poly, florid-faced elderly gentleman was sitting across the room with only a towel stretched across his large tummy.

Mandy smiled at me. 'Am I glad to see you. Wally's been waiting for ages.' She pointed to the roly-poly gentleman, who looked me up and down and grinned with approval.

Suddenly I was terrified. 'What do I do?' I asked with a quavering voice. 'You haven't trained me yet! I don't know the first thing about massaging.'

Mandy laughed. 'Look, Angie, guys do not come into places like this for a massage; they come in for some TLC and a good fuck. Now, get in there and give him one, okay? Hey! you'll be fine. It's always hard the first time . . . Oh, and he's had his shower.'

At that point I was on the verge of running out of the place. The only thing that stopped me was Wally.

Clutching the towel around his stomach, he said, 'So you are going to look after me today?' Taking my arm he led me into one of the de luxe rooms.

'Voila!' He beamed at me and dropped his towel to the floor. I hadn't seen a naked fat man before, so momentarily I forgot about the task that lay ahead and stared at his dangling little penis just visible below the bulbous stomach. His legs were skinny, and I remember thinking how much like a frog he looked. 'You're new to this, aren't you?' he said.

I nodded, and from then on Wally took over. He struggled onto the massage table. 'Now,' he said, 'take your clothes off and I'll show you how to massage. Come on, with a body like yours there's no need to be shy.'

Slowly I removed my clothes, while he looked on. My skin-tight top came over my head, taking with it what was left of my hairdo. I made a mental note to wear something easier to get out of in the future.

Wally lay on his large stomach, exposing a surprisingly small bottom. 'Right! Legs first. A couple of drops of oil on your hands.' He pointed to a bottle on the shelf behind the massage table. 'Now, slowly run your hands up and down my right leg, sensually, right up over the buttock . . . Ooh yes!' His bottom rose to meet my hands and he almost purred with ecstasy. Well, this bit was easy anyway, I thought. After I had massaged both legs for some time, he said, 'Okay, now do the same to my back, softly, sensually.'

After a few minutes of ooh-ing and aah-ing and wriggling about, Wally turned over onto his back exposing his erect penis, which was standing up vertically.

'Usually, at the end of the massage, the girls say something like, "Is there anything else I can do for you?"' he said, with a cheeky grin on his face.

'Is there anything else I can do for you?' I repeated, parrot fashion.

'Give me the works!' he replied.

'The works?'

'Oral and sex. Sixty dollars worth. Got your condoms?'

Condoms! In my bag. I scrabbled about in the bottom of my handbag until I found one. Ripping through the tinfoil, I pulled it out and peered at it intensely, trying to sort out which way was up.

Wally had eased himself up onto one elbow. 'You don't know much about these either, do you?' He took the condom from me. 'Now,' he pinched the bubble between the thumb and forefinger of his left hand and placed it on top of his penis, 'you roll it down . . . like so . . . See?'

I thought how clever he was to do that, because there was no way he could have seen what he was doing over his ample stomach. He must have read my mind. 'Many years of practice,' he said.

At this point, I must confess that I had never actually touched a penis, with my hand or anything else. Sure I'd had plenty of sex in my adult life, but I had never indulged in any seriously intimate foreplay. So giving oral was a new experience for me and I ran into a bit of a problem. Because I'm five feet two inches tall, and the massage table was waist high for someone five feet ten, my mouth wouldn't reach the man's penis; I couldn't even reach it with the tip of my tongue.

Meanwhile, Wally had relaxed back to enjoy it. Then I heard him sigh with frustration. 'No! No! You get on the table, between my legs, on your knees! Okay?' he said impatiently.

By this time I felt totally inadequate. I would get Wally over and done with, make my apologies and quit. This job was not for me.

I got up between his legs and put my mouth over his penis. Yuk! It was foul. A bitter, chemical-tasting substance was taking the skin off my palate. But I was not about to give up, and I sucked the putrid stuff off until my tongue stuck to the roof of my mouth. Then something told me it was time to do the sex.

It was very obvious to me that a massage table seventy-five centimetres wide by two hundred centimetres long does not lend itself to any imaginative sexual positions; even the good old missionary would have been extremely difficult. I looked at Wally, with his huge stomach and his little penis, and came to the conclusion that I should definitely be on top. I knelt astride him until the little penis disappeared into me. The width of the table didn't leave much room for my knees, and I knew I'd have to be quick. However, after bouncing up and down a couple of times I heard a kind of groan from Wally and it was all over, which was just as well, as I was about to fall off.

'Boy! I needed that,' he said as I hit the ground. He removed the condom with a tissue; 'I believe these go down the lav.' He handed it to me and got down off the table. 'It was a slow start, but I think you have the makings of a good working lady.' He pulled his wallet from his jacket and gave me sixty dollars in crisp new twenty-dollar bills. 'By the way, in future use Featherlite Durex. Gossamer are covered with a chemical called Monoxal. I've known girls to vomit on that stuff.'

While Wally was in the shower, I stuffed the money into my handbag and decided to stay and at least finish this shift before quitting. Then I had my shower and got dressed.

I said good-bye to Wally at the door, and went to meet the other girls at the bar. The first thing I noticed was they were not dressed like tarts, which immediately made me feel conspicuous in my shiny skin-tight outfit. They were all in smart little cocktail dresses that would have been acceptable anywhere. They wore their make-up subtly, elegantly, nothing like my heavy, slapped-on look. Mandy explained that girls only wore sexy, seductive clothing and make-up if a client requested it, and he was charged more for this.

We sat around the bar with a glass of wine each, for which the house charged us fifty cents a glass. There were only three of us working that afternoon and evening — Mandy, myself and a blonde girl called Sally. Mandy said we didn't have a receptionist that day, as Trish only worked occasionally. Apparently Trish had been a 'working lady', but had been 'busted' by the vice squad and therefore had a prostitution conviction. This meant that by law she was not allowed to work in a licensed massage parlour, not even as a receptionist. If she were caught by the police working on the premises, the owner would be prosecuted and lose his licence. A lot of ladies with convictions ended up working in either a 'rap parlour' or on the streets, which, according to Mandy, was a fate worse than death.

Sally rolled a cigarette, licked the paper and stuck it down. 'Fuck! Trish is still uptight about being busted by those cops. She really gives me the shits the way she acts sometimes!' she said.

'Uptight is an understatement,' said Mandy. 'The woman is a bundle of nerves. I don't know why she doesn't get a job in a rap parlour, at least she wouldn't be working with the fear of getting busted again, not if she sticks to receptionist work.'

'What's a rap parlour?' I asked.

Mandy lit a cigarette, offered the match to Sally, and looked thoughtful for a moment. 'A massage parlour is licensed to massage, and it can therefore advertise as much. Because it is licensed it becomes a public place, so the vice squad have entry by right and don't need a search warrant. The massage parlour bosses deny that any sexual activity takes place, and if anyone is caught indulging in sex, she is fired immediately; even the hint of a condom packet can get a girl fired in some establishments. But it adds a false sense of decency to the whole thing. Men generally prefer to visit a massage parlour because of this. Rap parlours are not allowed to do massaging. In short, they are just plain brothels; anyone going in is obviously after sex. And they do tend to be grotty places because, unlike massage parlours, they are not checked for cleanliness by the Health Department.'

'Trish was arrested by two Ds after telling a fucking undercover cop how much she charged!' said Sally, poking the tobacco into the end of her cigarette with the only long fingernail she had. 'He tricked her into it.'

*

The girls were very forthcoming with information about the job. They told me the vice squad were a worry. They checked all massage parlours regularly, sometimes even sending in undercover policemen. I was surprised to learn that prostitution was not illegal in New Zealand, but soliciting was. A girl had to be very careful when putting the subject of extras to a client. Asking if there was anything else she could do for him was a good approach, as it put it squarely on the shoulders of the client, leaving the girl innocent of any soliciting. The management of The Harem had installed a lighting system in all the rooms which was controlled by the receptionist. 'It's illegal to have warning lights,' said Mandy, 'but it's only a small fine if you're prosecuted for having them — a much better deal than being busted for soliciting.' If the squad arrived the receptionist could flick a switch and flash the lights on and off, warning the girls who were working at the time. If the lights flashed while you were working, you were to cover yourself and put a towel over the client's bum, and carry on massaging.

'But if we have no receptionist and everyone is working, what happens then?' I asked.

The girls looked at me with blank faces.

About two or three glasses of wine later, we had two men book in. One was a regular of Mandy's and the other was his friend, Ron.

'Grab your wine and come with me,' Mandy said. 'They want to watch a video before their massage. Ron has chosen you.'

The video room was tiny, with plush burgundy velvet couches that fitted around the walls giving it an oval appearance. The television and video machine were on a shelf that jutted out from the wall. I sat down next to Ron, feeling quite confident now, thanks to the Dutch courage. Mandy loaded the video and we all settled back to watch.

I knew full well we were not going to watch *The Sound of Music* or *The Ten Commandments*, but I was totally unprepared for what appeared on the screen. A beautiful blonde, wearing only a pearl necklace and a pair of high-heeled shoes, was on her hands and knees. A man with the biggest penis one could imagine was kneeling behind her and thrusting it into her vagina with considerable force and speed, while she groaned erotically. Then he withdrew and ejaculated over her bottom. I sat absolutely fascinated. I couldn't take my eyes off the screen. The set changed and an equally beautiful dark-haired woman was giving oral to a man with an equally long penis, and it disappeared right down her throat. I couldn't believe it. I took a sidelong glance at the others. The two men were watching avidly, while Mandy was puffing at her cigarette and picking at a thread on the hem of her skirt, not remotely interested in what was on the television.

Watching two human beings copulating was new to me, and it made me feel really loose. After his massage, Ron said he'd never had such a good time, and he gave me ten dollars over and above the sixty he owed me. But it took only a few days before I too got bored with porn videos, and would rather have watched *The Sound of Music.*

After Ron and his friend had gone, back to the bar we went for more wine. By this time I was feeling extremely happy. The job wasn't half as bad as I'd first thought. Money for old rope, I remember thinking to myself, while pouring yet another glass of wine. I giggled my way through the next massage. He was quite a young man, about twenty-three. He talked a lot about how he and his girlfriend had recently split up. I tried not to giggle, but it only made things worse. Anyway he seemed to enjoy the extras and left a happy man.

I went into the bar to find another man waiting for me. He was obviously drunk, and was all over me like a rash before we even got into the room. He refused to have a shower, and kept trying to play with my breasts while I was massaging his back. He wanted 'the works' but was unable to get an erection, and when he finally got that department under control, he couldn't ejaculate. We tried every position he knew and he ended up pounding away on top of me for what seemed like an age. His perspiration dripped into my hair and onto my face, but there was nothing I could do about it; I just had to lie there. Eventually he gave up, got off, got dressed, threw some money at me and left in a huff, mumbling something about it all being my fault. Sally was the only one at the bar when I went out. I told her about the problem I'd had with the last man.

'Oh,' she said. 'You get that at this time of night. They are too fucking drunk to do anything and they always blame the girl. You were lucky to get any money at all, most of them refuse to pay. If only they realised that coming in before they hit the booze would give them a far better time for their money and they'd remember it in the morning!'

That was not money for old rope, and I felt that I'd earned every cent of the sixty dollars the man had thrown at me. It was time for another drink.

Mandy came out with her client, we had a glass of wine for the road, and I drove home as pissed as a fart with two hundred and fifty dollars stuffed into my handbag. When I arrived, I went straight in to see if Emma was all right and found her peacefully sleeping. Then I sat down at the dining room table, pulled the wads of money out of my handbag and counted it again. I rolled into bed, and slept more soundly that night than I had for weeks.

The following morning I was up early, after only five hours' sleep. At breakfast Emma was full of questions. Was it too awful? Did the other girls have tattoos? Would I be going again tonight? And, 'Oh yes, Nana called last night and wanted to know where you were!'

'Oh! What did you tell her?' I asked.

'I said you'd gone to work in a massage parlour of course.' She grinned at me. 'No, just joking. I told her you were at the movies with Carol.'

I gave Emma a hug. 'Well done, sweetheart.' It was difficult to believe she was taking all this so well.

I pulled my earnings from the night before out of my purse and waved it under her nose. 'Two hundred and fifty dollars,' I said. 'In just a few hours I've earned more than most people get in a week.'

Emma took the money from me, flicked it through her fingers and said, 'Wow!'

'I'll pick you up after work and we'll do some shopping,' I said as I drove Emma to her part-time holiday job. I then returned home to concoct a suitable story to keep friends and relatives happy. It was becoming obvious that leading a double life was not going to be easy.

CHAPTER 4

I decided to tell everyone that I was working in a club behind the bar. I thought it would explain why I went out wearing a cocktail dress so often. I phoned my mother to tell her the news.

'Oh Angela, how could you?' she said. 'Your father's not going to like it. I don't know why you had to give up a perfectly good job in a salon to work in a common bar. And what about Emma? I hope you're not going to leave her on her own night after night.'

I tried to tell Mum that my neighbour, Carol, was going to keep an eye on Emma, and that Emma was ten weeks off her fifteenth birthday and old enough to babysit herself, but to no avail. My mother was determined to worry herself into a spin.

'There are all sorts of undesirables wandering the streets at night . . . ' The lecture went on and on, and I listened to it dutifully, putting in the odd 'Yes, Mum' and 'No, Mum' every so often. Then eventually she said, 'Well, dear, I must go because Betty's coming over for afternoon tea,' and I was dismissed.

For the rest of the afternoon, until it was time to pick up Emma from her job, I got into some serious housework, which I hated with a vengeance. As I tipped the bucket of dirty water I'd just washed the floors with into the wash tub, I made myself a promise to hire a cleaner as soon as I could afford one. Looking at my watch I realised it was time to go, and was about to walk out the door when the phone rang. It was Trish.

'I've just finished the rosters. You will be working New Year's Eve and the two following nights, okay?'

'I can't work New Year's Eve,' I said. 'I'm going to a party. Sorry.'

'I'm afraid you'll have to, you have no choice in the matter,' she said. 'If I let everyone have the days and nights they want, there would be no one here Friday and Saturday nights or Sunday and

Monday days. I try to be as fair as possible, and as you are the last one to join us, you have to work.'

I felt really bitter about it. I had been looking forward to the party for so long. It was at the home of a friend who was in show business, and there were going to be some celebrities attending. However, I had chosen to work at The Harem and was therefore obliged to stand by their rules.

'Oh! Angie, apparently you wore trousers to work last night. We don't allow trousers of any type to be worn on shift. Okay? We'll see you tomorrow. Bye.'

Still feeling angry, I almost slammed the receiver down.

Emma came running along the footpath at full pelt, her raincoat flapping behind her. She took it off and threw it in the back with her bag. 'Where are we going?' she said.

We went into the city. I parked in the Britomart carpark and we walked up to High Street to have a cup of coffee at Nicholas Nickleby's.

'I have to buy a cocktail dress,' I said to Emma. 'I think we'll pop back to Queen's, they have some nice after-five stuff.'

Queen's was on the corner of Queen's Arcade and Queen Street, a delightful shop. But it had one problem; all the staff were trained in the art of 'hard sell', and from the moment you set foot in the place you were continuously hounded by salespersons. Yet because the clothes they sold were well made, up to the minute fashion and affordable, they were never short of customers. About this time, Princess Diana had dared to wear a strapless red taffeta frock with ruffles around the top to a royal function. It had caused quite a stir in some circles. And there in the window of Queen's was a replica of that frock.

We went in, and immediately a salesperson was at my elbow. She smiled a 'toothpaste ad' smile. 'I see you're interested in the Lady Di number. It would look perfect on Madam. You have the same colouring.'

Emma was standing behind the assistant miming her.

'Do you have a size ten please?' I asked.

The salesperson sped through the rack of dresses. 'No, but we do have a twelve. It's a small cut and worth a try.' She bustled me into a changing cubicle. 'There you go. I'll be back in a minute to see how you're doing.'

I'd barely got the frock on when she was back. Whipping open the curtain for all the world to see, she said, 'Oh yes, it's perfect for Madam.'

I looked in the mirror. It was far too big and hung on me like a lamp shade. The waistline rested on my hips, which made the well-boned bodice stand up like a huge drainpipe around my breasts. The skirt, which should have been knee-length, came right down to my lower calves, giving the impression they were super-skinny and my feet were super-big. I looked more like Mary Poppins than Princess Diana. Meanwhile, the assistant, realising I wasn't quite that gullible, had gone to fetch more dresses. She came back with a selection, and I was eventually pressured into one I didn't really like, but would do.

Leaving Queen's, I said to Emma, 'Now it's your turn, what would you like.'

She didn't hesitate. 'There's this neat skirt in Hullabaloo.'

So up Queen Street we went and bought Emma the most awful grey skirt I'd ever set eyes on. But she loved it, so that was all right.

We drove home and got changed, then went out to dinner at the Jade Garden restaurant and ate up large — something we hadn't been able to afford to do for months.

The next day was New Year's Eve. Emma came into my bedroom with a cup of tea for us both about eight o'clock and she got into bed with me. 'What shall we do today?' she asked, dunking a gingernut into her tea.

'I have to work tonight,' I said, 'so we can't go too far.'

We took a picnic to the Domain and went for a long walk.

I arrived at The Harem at ten-to-seven. It was very different from my first night. The place was bustling with the shift change over.

Sally was sitting at the bar, so I went over to join her. 'I'm fucked off having to work tonight,' she said. 'My man is riding up from down south and should be here around ten, so if it's quiet I'm going to fuck off. New Year's Eve is always quiet, everybody's out celebrating, and those that do come in are too drunk to do anything.' She told me her man was a Hell's Angel and was riding up from Wellington with a pack of them. 'If he gets to Auckland and I'm working, he'll just get drunk and fuck someone else. I'd just die if he went with someone else.' She looked extremely worried about it.

Sally was an angelic-looking girl of nineteen. She had a two-year-old son, who was looked after by his grandmother while she worked. She had long, fine, straight hair; it was almost flaxen, and natural by the look of it. Her skin was flawless and her eyes were the most beautiful blue. But what let Sally down was her figure. At the age of nineteen she had a matronly, pear-shaped body, with a wide, angular bottom that comes with childbearing. And I couldn't help being amazed at the profanities that came from her angelic-looking mouth. The words 'fuck' and 'cunt' rolled out as regularly as 'if' and 'but'.

She was in the middle of telling me about her son when the phone rang. 'Would you mind answering that?' she said. 'We don't have a receptionist, so we take the phone in turns. Just say, "Harem. Can I help you?" '

I hurried over to the phone, which was situated by the entrance, and picked up the receiver. 'The Harem. Can I help you?'

'Who do you have working tonight?' asked a well-spoken male voice.

'Just a moment,' I said, and rushed over to Sally. 'He wants to know who's working tonight.'

'Oh, fucked if I know. You'll have to grab the roster from the office,' she said.

I did as she suggested and went back to the phone. 'Umm . . . Jana, Sally, Karen and Angela,' I said.

'And what would they look like?' said the voice.

I described Sally and I, then told him that the other ladies had not arrived and I was new, so I wasn't able to tell him about Jana and Karen.'

'And what would Sally be wearing?' he asked, and I described her clothes. 'And what would her underwear be like?' I said I didn't know. 'And what would Angela be wearing?' I described my clothes. 'And what would her underwear be like?' I told him it was black. 'And is she dominant?' he said. I told him I didn't think so.

'Do you have any dominant ladies working tonight?' he asked.

I told him he'd have to phone back later because I didn't know, and I hung up.

Back at the bar, I told Sally about the call.

'Oh, that guy. He calls himself John and phones up all the parlours asking the same questions. You get lots like that. They're a fucking nuisance.'

The phone started ringing again. 'Would you mind?' said Sally.

'The Harem, can I help you?'

'Who's working tonight,' said another male voice.

'Jana, Karen, Sally and Angela,' I replied.

'Oh, can I make an appointment with Angela at nine-thirty please,' said the voice.

I didn't know if it was possible to make appointments, so I told him to just come on in.

'Is that Angela I'm speaking to?' he asked. I said it was. 'It's me, Mark. I came in to see you the night before last, do you remember? You really cheered me up and I'd like to see you again.'

It was the young man who had told me his relationship had broken up and I had kept on giggling while he was telling me about it. I said I'd love to see him again and he was welcome to pop in any time.

I had just replaced the receiver when three men arrived, all talking in a foreign language. They went into the office and closed the door.

'That's Mel and his mates,' said Sally. 'I expect he'll want to try you out later. He tries us all out. Except Mandy — she told him to get fucked.' She laughed, then added, 'But the next girl who told him to get fucked got fired. Anyway, make him pay. He won't if he can get away with it, so get your money first.'

Ten minutes later, Mel's friends left and he came over to me.

'You take me for a massage,' he said in broken English, and led me into one of the de luxe rooms. Mel was a pathetic little man. He was in his forties, with dark hair, olive complexion and eyes like a spaniel. He moaned about his wife, from whom he was separated. He moaned that no other woman wanted him because he owned a 'sauna' — many people called massage parlours saunas back then. He moaned about not getting the right girls working for him. In fact, he spent the whole time I was massaging him moaning about something or other.

After the massage he said, 'You give me extras. I will pay later.' I didn't feel free to argue with him — he was the boss after all — so I started doing all the things Wally had taught me. But when I tried to put the condom on he said, 'No joe. You do it without.'

'But you have to use one!' I said.

'Other girls — Sally, Jana, all of them — they don't use joe.' I could see he was getting agitated. He hadn't had a shower, and there was a nasty smell coming from his scrotal area. There was no way I could give him any oral.

Luckily for me he said, 'You lie down.' He moved to the end of the table, and I lay down and opened my legs. As he entered my vagina, I screwed up my eyes tightly. I could feel him breathing into my hair, the massage table started to squeak as the rhythm got harder and faster. My fists were clenched so tightly I could feel my nails digging into my palms, and when he finally ejaculated into me I desperately wanted to cry. He got down from the table, grabbed a towel and went into the shower.

I sat up, pulled a tissue from the box and blew my nose. His semen was running out of me, all over the towel I was sitting on. I pulled some more tissues from the box to mop it up. Mel came out of the ensuite and started to dress. I hurried into it, ran a shower and tried to wash away the smell of him. I now knew what the phrase 'feeling dirty' meant.

After dressing and tidying the room, I went out to the bar for a drink. I needed one.

Sally had been joined by Jana, a curvaceous blonde in her mid to late twenties, and Karen, a brunette of about thirty-five. I noticed Karen wasn't drinking, and asked if she'd like a glass of wine.

'No thanks,' she said. 'I'm allergic to alcohol. I'll pop out to the garage next door for some coke.'

'How did you get on with old fuck-face?' asked Sally. 'I hope you got some money out of him, because you missed out on a guy called Mark.'

I lied and said I did. Ten minutes later, Mel called me into the office and gave me thirty-five dollars. I could not look the man in the eyes.

*

When I got back to the bar, Sally had 'gone through' with a client, Karen had gone down to the garage for some coke, and I was left talking to Jana. She told me that she and her husband were hoping to go into business pretty soon. They were a few thousand dollars short of what they needed to get going, so she had started 'working' to get it as quickly as possible.

'I worked at Fleure's for about a month,' she said, 'but I was fired because I left a condom packet in my room. Anyway, there were far too many rules — and the endless cleaning! So I wasn't too unhappy about it. There was one thing I liked about the place, though. You didn't have to sleep with the boss to keep your job.'

Before very long, Karen came back from the garage, Sally finished her massage, and we all sat around the bar drinking glass after glass of wine. Not one person came through the door, nor did the phone ring, for four hours.

'It's always like this on public holidays,' Sally said just after ten, 'and I'm fucked if I'm hanging around here. If Mel asks, I've gone home sick, okay?' We all nodded and off she went.

Karen had worked at The Harem since it opened. She and Mandy had worked together at a parlour called Hostess somewhere near Symonds Street, in the city. They had both left Hostess because the place had become old and shabby, and clientèle had dropped off dramatically. 'A lot of our clients followed us here,' she said. 'Mel's doing very well out of Mandy and I, and still he hits on me for sex. I wish I'd stopped him from the start, like Mandy did. I wouldn't mind, but I always miss out on a good payer while I'm keeping that bastard happy, like you did earlier.'

'He won't wear a rubber,' said Jana, 'and he stinks!'

'Do you ever do men without a condom?' I asked.

'Oh yes,' said Karen, 'but only special clients. It's okay as long as you have regular STD checks. I go every two weeks, unless a joe breaks, then I go ASAP.'

Mel went out at eleven-thirty, and at midnight we linked arms and sang 'Auld Lang Syne'. We could hear the ships' foghorns hooting from the docks, and I wondered what my friends were doing at the party.

'It could get busy now.' said Jana. 'Be prepared for a late night.'

*

At a quarter-to-one, a man arrived at the door. He wanted to know who was working, and to meet them all. He stood, looking us up and down. 'I'll have you,' he said, pointing to me, and I took him through to one of the cushion rooms. He took off his clothes and went across the corridor to the shower. As soon as he arrived back he said, 'How much do you charge for sex?'

'Sixty with oral, fifty without,' I replied.

He nodded. 'Sixty. No massage, just get into it.'

I'd drunk a fair quantity of alcohol, and was not too steady on my feet. I nearly fell over taking off my knickers, and found it difficult to undo my bra. I ripped open the condom packet and immediately dropped the condom on the floor. I eventually performed my task, and the man got up to have his shower. When he came back, I went to have mine, and when I came back, he was gone!

I thought he might be waiting for me at the bar. He wasn't. 'You've been ripped off,' said Karen, who was, of course, as sober as a judge. 'I saw the man leave. I didn't realise he was doing a runner. Look, they do not go together, working and drinking. When you're drunk, you make too many mistakes and lose too much money. Guys like that are looking for someone easy to rip off. Christ! We work too hard to give it away. Another thing, get your money before you start performing, unless you know the guy. Regulars are different.'

For the second time that night I felt as though I'd been raped.

From then on, we were busy. I drank heaps of water to sober up. Most of our clients were drunk, but jolly with it.

I couldn't help noticing how amazing Karen was. She was telling us about her marriage break-up, and how her husband had taken custody of their children, whom she missed dearly. Her eyes were brimming with tears, and I felt very sorry for her. Then a client arrived at the door, and it was her turn to 'do the desk'. In a fraction of a second her face had changed. A beaming smile spread across it as she ushered the man to the bar. She joked and flirted with him, and, of course, he chose her. She took him into a de luxe room. Then she came out to the bar for her purse, and I noticed the pain had returned to her face. She picked up the purse, breathed deeply, showed us a sunny smile, and went back into the de luxe room. The show must go on.

I did two men who were relatively easy, then one who could hardly stand up and admitted he was unable to have sex but paid me twenty-five dollars anyway. Then I did another man, who wanted the works and took an hour to finish it. I walked out of that room looking a wreck, my hair soaked with sweat, lipstick spread from one ear to another and my inner thighs bruised with his attempts to 'do it doggie style', as his knees kept hitting them with every thrust. I would have liked to have gone home at that point. The alcohol was catching up with me, my head was pounding, and I was aware that I still smelled of Mel.

But another man came through the door, and into one of the cushion rooms we went. This man was full of the joys of spring. He told me filthy jokes and roared with laughter before he got the punch line out. He pulled some postcards from his pocket showing pictures of white women having sex with black men and vice versa.

Then he produced a condom from his wallet that was black and made of quite heavy rubber, with some red tentacle-like things protruding from the end. 'This'll tickle your fancy,' he said, trying to stick the index finger of his other hand into my vagina. 'This'll tickle your little pussy, eh!' But by the time he got around to having sex his penis had gone down, and the ghastly black condom was hanging off it. 'Oh, you will have to cheer him up, won't you. Come on, give him a little lick!' I just wanted to die, I felt so dreadful. 'You're a serious little thing,' he went on, and pinched my bottom.

He started masturbating until his erection reappeared and he was able to slide the condom on again. He was about to take up the missionary position, when he ejaculated and it was all over. I have never been so pleased about anything in my life. Good-naturedly he tottered off to the shower, and I in turn had mine. The whole time he was telling me jokes and roaring with laughter himself. I wouldn't have minded if he had walked out without paying, because I didn't deserve to be paid. But he sorted through his wallet and gave me eighty dollars, and said, 'I'll be back to see you again.'

We closed up just after five a.m. I drove home very carefully and went straight to bed without even counting my money.

CHAPTER 5

I awoke at eleven in the morning with the most awful hangover. Emma brought me a cup of tea and a packet of Aspirin. My head pounded, my mouth felt like a piece of blotting paper and I wanted to throw up. The thought of going to work that night made my skin crawl.

'I know what you need,' said Emma. 'Berocca, they're really good for hangovers. Shall I go and buy some?'

I was desperate enough to try anything. 'Oh, yes please, love, my bag's on the dining room table.' I remember wondering how she knew about this stuff. I wasn't a habitual drinker, and couldn't even recall the last hangover I had. How did she know about the benefits of Berocca?

I dozed a little and woke up when Emma arrived home. She threw the Berocca on the bed and went to fetch a glass of water. 'You must have done well last night,' she said, dropping the tablet into the water. 'I opened your purse in the chemist's shop and all these wads of money spewed out over the counter.' She opened it again and tipped them onto the bed. I finished drinking the Berocca, picked up the wads and straightened them. A couple of orange fifties stood out amongst the pile. I counted it — three hundred and twenty dollars. I gave the pile to Emma and she counted it. 'Three hundred and twenty dollars,' she announced.

I suddenly felt a lot better. 'Emm, give me an hour to sleep this off, twenty minutes to have a shower, and then I'll take you out for a slap-up lunch.'

At one-thirty we were sitting in the Steam Biscuit Factory restaurant, in the Sheraton Hotel. The Berocca had done its stuff, and I ate heartily.

*

All too soon it was time to get ready for work, and although I still felt a bit fragile, the thought of it did not make me feel as bad as it had done that morning. I met Mandy at the foot of the stairs. 'How's your head?' she asked.

'Much better than it was this morning,' I replied. 'I've brought some orange juice to drink tonight.'

Mandy laughed. 'I phoned Karen this morning. She told me how you and Jana got into the turps last night. I bet she's feeling rough too.'

Once inside The Harem I was told a client was waiting for me in one of the cushion rooms. I went in to find Mark stretched out among the pillows. During the session he asked me about my life, and I told him of Emma and how I was working to pay our mortgage arrears. I found Mark to be pleasant company. He had a very good sense of humour and made me laugh a lot. Afterwards, while giving me my money, Mark asked me to go out to dinner with him. I was really flattered because he was good fifteen years my junior, but I didn't really want to. I thanked him for asking me and refused as politely as possible. He left, still smiling, and promised to see me next week.

I told the girls how chuffed I was with such a young man asking me out for dinner.

'You get those all the time,' said Mandy. 'And if you'd accepted, you would have ended up at his place with a plate of stir-fry veggies, and him groping and mauling you, hoping to get a freebee. Some weeks I could go out to dinner every night of the week with one client or another. You didn't accept did you?' I told her no. 'You never tell clients anything about yourself or your family, and never tell them where you live because you'll have them turning up to see you at all hours of the day and night for a "bit of business".'

I said nothing. It made a lot of sense to me, but it was too late to do anything about it. I only hoped Mark wasn't the sort of man to cause problems. I didn't think he was the type, but then who is? I wasn't going to be so stupid again.

'Fuck! I never get anyone asking me out,' said Sally, slurping loudly on a mug of coffee.

Mandy slipped down from her stool and looked at Sally. 'I wonder why that is?' she said, and went into the office.

The remark went right over Sally's head. She lit a cigarette, drew deeply and grinned at me. 'Mandy's neat, eh,' she said.

The phone rang and I went to answer it.

It was Trish. 'Is that you, Angie?' she said. 'I'm rostering you on two days and two nights next week. You won't mind a couple of day shifts, will you?' I said it was fine by me, knowing full well that to complain wouldn't make a scrap of difference anyway. She went on, 'Monday and Tuesday days, Thursday and Saturday nights. We're a day girl short for the next two weeks, so the night girls will have to fill in.'

About eight-thirty, a man appeared at the door. 'Oh fuck! It's old Henry,' said Sally, disappearing into the kitchen. Thinking something really bad was about to happen, I followed her.

'What's wrong with him?' I asked.

'He's a boring old cunt. He books in for an hour, he won't have a massage and he only has a twenty-five dollar hand job,' she whispered. 'He's real hard work, and he always asks for me. Today he can get fucked!'

Mandy came storming into the kitchen. 'What are you two doing in here? Sally, Henry is here to see you.' She raised her eyebrows and looked deliberately at Sally, who was pulling a face. 'I know he's a pain, but he's also the only regular you have managed to get since starting here. Now, if you still want a job at The Harem, get out there and make the old guy happy. NOW!' Reluctantly, Sally dawdled out to Henry, who was standing at the bar grinning from ear to ear.

'What's hand relief?' I asked, as Sally disappeared into a cushion room with the still grinning Henry hot on her tail.

'Haven't you done one yet?' Mandy asked, looking surprised. I shook my head. 'Well, instead of having conventional sex, some men, for one reason or another, prefer you to put some oil on their penis and masturbate them, you know, with your hand.' She made a milking motion with her right hand. 'It's only twenty-five to thirty dollars, and all a lot of men can afford. We do quite a few.'

My second client booked in for half an hour. He had come in to see Karen, who was not working that night. Mandy talked him into seeing me instead. 'He's a very wealthy businessman,' she said, 'one of Karen's specials.'

I went through to a de luxe room with him. He was cold and business-like. After his shower, he lay on his back and said, 'A quick blow job please.'

'You don't want a massage?' I asked.

'No thank you, just the blow job, and I'm in a hurry as I must be out at the airport in an hour.' I pulled out a condom and started to tear the wrapper. 'No condom, thank you. Karen doesn't use one on me!'

I peered at his flaccid penis; a clear discharge was just visible at the end. Well, I thought, it's now or never, and I picked it up between my thumb and forefinger. The penis started to stiffen, making it easier to put in my mouth. It tasted salty and increased in size as my tongue slid up and down its shaft. My mouth started to ache as his breathing came in short bursts. His hands clasped the back of my head and he gasped. I could feel his penis pulsating gently in my mouth, and my mouth filled with a salty, foul-tasting liquid. I wanted to vomit. I grabbed a handful of tissues and spat out the semen, then turned my head away and dry-retched a couple of times. Luckily my client was relaxing with his eyes closed.

'I'll pop out now and have my shower,' I said. 'We don't want you missing your plane.'

In the shower, I filled my mouth with the warm water and spat it out time and time again, trying to rid it of the awful taste. When I returned to the room, my client was almost dressed, and four twenty-dollar bills were spread out on the massage table. He finished tying his shoelaces and picked up his briefcase. 'Thank you and good-bye,' he said, and walked briskly out. I put the money into my purse and thought that eighty dollars, earned in half an hour, was almost half a week's wages at the salon. I'd soon get used to the awful taste.

Mel and his mates were sitting around the bar when I went out. Mel pulled me aside. 'You take Ali for massage, you do special price for my friend.'

Ali was a prize bastard. He didn't want a shower, he didn't want a massage, he didn't want a condom. But he did want sex — on the floor, against the wall, sideways, over the chair, in the shower; in fact in every position one could imagine. I was glad there was no chandelier hanging from the ceiling. He would have done the *Kama Sutra* proud. He was like an octopus; he stuck his tongue and fingers into every orifice I had. At the end of it all, he got dressed and paid me thirty-five dollars, telling me in his irritating accent not to spend it all at once. Again I felt I'd been raped, and I thought maybe this was what prostitution was all about — that not getting paid for half the work you do was a part of it. Later that evening I had a talk to Mandy.

'You do get ripped off a bit at the beginning,' she said. 'To be able to recognise a situation before it happens comes with experience. For instance, I could tell Mel was a sleaze-bag when I first met him. He was the sort of boss who would hit on the girls for sex. So before I started, I told him that I did *not* sleep with the boss, and if that was what he wanted, I'd work elsewhere. He agreed to leave me alone. Karen on the other hand, being a real pushover, didn't make it clear to him, and he's using her all the time. Sometimes he has sex with several girls in one day, and very rarely does he pay.'

We were then interrupted by two men dressed in suits, who were waiting by the door. Mandy booked them in and brought them over to the bar. 'Angie, I'd like you to meet David and John. David is an old friend of ours, and John is his colleague from Wellington. If you would like to take John through to a de luxe room for his massage, we'll see you back here in an hour.' She poured John a glass of wine and through we went.

John was a true gentleman and handsome with it. He was tall and slim, with a mop of iron-grey hair. His eyes looked very blue against his tanned face. After his shower he stood awkwardly by the table, clutching his towel around him. 'I haven't done this before,' he said. I told him not to be shy. 'Just drop your towel, and lie tummy down on the massage table and relax.' He was a well-muscled man, his back strong and tanned, his legs long and well-proportioned. In fact the guy was a real spunk. As I massaged him I felt a tingle down my spine and hoped he would have the works for extras, as I was going to enjoy every minute of it. I gave John the best massage I knew how to do at the time, and when he turned over, he had the most beautiful penis I'd seen. It was big and straight and hard as a rock.

'Is there anything else I can do for you?' I tried to say, but it came out as a croak. I cleared my throat and said it again. 'Is there anything else I can do for you?'

John sat up, covered his frontal area with a towel and said, 'That was an enjoyable massage, and you are a very sexy lady. But I have to tell you, Angie, I am a very happily married man and I do not want to do anything to spoil it. So I'm sorry, but no thank you. I'm tempted, but I could never forgive myself if I did.' He looked at his watch and laughed. 'I think a cold shower would be the order of the day.' He looked down at his still erect penis protruding through the front of his towel. 'Don't you agree?'

As he ambled into the ensuite I sat on the table and whispered under my breath, 'Oh damn!' And I thought what a lucky woman his wife was.

While we dressed, John confessed he had not wanted to come into a parlour in the first place. 'But Dave has a very persuasive tongue,' he said. Just as we were about to leave the room, John hesitated. 'Look, I must pay you something.' He got his wallet from the inside pocket of his jacket and pulled out some twenty-dollar bills. 'I think Dave said something about sixty dollars.'

'Oh no! I couldn't possibly accept it,' I said. 'I didn't do anything.'

John pressed the money into my hand. 'It was a fine massage, and I insist.' I thanked him profusely and accompanied him back to the bar to wait for David and Mandy. We talked about politics and travel. John had been to several places I knew well. He had a daughter the same age as Emma, and we laughed at their strange fashion preferences. Sally sat quietly at the end of the bar. I tried several times to bring her into the conversation, but she refused to respond to my efforts. When David and John had gone, Sally said, 'I hate fucking yuppies!'

'Perhaps that's why you don't make much money!' said Mandy. Once again it went right over Sally's head.

Just before midnight, Mark came back to the parlour with two friends. They had been drinking, but did not seem to be too worse for wear. They wanted a game of snooker, then Mark's friends would book in with Mandy and Sally.

'Do you mind spending another hour with me?' asked Mark. I said I didn't mind and we went through to a cushion room.

This time was different. Mark had been drinking since he left The Harem earlier, and was feeling sorry for himself. He begged me to go out to dinner with him, and when I said no, he cried. He said all women were bitches, then he said he was sorry he said that and begged my forgiveness. He then tried to have sex with me and couldn't manage it. He tried again, and couldn't manage it again. He went into the shower and demanded I wash his back. I did it to humour him. He then told me he didn't have any money.

'I just had to see you again,' he whined. 'I want to have sex with you.' He started taking his trousers off. I knew I was over my time, but this guy was impossible, and I couldn't see me ever getting him out of the room. As a last resort, I put a towel around myself and went out to the bar, where Mandy and Sally sat on their own waiting for the guys to finish their game.

'What's wrong?' asked Mandy.

'Mark is drunk and disorderly, he will not do as he's told, and I can't get him out of the room,' I admitted.

Mandy marched into the cushion room where, by this time, Mark had taken all his clothes off again and was lying on the mattress masturbating. She picked up his clothes and threw them at him. 'If you are not dressed and out of here in five minutes, I'm calling security. I cannot guarantee your safety when they get here.' She looked at her watch. 'You now have four-and-a-half minutes.' She turned on her heels and went into the snooker room and said to Mark's friends, 'Your mate is causing us some serious bother, so I'm calling security unless you're all out of here in five minutes.'

In a very short time they were gone, Mark running after his mates, carrying his shoes and socks.

'What security?' I asked.

'Angie, we have no protection here whatsoever. If a client starts getting rough, we would be at his mercy. Mel is never around to do anything to help, which breaks the terms of his licence. If the police knew, he'd lose it. So I invented a security system, and so far it's worked.'

I thanked her very much, went for a shower and got dressed.

*

The rest of the shift was uneventful. We all did another one each, had a cup of coffee, did the cleaning and went home on the dot of one o'clock.

I was not tired when I got home, mainly because I'd consumed nothing but orange juice and coffee. So at one-fifteen in the morning, I sat wide awake and wondering what to do. There was no television on at that time, and in those days the radio stations were boring. I'd read everything there was to read. I thought of what I did when returning home from my job at the salon. Cooking and cleaning came to mind, but one cannot cook and clean at one-fifteen in the morning because the noise would upset the neighbours. I emptied out my purse onto the dining room table and counted the pile of notes. Two hundred and seventy dollars. From a mung-bean jar in the pantry, I fished out an envelope that contained the rest of my week's earnings. I put the whole lot into some sort of order — fifties, twenties, tens, fives and twos. I counted it again. Six hundred and forty dollars in total, and that wasn't counting the one hundred and eighty I'd spent on the cocktail dress, Emma's skirt and the meals out. Tomorrow I would do some grocery shopping, get some of Emma's favourite biscuits and some special cheeses. Life was certainly looking up. I stashed the money back in the pantry and made a list of things we needed.

What to do next? I went through the book-case and there was nothing in it I hadn't read. I peeped in on Emma again. She was still sleeping peacefully, and I envied her. I noticed the book she was currently reading on her bedside table, and I picked it up and took it out with me. *Flowers in the Attic*, it was called. I made a cup of hot chocolate, put my pyjamas on, cleaned my teeth, took off my make-up — what was left of it — and went to bed with Emma's book. Fluffing up the pillows, I settled down for a good read. *Flowers in the Attic* boasted of being a bestseller, but proved to be a symphony of badly written emotional rot that only adolescents would read. I struggled to the end of chapter one and put it down. Not even my state of utter and complete boredom could persuade me to suffer one more page. I looked at the clock. A quarter-past-two, and I was still wide awake. I got out of bed, went back into the kitchen and wrote 'library' on the end of my grocery list.

I had to find something to do in the time I had after work. Embroidery? No, not me. Knitting? That wasn't me either. Writing? That gave me an idea. I would keep a kind of diary, a secret one. I would hand-write it and keep it hidden somewhere safe, for who knew what could come of it later? Sorting through Emma's school bag, I found a spare refill. I took it back to the dining room table and started to write about my last few days. An hour-and-a-quarter later, I put my pen down, hid the refill, went to bed and fell asleep.

CHAPTER 6

Emma woke me at eight o'clock with a cup of tea. 'You look so tired,' she said.

I felt tired and had to drag myself out of bed to go to the loo. While washing my hands I glanced in the mirror. An old hag looked back at me; my skin was pale even through the tan, and the crows' feet around my dark, hollow eyes looked more like chickens' feet. The fact that my hair was standing on end didn't help the situation either.

'I think I'll take you to work, then come home for some more sleep,' I said to Emma. 'I can't go to work tonight feeling and looking like this.'

That turned out to be easier said than done. I returned home, went to bed and drifted off into the most wondrous sleep. But the phone rang, and rang and rang. I got up to answer it. A child's voice asked to speak to Nana. I told her she had the wrong number, hung up and went back to bed. The phone rang again, and again it was the same child wanting to speak to Nana. This time I left the receiver off the hook. Back to bed I went and straight to sleep. Then I awoke to the sound of banging. It was somebody at the front door. I hoped like anything they'd go away, and just when I thought they had, it started again. I got up and put a robe on and went to the door. A taxi driver stood there.

'Cab for apartment two,' he said. I pointed to the large '1' stuck to the front door. 'Oh, sorry!' he said and toddled off to apartment two.

Back in bed, I lay there wondering what would happen next. Nothing did, and I drifted off once more.

Way, way back in my subconscious, someone was screaming. It got louder and louder. I opened my eyes and realised that it was Thursday and the property maintenance men had arrived to do the lawns. I got up and switched the jug on. No rest for the wicked!

After my shower I pulled on a pair of jeans and a cotton blouse, covered my eyes with a pair of large dark glasses, and went out to buy some more condoms. I drove out to Panmure, parked the car and went to the first chemist I came to. Without hesitation I walked up to the counter and said to the assistant, who looked no more than fourteen, 'Twelve Featherlite Durex please.'

She looked at me blankly and started sorting among the pain killers. 'For a headache?' she asked.

'No. They're condoms,' I replied.

She looked a bit embarrassed and pulled a drawer out from under the counter. I spotted them immediately and picked up a packet. She gave me a sheepish smile and held a bag open for me to put them in. I paid for them and left the shop. Well, that was a bit easier.

Before getting ready for work, I took a long look at myself in the mirror. Nothing had changed; the old hag was still there, which is not good when your livelihood depends on looking beautiful. This calls for drastic action, I said to myself, and slapped on a bright green, mud-textured face-pack plus a piece of cucumber for each of my eyes. I then lay on my bed for the twenty minutes recommended by the face-pack manufacturers. It made not a jot of difference. Nor did the toner, the vitamin E cream, or the anti-wrinkle moisturiser, and no amount of foundation would cover up the dark hollows around my eyes. The chickens' feet suggested a facelift was well overdue, and I felt so tired.

At work I poured myself a glass of wine. I figured it would pick me up a bit, but it only served to make me feel more tired than I already was. A man arrived at the door, and one of the day girls checked him in.

'He's paid for an hour in one of the de luxe suites,' she said. 'You can take him through now if you like. No one else has arrived yet. His name is Trevor.'

While Trevor was lying on the massage table having his massage, he chatted on about this and that. Then he suddenly went quiet. I assumed he was totally relaxed and just wanted to doze. But then I felt his shoulders start to shake and shudder, and I thought he must be having some kind of seizure.

'Are you okay, Trevor?' I asked. He said nothing. His whole body was now shuddering, almost violently. 'Trevor, please tell me what's wrong?' His breathing was all right; he was taking in great lungfuls of air. It was then I realised he was crying.

He sat up, his face streaming with tears. He was sobbing uncontrollably. I held him to me.

'Hey, what's wrong?' I said. He clung to me, his whole body heaving with emotion. I must confess to being a bit frightened. We sat on the massage table locked in each others' arms for a good ten minutes before his sobbing subsided. 'Would you like me to make you a cup of tea?' I said. 'Or perhaps something stronger from the bar?'

'Tea would be fine,' he said quietly. I wrapped a towel around myself and went out to the kitchen.

'What's wrong,' asked Karen as I passed her with the tea.

'I've got a man in my room crying his eyes out. Karen, I don't know what to do!'

'Is he drunk?' she asked.

'No,' I said, 'this man is hurting!'

'All you can do is get him to talk and listen to what he has to say. It happens every now and again. Good luck.'

I arrived back in the room to find Trevor still sitting in the same position. 'I'm sorry,' he said. 'I'm making a real fool of myself, aren't I?'

I gave him his tea and asked him to tell me what was wrong, which only served to make him cry again. I put his tea down and held him to me. I could feel his tears running down my back. I stroked his hair as one would a child. 'Crying is good for you, you know, and we have plenty of time, so let it out.'

'I'm so sorry,' he gasped between sobs. 'I just need to talk to someone. My family have gone to pieces, and my staff would think I'd gone mad. Everyone thinks I'm strong, and I was until today. But when they'd all gone and I was on my own, I couldn't cope.'

'Well, you can tell me,' I said. 'What hit you?'

Trevor breathed in deeply. 'My wife died of breast cancer on Monday. She was buried today.' He looked up at the ceiling and

50

blinked back the tears. 'I loved my wife . . . I still do. She was thirty-nine last week.'

Now it was my turn to cry. I couldn't help it. 'Were you happy?' I asked, grabbing a tissue to blow my nose.

He nodded. 'We had a wonderful relationship. She had a way of turning any tiff we had into a humorous series of events, and no one could stay angry with her for long. She made me laugh. I don't know how I'll live without her. When everyone left the house after the funeral, it was cold and empty. I felt I had to get out, and I don't want to go back there.'

'Do you have any family?' I asked.

'Yes,' he said. 'A boy of fifteen and a girl of twelve. They are staying with my sister in Takapuna.'

'Can't you stay with your sister for a while?'

'She wanted me to, but I felt she'd done enough looking after the kids. And anyway, I can't talk to her because she gets all upset, and then I have to comfort her. It makes me want to shake her and yell that it's me who's hurting,' he said.

'Trevor, I think you should stay tonight with your sister and your children. Tomorrow is another day, you can start sorting things out then. Just get today over with first.'

Trevor nodded, and started to get dressed. 'Thank you for being so understanding,' he said.

I often wondered if Trevor went to stay with his sister that night, and how he coped without his wife. The fact that he had had a happy marriage made it a particularly sad story. In the sex industry I met so many men who were in unhappy marriages, bound to their wives by guilt and loyalty to children. It seemed so unfair that Trevor's happy relationship had to end that way.

It seemed only Karen and I were working that night. Sally had phoned in to say her mother was sick and she was obliged to look after her and the boy.

'It won't be any great loss,' said Karen. 'Sally is more street material than anything. Mel was short of staff when he hired her. At the time he was grateful for anyone.'

At about nine o'clock, Mel and his mates arrived. 'Uh oh!' said Karen. 'Here comes Stinky and the Octopuses.'

It wasn't long before Mel was over to us. 'Angie to do massage for my friend Paulo. Karen you take Michael. De luxe please. You do a good deal.'

Here we go again, I thought, and led Paulo into one of the rooms. 'I will have a shower if you would like to finish your coffee in the lounge,' said Paulo, and for the first time I looked at him. He was quite young, about thirty-two, and he was smiling, his teeth white and even against his rugged olive face.

'I hoped to get you,' he said. 'I like mature ladies.' He ambled into the ensuite and came out with a towel around his waist, drying his back with another. 'You give me good massage and sex, I pay you fifty dollars, okay?' I nodded, and he lay down on the table.

While I massaged him, Paulo talked about his home in the Middle East, and the different cultures and ways of life there. He asked me about my life and why I worked. He turned out to be a very charming man, almost boyish in some respects. When it was time for the extras, he did not complain about using a condom and was very gentlemanly about the whole thing, to the point of asking me if I was comfortable during the missionary position. This man did not have sex, he made love, and I'm sure I'd have enjoyed it immensely had I not been so tired. Afterwards, Paulo took off his own condom, wrapped it in tissues and put it down the loo. 'You have a shower,' he said, handing me fifty dollars. 'You might miss other man, no good for business.' He grinned and winked at me. When we left the room he went into the office with Mel, and I went back to my coffee, which by this time was cold.

Karen was soon out. She sat down and sighed. 'What do they think we are? They have no idea when it comes to sex. No wonder they have to pay for it.'

'Well, mine was lovely,' I said, 'and he paid me well. He can put his shoes under my massage table any time he likes. I suppose Mel will want his share soon.'

'I don't think he will tonight. Apparently he made a pig of himself earlier with the day girls.' Karen lowered her voice to a whisper. 'He went through with all of them between one o'clock and five. The last girl couldn't get even a flicker out of his cock, and gave it away.'

The phone rang and I went to answer it.

'What are your charges please?' said a male voice.

'Thirty-five dollars for an hour in one of our de luxe suites; twenty-five for a cushion room.'

'And how many ladies do you have working,' asked the voice.

'Two this evening.'

'What's your name?'

'Angie.'

'You sound nice,' said the voice.

'Thank you,' I replied.

'Are you one of the girls?'

'Yes.'

'That's nice,' he said. 'What do you look like?' I told him. 'Have you got a big bosom?' I told him it was average. 'That's nice,' he said. 'What colour panties are you wearing, Angie?' He seemed to be running short of breath.

'Black ones,' I said.

'That's nice,' he said. 'I bet you've got a pretty pussy. I bet it gets wet when you're . . .' I hung up. I could not believe I'd let myself get drawn into that one.

Karen roared with laughter when I told her. 'He'd have been wanking himself off while talking to you. It happens all the time. Nine out of ten calls we get are from idiots like that one. Mandy has a wonderful way of dealing with them, ask her about it.'

Three men then appeared at the door. They wanted a lady each and all at the same time. As there were only two of us, we could not oblige, and they went away.

Karen sat reading a book, and I read a magazine from the coffee table in the lounge. The boredom was endless, and even the odd phone call from some heavy-breathing fool was welcome. Anything was better than reading the *Rugby Times* for two hours.

Then suddenly two men came to the door. Karen went to book them in. She talked to them for a minute or two, then brought them over to the bar. 'Angie, this is Brian and John, they are visitors to Auckland.'

They said nothing, just stood there looking Karen and I up and down. Then, at exactly the same moment, they turned on their heels and walked out as if choreographed to do so. 'You win some, you lose some!' said Karen, and went back to her book.

We sat there for another two hours. 'If nothing happens by one-thirty, I think we'll do the cleaning and go home,' said Karen. 'I can't be bothered working after sitting around for hours. I get stale.'

At ten-minutes-to-two, we were practically finished with the cleaning. I had only the last ensuite to do, and Karen was almost through with the vacuuming. I could hear voices in the lounge, and thought it was Mel and his mates leaving. I picked up the bucket and mop, turned round and came face to face with a man in a suit.

'Hello, there,' he said. 'The chap out there said you'd take care of me. My name's John.'

I did not feel like working after having sat around most of the night being bored out of my brain. So it was with rather bad grace that I put away my cleaning things and started being nice to the gentleman. I found it extremely hard to smile at him, or to even speak to him. But he chatted away pleasantly about his flight from England — he was an engineer working on a huge project down south, and he flew back and forth to New Zealand frequently. 'As soon as I land,' he said, 'I make straight for the nearest knock shop for a bit of "how's your father". Gets you over jet lag just like that.' He clicked his fingers and hooted with laughter. He didn't seem to notice my hostility at all. Why do I always get these larger-than-life characters at the end of the shift, I asked myself.

John had sixty-dollars worth, and spun it out as long as he could.

'Can I see your fanny?' he said. 'I like to see what I'm dipping my wick into.' He put on his glasses and peered intently between my legs. 'That's a nice little clitty.' He rubbed it with his forefinger as though he were trying to remove a stain. Still peering intently, he said, 'How's that? Turn you on, does it?'

It was extremely uncomfortable, but I nodded, wishing he'd get on with it. He stuck his finger into my vagina and wiggled it about. 'Let me see you orgasm.' He wiggled his finger about some more.

Okay, Angie, I said to myself, if you don't do something, you'll be here all night with this clown. I closed my eyes and moaned softly, and before you could say 'Jack Robinson' he was on top, trying to get into the missionary position. But it was too late; it was all over for him, and he hadn't even entered me. I looked up at the ceiling and said a little prayer of thanks, because by this time I could barely keep my eyes open.

'I won't stay for a shower,' he said. 'I'll have one in my hotel.'

I was very pleased about that and walked him to the door. At last I could go home to sleep, and the thought of only making one hundred and ten dollars didn't worry me at all.

But I couldn't find Karen! I thought perhaps she'd gone home, so I went into the office to ask Mel if I could go too. 'She working, you will have to stay until she finish,' he said, looking at his watch. 'Thirty-five minutes.'

It was the longest thirty-five minutes in history.

I eventually arrived home at three-thirty. I went straight to the kitchen for a drink of orange juice and nearly fell over a bucket of water containing the biggest bunch of flowers imaginable. There was a card attached to it. 'My sincerest apologies for my behaviour Tuesday night. Mark.' I put the card on the bench and went to bed.

I slept for nine hours and awoke feeling wonderful. It's amazing what a good night's sleep can do.

'Who's Mark?' Emma wanted to know at breakfast. 'And what did he do on Tuesday night to warrant such a big bunch of flowers?' I told her the story, well, most of it anyway. I wondered how he knew where I lived. I'd told him the name of the road, but not the number. It was a long road. Surely he hadn't walked the entire length of it asking for me.

'They must have come as soon as you'd gone,' said Emma. 'They weren't on the doorstep when you left, but they were there five minutes later when I went out to get the milk.'

We put the flowers into vases and forgot about them. I had three days off ahead of me, no work until eleven on Monday morning, and a mung-bean jar full of money.

'Okay, Emm, let's enjoy ourselves,' I said. 'What shall we do first?'

'Let's get a kitten! We can go to the SPCA this afternoon. Go on, Mum. Please.'

I explained to her that to take on an animal, no matter what it was, you had to take the responsibility of it for its entire life. 'Cats can live till they're fifteen or sixteen. Are you going to be here in fifteen years to feed it?' I said.

'Mum, the SPCA are overcrowded with kittens and are having to put lots of them down because they have no room. We can offer a kitten a lovely home here and we can afford to look after it properly. It would be selfish of us not to.' Emma always sounded so logical about everything.

'Oh, all right,' I said, against my better judgement.

We drove out to the SPCA that afternoon. I didn't want to pick one out myself, because I would have taken them all home. 'Can you pick one for us?' I asked the assistant. 'It doesn't matter what sex or colour.'

She came out with a little male tabby. 'He was found in a sack with four other kittens,' she told us.

We had already been to a pet shop and bought a carrying cage, dirt box, play-things and food. So we drove straight home to get to know the new member of our family.

CHAPTER 7

Massage parlours are timeless places. Even at eleven o'clock in the morning The Harem had a night-time feel about it. All the windows were blacked out and covered with plush drapes. The lighting in reception had a subtle, intimate glow, and the cushion rooms were soaked with a warm pink that made your skin look beautiful. Red or pink lighting covered a multitude of sins without making the room too dark. Stretch marks, cellulite, moles, spots and pimples disappeared as if by magic, and the lights in the cushion rooms gave our faces an exotic sexy glow and highlighted eyes and cheekbones. But the de luxe rooms were harshly lit, and because of this, the girls hated using them.

I found it strange walking from the morning sun into instant night-time. Once inside, one lost track of the hour, and midday could have been midnight for all one knew.

I was surprised to find Mandy in the kitchen making a cup of coffee. Instead of the cocktail dress she usually wore in the evening, she was dressed in a beautifully fitting black suit, white silk shirt, black stockings and gorgeous Italian court shoes. She wore her auburn hair in a Cleopatra bob, and looked absolutely stunning. No one would ever have guessed her occupation.

'Like a coffee?' she asked.

'What are you doing here at this time of day?' I wanted to know.

'A double shift. One of the day girls is on holiday and another has quit. I'm a bit cheesed off about it really. I have just bought my own house, settlement day is today and I've got a heap of stuff that needs doing to prepare for the shift. My new bedroom and lounge suites are arriving this afternoon, and I dearly wanted to be there. Still, business is business!'

We sat down with our coffee and Mandy went on to say that she had arrived in Auckland five years back from Palmerston North with a brand new secretarial diploma and a head full of dreams. She took a room in a smart house in Epsom with four other girls and soon found that life in Auckland was no easier than it was in Palmerston. She was only able to find a job as a clerk with the city council, and her pay barely covered her rent, power, food and phone. New clothes were totally out of the question. One of her flatmates, who not only drove a Mercedes sports car but also owned the house they lived in, confided that she worked in a massage parlour. Mandy immediately applied for a job there, two nights a week to start with. Once the money started to roll in, Mandy decided it was a waste of time at the council, as she was earning twice as much money doing only two shifts at the parlour, so she went into prostitution seriously, making a career of it. She said her only concern was that her family would find out, as they were under the impression she was a private secretary to a director in a big company. I noticed she always referred to her occupation as a masseuse, and would frown at the word prostitute.

Our conversation came to a halt when a man came to the door. He was wearing a suit and carrying a briefcase. The rule was, whoever arrived first took the first client, unless he requested someone else. So Mandy went through, leaving me to drink my coffee.

But my peace was short-lived. From one of the small rooms out the back, came Mel. Obviously just out of bed, and wearing only a pair of striped pyjama pants, he was unshaven, unwashed and undesirable. 'I have a shower, then you do me a massage,' he said, and disappeared into the unoccupied de luxe room. If he had walked out a few seconds earlier, Mandy's client would have run a mile. I didn't realise Mel actually lived on the premises at that time.

The hour with Mel was not as bad as our first session, or maybe I had become hardened to some aspects of the job. I reluctantly massaged him, listening to him whinge away about staff shortages, his wife and how bad business was again. Sex was pretty straight-forward and quick, but I did not like having to do it without a condom. This time he did not pay me anything. In the shower afterwards, I realised that my period had started.

I found Mandy in one of the de luxe rooms stacking some towels. 'What do you do when you've got your period?' I asked, thinking she might send me home. 'Mine's just started.'

'You'll have to go out to the chemist and buy a small natural sea sponge,' she said. 'You use it like a tampon. They soak up the blood much better than a tampon, and you can wash them out between massages.'

'Oh, really! How do you get it out?' I asked. This sounded awful!

'You just put your fingers up and pull. Sometimes it's a bit difficult to reach, but if you bear down at the same time it's okay.' She was so matter of fact about it, as though people stuffed sea sponges into their vaginas all the time.

I walked to the Downtown Pharmacy and bought three sea sponges from Shirl, who luckily didn't seem to recognise me from the condom fiasco. Back at The Harem, Mandy told me to wash one out in hot salt water. 'To kill any germs,' she said.

Once wet, the sponge softened, and I went into the loo to insert it. I could not believe how comfortable it felt. 'Are you sure the clients won't be able to feel it?' I asked, feeling a lot happier.

'Not a chance!' she said. 'It just feels like a part of your insides.'

I was pleased that I wasn't obliged to take the whole week off work when I had only just started on the job.

My first client of the day was an elderly gentleman called George. 'I always ask for a mature lady,' he said. 'These youngsters wouldn't know what time of day it was. They've had no experience with old codgers like me. We have special needs to be met.' He winked at me. 'Know what I mean?' I didn't know what he meant, but nodded anyway.

Half an hour later I did know what he meant.

'Is there anything else I can do for you?' I asked sweetly.

'You certainly can,' he said. 'A hand relief will be very nice, and I like a bit of a kiss and cuddle as well. I pay the thirty.' He said it as though he were ordering afternoon tea in a café. He was a lovely old man, so I agreed.

This was my first hand relief, and I remembered Mandy saying something about oil on the penis and her making a milking motion with her hand, which at the time seemed reasonable when I thought of doing it to an erect penis. George's was not erect, far from it. It lay like a dead worm on top of his testicles. I spread some oil on my hands and picked it up. Not a flicker! It was impossible to get any motion into it because the penis went up and down with my hand, and flopped about like a raw, half-empty sausage. I put more oil on. Still nothing. George was lying on the mattress amongst the cushions looking happy enough, so I lay down beside him, he put his arm around me and gave me a kiss. I felt a movement down below, so I kissed him back. After a barrage of kisses, George had the most beautiful erection, and I was able to slide my hand along its shaft without any problem.

'May I touch your breasts?' he whispered.

'Of course you can,' I whispered back, and he cupped one gently in his hand. His breathing started to get faster and suddenly his body stiffened. I could feel his penis pulsating slightly in my hand. Then he ejaculated.

'Ooh! That was good, I'll come and see you again,' he said, all red in the face and grinning. 'Those youngsters won't let you kiss or cuddle them, you know, and they don't like you touching their breasts either. That's no good to an old guy like me.'

I came to the conclusion there was a bit to learn about this job after all.

Mandy booked a client in and brought him over to meet me. 'Angie, this is Percy. He would like you to give him a nice massage. Cushion room, please.'

Percy was no oil painting. He looked to be well into his seventies and didn't have a tooth in his head. He was tall and stringy, with a slight stoop. We went through to one of the cushion rooms, where he had his shower and lay down on the mattress. 'We like a good massage,' he said. 'We have never been married, but we are not homosexual and do like the company of a pretty girl.' The way he used the royal 'we' fascinated me. He told me he owned a small farm just out of Whangarei and still worked in a quarry close by. He came by bus to Auckland once a month for a little bit of fun.

I started to massage him, and as my hands ran up his back all the skin went with them, forming a mountain of wrinkles at the base of his neck; it was the same going down. His shoulders were so bony it was almost impossible to do anything with them. But he appreciated everything I did for him. Massage finished, I asked if there was anything else I could do. He said yes, he'd like to massage me and then 'make love', but he didn't have any money with him! However, if I would trust him, he was staying at a motel in Parnell — he told me his room number — and I could pick the money up from there before check-out time the following morning. Rashly, I agreed.

He massaged me with gentle care, his rough work-worn hands, softened with oil, hardly touching me. 'In case they mark your lovely skin,' he said, standing up and stretching because his legs were aching crouched on the floor.

'Making love' with Percy was not easy. His knees not being what they were, he was only able to have sex standing up! His penis would not get totally erect, and it was difficult to keep the condom on it. We tried all sorts of ways to combat this, and eventually piled some of the large pillows onto the mattress, which was folded in half, and covered them with a towel. When stretched across this mountain of kapok and foam rubber, it brought me up to penis level, and with my legs spread out and up in the air, I guided him in. He had to bend over me with his hands on the cushions behind my head, but at least his legs were straight. We must have looked hilarious, but it worked, and Percy was a happy man. I didn't tell Mandy about picking the money up from Percy's motel because I knew it was a risk, and she'd say I was a fool.

I said good-bye to Percy, and Mandy told me there was some-one waiting in one of the de luxe rooms. It was Ron, the man I saw on my first night. This time dressed in a suit and tie, he said he was between meetings and only had limited time. He had a quick shower, quick sex, another quick shower, slapped sixty dollars on the massage table and asked me out for dinner one evening. I said I was unable to accept his invitation at this time. 'I'll talk to you about it next time,' he said, and left.

About two forty-five, two suit-clad men came to the door. They com-plained that all the girls at Fleure's, the parlour the other end of town, were booked out for the day, so they thought they'd try us. Mel was still wandering around like a derelict, unshaven and in his pyjama pants, drinking a cup of coffee from a badly chipped mug. Not the kind of situation one would want new clients to walk in on, and it was embarrassing for us to have him hanging around. The man I got was called John. He talked continuously about Fleure's and the lady he usually saw there. 'Francy's the best in the business,' he said. 'Mind you, Don Springfield only has the best working for him. He runs a tight ship.' John told me that this 'Don Springfield' owned three parlours and Fleure's was the best of them. 'Big round beds that you can get up to all sorts on,' he said with a knowing smirk on his face, 'and mirrors all around, even on the ceiling.'

At the end of the massage, when I asked if there was anything more I could do, he said, 'It was a very nice massage, thank you, I won't bother with anything else at the moment. You see, Francy and I have a special relationship, and you couldn't get up to much on this table anyway.' I suggested that a cushion room might be more comfortable, but he didn't want to know. 'No offence you understand. I only ever go with Francy. I wouldn't have come here today, only my partner, Bob, insisted. Thanks anyway.'

That Francy must be something else, I thought.

When both the men had gone, I asked Mandy about Fleure's. 'I wouldn't work for Don Springfield if his parlours were the only ones left in the whole of New Zealand,' she said. 'He's a cruel, thoughtless, foul-mouthed pig!' She lit a cigarette and sat silently for a moment or two, then said, 'He runs three parlours — Fleure's, The Tokyo and Executive House. He treats his girls like shit, sometimes firing a whole shift in one go. He works the girls till they drop, and because a lot of them are forced to work when they're sick, they often do drop. Clients are admitted into his parlours no matter how drunk they are, and girls are regularly abused by them; but because of the strict rules, they can't complain.' I could not imagine how anyone could be so callous, but Mandy seemed to know what she was talking about and I believed her.

The rest of the day went by quickly, and we did ten clients between us. I felt pretty upset about spending all that time in the room with John listening to him raving on about Fleure's, and not getting any money out of it. Mandy said it was the luck of the draw. They paid for a massage at the door, and if that was all they wanted, it was tough on us. Luckily it didn't happen often. I couldn't help thinking that this is where the rap parlours had it over licensed massage parlours.

We then had four 'dirty phone calls' in a row, all from the same man, and I was unfortunate enough to take them. Mandy noticed me continually hanging up on him and came over. 'Here, let me take the next one,' she said. Sure enough, it rang again. 'The Harem, can I help you?' Mandy pulled a sickly-sweet face at me and went on, 'I'm sorry, sir, this is a dreadful line. Can you please speak up . . . Are you there? . . . Are you there? . . . I'm sorry sir, I still can't hear you, you will have to talk louder . . . Sir, can I ask you to speak a little louder, there is something wrong with the phone!'

She beckoned me over, and put the receiver between us, so I could hear as well. 'HAVE YOU GOT A NICE WET PUSSY?' shouted the man on the other end.

'I'm sorry, sir, I still can't hear you properly.' There was a click and he hung up. 'The words don't have the same impact when they're being shouted loudly,' she said. 'He won't call back now.' And he didn't!

Because Mandy was working a double shift, and the other night girls came in early, I was allowed to leave at six forty-five. Emma was already home and had dinner started. I counted my earnings for the day — one hundred and forty dollars — and stashed it in the mung-bean jar hoping like anything I could find Percy in his motel room the next morning, so I could collect the sixty dollars owing.

We sat down to dinner at around seven forty-five, and Emma said, 'Aunty Kath phoned. She and Uncle Roy are coming to Auckland for a few days, and wanted to know which club you're working at. They want to pop in, have a drink and say hello. I told them I couldn't remember the name of the place. Anyway, she's calling back later . . . Oh! and Mr Clarke phoned, will you please contact him ASAP.'

Kath and Roy were friends from the small Waikato town where I was brought up. They were lovely people, except Kath had a mouth that could have out-shouted a town crier. She wasn't in any way malicious, but she just could not keep a secret, not even if her life depended on it.

The phone rang and it was Kath. 'We're coming up for a few

days and thought we'd like a night out on the town. What's that club you work at like?'

'Oh, it's okay. More for teenagers — you know, Boy George and that kind of music,' I said, trying to put her off.

'Oh that's all right, you know Roy and me, we'll dance to anything.'

'Umm, when are you up here?' I was desperately trying to think of excuses to keep her happy, because if she got wind that anything underhand was going on in my life, my mother and the rest of the township would know within a matter of hours.

'We're booked into the Sheraton Thursday, Friday and Saturday of next week. Roy's at a conference and I'm doing all the wives' days out and such. We have a cocktail party that finishes at seven-thirty on Saturday night, then we're free for the rest of the evening.'

'Kath, I'm so sorry, but Thursday, Friday and Saturday nights are my nights off next week. Look, why don't we go somewhere for dinner instead?'

Kath thought that was a wonderful idea. 'We could go to your club after dinner.'

I thought that was a jolly good idea too, and we said good-bye, promising to be in touch before the weekend.

Emma was in fits of laughter when I hung up. 'Can you imagine what would happen if Aunty Kath found out?'

Yes, I could imagine, and it worried me. If I could only keep up the pretence of working in a club until I got the mortgage up to date, and a little put by! Perhaps then I could buy a salon of my own and there would be no need to tell lies. Up till now, with only one or two exceptions, my job as a prostitute had not been as bad as I'd first thought. The girls I worked with were not 'tarts'. They were normal everyday women you'd pass in the street and not look twice at. Mandy was the exception there. She was always beautifully and expensively dressed. In the street, heads turned as she walked by looking for all the world as though she'd stepped off the front page of *Vogue* magazine. With the exception of Sally, the girls I worked with were well-spoken, articulate and swore very little, which was a pleasant change from the young girls and boys I worked with at the salon. Among young people, bad language was as trendy then as it is now.

Prostitution has been practised since the year dot; yet it is still socially unacceptable, after all this time. I was well aware that if it became widely known to friends and family that I was working as a prostitute I could end up a social outcast, perhaps for the rest of my life. It was one hell of a risk, especially when you had a mother who cared a lot about what the neighbours thought.

Emma and I sat watching television and playing with Minty, our kitten, and after Emma had gone to bed I wrote up my journal.

I thought maybe I'd work nights for a couple of weeks, then ask to go on days. Today was a breeze, not a drunk in sight. The men were either kindly old gentlemen or businessmen, and although John — the 'straight' guy — was not financially productive, he wasn't hard work. I didn't leave his room feeling like the dish rag that most night clients made you feel.

I was up early the following morning, took Emma to work, then came home to do some cleaning. Halfway through I stopped, hauled out an old *Courier* newspaper from a pile of papers we kept in the broom cupboard, and turned to the 'work wanted' column. Today was the last day I was going to do housework. In ten minutes I had two ladies coming for interviews on Thursday.

After the cleaning was finished I got ready for work, then phoned Mr Clarke. 'Has there been any interest in your property yet, Mrs Blake?' he wanted to know.

'No, there hasn't, Mr Clarke, but I've decided not to sell. I have a good job now and I think perhaps I can afford . . .'

'Mrs Blake! With all due respect, you are now two thousand five hundred dollars in arrears. I cannot see how you could possibly repay that sum working as a hairdresser, no matter at what level. If it is not repaid soon we will have no option but to put the property up for mortgagee sale.'

Clarkie's attitude called for some drastic action. 'Mr Clarke, can I come in to see you tomorrow morning about nine?'

'I think that would be a very good idea, Mrs Blake. I'll see you then. Good-bye.' I could tell he was losing patience with me.

On the way to work I parked the car on Parnell Road, and made my way to the motel Percy was staying at. It was a large building, which is now a block of expensive apartments. I found the room and knocked on the door. Percy opened it, and greeted me like a long-lost friend. He asked if I'd like some coffee, but I had to say no because I was due at work. Without hesitation he gave me an envelope with 'Angela' written on it. Percy insisted that I open the envelope and count the money in front of him. He gave me a quick peck on the cheek, and I left.

At work a strange face greeted me. 'Hi, my name's Jaqueline,' said a petite brunette with large hazel eyes. She looked to be in her late thirties and was very thin. 'I'm making some coffee. How do you like yours?' I thanked her and said I'd like it black. 'Mandy's going to be late, she did a double yesterday, and is doing another today. They weren't able to do the cleaning last night, so if you do the showers, I'll do the vacuuming. But we'll have a quick coffee first.' This lady was full on.

Jaqueline was an organiser. She insisted on answering the phone and she would rush to the door whenever a client arrived, running along and almost elbowing us out of the way to be first.

It wasn't until halfway through the shift that Mandy told me Jaqueline had only just started that morning. 'I don't think she's dirty hustling,' said Mandy, though she was quite obviously irritated by Jaqueline. 'I think she's just super keen.'

The day was a steady one. I did four well-paying clients, all clean, considerate men, nice and easy with no problems. But the fifth made up for them all.

An escort was wanted at six o'clock in an office on Vulcan Lane. He was paying cash, and I was told to get the money as soon as I got there. I was to take a taxi, which the client would pay for, and on arrival I was to phone the parlour to tell them all was well. When the business was done I had to call the parlour to say I was on my way back.

I arrived to find the office empty except for my escort, who was so drunk he could barely stand up. His words were so slurred it was difficult to understand him, and I wondered how he had been able to make the escort arrangements to start with.

I called The Harem to find the line engaged. The client demanded I take off all my clothes before he would hand over any money. He was swaying back and forth, his shirt undone to the waist and his tie hanging sideways around his neck. I obliged and, true to his word, he paid up.

Still swaying about, he undressed with difficulty and eventually fell onto the floor, where he removed his socks. We had to lie on the floor, as there was nowhere else. He groped and fumbled, kissing me passionately with a wet, alcohol-tasting mouth. He wanted to give me some oral. I said I didn't do that, but he started to get nasty and belligerent, so I gave in. He slobbered all over me, sticking his sloppy wet tongue in my naval, vagina, ears and mouth. He wanted sex but was unable to get an erection. He said he'd be okay once the condom was on, but it was impossible to get it onto his soft, floppy penis. He was getting nasty again, saying he'd paid top dollar for me and he wanted satisfaction. I started to get frightened, and he must have sensed it.

'Take your money and piss off!' he bellowed at me. I didn't need telling twice and began to get dressed. 'You're a no-good little tart!' He looked a pathetic sight, sitting on the floor naked but for a pair of horn-rimmed glasses. 'My wife's a no-good whore, and you're just like her, a whore!' Suddenly he was crying and mumbling to himself incoherently. I left, not even staying long enough to call a taxi, as I knew there would be one on Queen Street somewhere.

Back at The Harem, I tried to tell them about the man, but nobody was listening. It was shift change-over, and Mandy was more concerned with the way Jaqueline had tried to take over the running of the place. So I went home.

CHAPTER 8

'You're quiet tonight,' said Emma.

I laid my knife and fork down, covered my face with my hands and burst into tears.

'Oh Mum! Don't cry.' She held me to her, patting my back. 'Did something awful happen today?'

That made me worse and I started sobbing uncontrollably. I didn't want to tell her about the drunk man in Vulcan Lane, and how much being called a tart and a whore had hurt me. If I was going to do this job, these names were part and parcel of it, and I was jolly well going to have to get used to it.

'Would you like a glass of wine?' she said. 'That'll cheer you up.'

I nodded, trying hard to stop the tears. 'Angela, stop this silly nonsense or you'll frighten the hell out of Emma,' I said to myself, and after a couple of deep breaths, I was able to sip the wine. 'I'm sorry, darling. PMT, I think. That time of the month and everything. Plus the thought of the meeting with old Clarkie tomorrow morning — he has that effect on people.' Emma laughed, and I felt much better.

After Emma went to bed, I took the mung-bean jar from the pantry, pulled out the large wad of money and counted it. Despite all I'd spent over the last ten days, eleven hundred and forty dollars remained. I replaced one hundred and forty in the jar, and put the rest into an envelope, sealed it and hid it in my handbag.

I sat in Mr Clarke's office the next morning, waiting for him to say something. He did his usual paper shuffling, and eventually, peering over his glasses, he said, 'Mrs Blake, I know this is a very difficult time for you, but you must be sensible about this property of yours. Your income cannot support your outgoings, and I strongly advise . . .'

A thousand dollars in fifties, twenties, tens and fives came snaking its way across his desk and stopped just before the first fifty fell into his lap.

'Mrs Blake! What is this?'

'It's money, Mr Clarke, a thousand dollars of it. There was a lot more, but I spent it on clothes and food. You can count it if you like.'

Mr Clarke looked at the money through his glasses, then at me over the top of them. 'Where did you get this money, Mrs Blake?'

'I'm working in a massage parlour, Mr Clarke. It's taken ten days to save a thousand dollars, so there is now no reason to sell my property. I should have the mortgage arrears paid off by the end of the month and a large proportion of the principal in one year.'

Mr Clarke leant back in his huge leather chair and linked his hands behind his head. 'Would you like a cup of coffee, Mrs Blake?'

'Yes please, Mr Clarke.'

He picked up the phone and ordered the coffee. 'So, in this . . . er . . . massage parlour you . . .?' He grimaced and made a rolling motion with the forefinger of his right hand.

'Yes Mr Clarke, I do.'

'And you find it . . . all right, do you? Not upsetting in any way?'

'Most of the time I enjoy the job very much, Mr Clarke. Of course there are moments that are not so enjoyable, but on the whole . . . Our clients are professional gentlemen like yourself.' I could see he was embarrassed, but was saved from comment by the arrival of the coffee. As quick as a whizz he scooped the money up off the table, folded it and secured it with a rubber band from a drawer in his desk.

When his secretary had poured the coffee and gone, Mr Clarke said, 'This has come as a surprise to me, Mrs Blake. But I think you have great courage and I admire your strength. Many people in the same circumstances as yourself would have gone to pieces. Forcing a mortgagee sale is a part of my job that I detest, but you must understand that I have a responsibility to my investors. Which brings me to some advice you may or may not wish to take.'

'I would be pleased with any advice you have to offer,' I said in all sincerity.

He leant forward, sorted through the file and came up with a document. 'Your mortgage has to be refinanced on the third of

December this year. I would suggest you try for a bank loan. It would be at a far lower interest rate than it is at the moment. And any spare money you have, invest it with me at a higher rate. You could do rather well out of it at the end of the day.' He was smiling at me, not the squeezed, painful smile I knew so well, but a broad full smile which made him look quite attractive.

'Thank you, Mr Clarke,' I said, getting ready to leave. 'I'll keep that in mind.'

Back at home, I put the jug on for a cup of tea and the phone rang. 'Hello . . . Angie?' It was Trish. 'Look, something's happened this morning that you should know about.' She sounded serious.

'What's wrong?' I asked, and the old 'going to the dentist' feeling hit my stomach.

'That escort you did last night . . . John, was it? Anyway, he phoned the parlour a few minutes ago.' She didn't say anything for a moment or two.

'Trish, what's going on?' I said.

'Angie, he said that you've given him herpes! We know the man's a nutter, but it might be as well to have a check before work tomorrow.'

I couldn't believe it. 'What do you mean, I've given him herpes? Trish, the man was a belligerent drunk, and he would have raped me if he could have. I tried to tell Mandy all about it, but she was too busy to listen. And, I do not have herpes.'

'Angie, don't panic! The sex industry is full of nutters. But I do think you should go to the STD clinic for a check-up . . .'

'Trish, I am telling you that I do not have, nor have I ever had, herpes. Got that?' I shouted at her.

'Perhaps not,' she shouted back at me, 'but he might have, and if he's given it to you, it's incurable! Now, have you got a pen handy?' She gave me the number of a private clinic on Konini Road in Parnell. 'Ask to see Mike Wallace, you can tell him anything, he specialises in STD cases and does the testing for most of the working ladies in Auckland. It costs about twelve dollars. Would you like me to come with you? I'm at home at the moment, but I could be at your place in twenty minutes.'

I thanked her very much, but declined her offer.

*

The clinic said they couldn't see me until Friday, but when I explained that I needed to see Dr Wallace that day, the receptionist put me on hold for a while, then asked if I could be there in fifteen minutes. On arrival, I checked in at the desk, and was shown into the waiting room. There were tea- and coffee-making facilities, so I made a cup of coffee and sat down to wait. I was halfway through drinking it when a nurse asked me to go through to the surgery. 'Bring your coffee with you,' she said.

A very trendy young man with glasses shook my hand. 'Hi, Angela. I'm Mike Wallace. Please sit down. How can I help you?'

This being my first-ever experience in an STD clinic, it did not come easily to start with, but after a lot of stuttering and stammering I was able to tell him about the drunk escort accusing me of giving him herpes. He asked if the man had any sores around his mouth, or on his genitals. I said there weren't any noticeable. He asked me to remove my knickers and hop up on the examination table, and would I like him to give me a routine check while I was there. I said yes. First he ran the hot tap and warmed a contraption that looked like two metal shoe-horns hinged together. Then he slid this contraption into my vagina and cranked it open. He and his nurse chatted away to me right through the examination, and gave me a quick talk on the use of condoms. He took two swabs, the first of which went into a tube; the second was smeared onto a glass slide, the type that fitted under a microscope.

'It all looks very healthy in there,' he said, peering in between my legs with a long skinny torch thing. He removed the shoe-horns and said, 'You can get dressed now.' I put my knickers back on and sat down by his desk. 'Now, just a swab from your throat. Open wide.' He pushed my tongue down with a wooden spatula and quickly wiped the back of my throat with a swab. 'And a little sample of blood.' He bound my upper arm with a thick round tie, and told me to open and close my fist. I felt a sharp prick and watched an enormous syringe fill with blood. 'There, that's all there is to it. Now, about this genital herpes, Angela, you certainly show no signs of it at the moment, and if you've had no symptoms in the past the likelihood of having it at all is minimal. Even if you did have it and were covered in sores, there is no way that anyone you had been in contact with would come up with any symptoms in such a short space of time. I should forget about it. Should anything untoward show up in the test results, we will let you know.'

I thanked him kindly, paid my bill and made an appointment for nine o'clock Friday in two weeks' time. I left the Konini Clinic a lot happier.

I'd always had a fear and abhorrence of sexually transmitted diseases — or venereal disease, as it used to be called. Catching one was almost as bad as having a baby out of wedlock. It proved beyond all doubt you'd been up to no good. But at the clinic Dr Mike and co. talked about gonorrhoea and syphilis as though they were no worse than the common cold, and genital warts as though they were an everyday occurrence, and I suppose at the clinic they were.

Thursday morning at ten-fifteen, Mrs Franklin arrived to be interviewed for a position as our housekeeper. She was in her sixties, with dyed black hair and make-up which looked as though it had been applied with a trowel. She sat bolt upright at the dining-room table, clutching her handbag as though someone were about to steal it. 'The bus stop is too far away!' she said, 'and I don't like all those stairs. Now, I don't do ovens, fridges, ironing or scrubbing floors. Just vacuuming and dusting, and I can only come on Monday mornings.' I could tell that Mrs Franklin and I would not see eye to eye, and told her that cleaning fridges and ovens was definitely an important part of the job and I was sorry to have wasted her time. At eleven o'clock Sheryl arrived, and yes, she did fridges, ovens, scrubbing floors and anything else I wanted her to do. She could come Monday and Friday mornings for three hours. She was neat, bright and cheery. I hired her on the spot. Yippee! No more cleaning!

When I got to work on Thursday night my very first job was an escort! It was with much trepidation that I walked into the lobby of the Sheraton Hotel in Symonds Street. In the elevator on the way up to the sixth floor, I wondered who waited for me in room 634 and whether he would be drunk? I found the room easily. There was a room-service tray with the remains of a steak meal outside the door. I knocked and waited. The door was opened by a short fat man of about forty.

'Hello, my name's Angie,' I said.

'Hello Angie, I'm Peter. Come on in. Would you like a drink?' I noticed he had a Scotch on the rocks sitting on the table by the bed, but he was nowhere near drunk. I said a glass of wine would go down nicely, and he poured me one from a small bottle out of the mini-bar and handed it to me. 'Cheers!' he said and took a gulp of his Scotch. He held his glass up and said, 'Dutch courage. I haven't done this before and I'm a bit nervous. What do we do now?'

'Well, let's get the money sorted out, then we can relax,' I said. He paid me in cash. 'How about we start by giving you a nice massage?' I spread a towel on the bed and asked him to lie down on his stomach. He was so nervous that his bottom was trembling. He had paid for the works, so when he had turned over and his front was finished, I pulled the condom from its packet. I just about had it on when he ejaculated into it. He was so embarrassed that I felt embarrassed as well. It was an awkward situation. I wasn't sure what to do next, and there was still half an hour to go. 'Look, I'll massage you again, and we'll have another go, okay?' I suggested, and he agreed.

Because of the time factor, I kept it short but as sensuous as possible, and it wasn't long before his penis was rock hard once again. I applied the condom carefully, as I didn't want a repeat of last time, and I didn't want him asking for his money back. As I slid my tongue up and down the shaft of his penis, he moaned with pleasure.

'Let me do the same to you,' he said, and we swapped places. After the experience I'd had with 'Drunk John' on Tuesday, I wasn't too keen. Peter gently caressed my clitoris with his tongue, and although I found it pleasant enough, it didn't do a thing for me sexually. But when I felt his penis move into my vagina, something stirred within. He kissed my breasts, my neck, my lips. I lifted my legs and wrapped them around his body. He started thrusting deeply into me and I could feel every nerve in my body tingle. Something inside me started to bubble, I was going to explode! I was right on the verge of a beautiful orgasm, when he stopped, got up off the bed and said, 'Oh! That was excellent, thank you.' I had to remind myself that 'he who pays the piper calls the tune', because I had an almost irresistible urge to pull him back on the bed and make him finish what he'd started. Instead I smiled weakly, feeling unfulfilled, let down and irritable. In the taxi on the way back to work I thought how funny it was that a short, fat, unattractive man could make me feel like that.

I did two more escorts that night, and quite enjoyed them. I made a mental note to bring a coat to wear over my work clothes. It looked a bit suspicious, a single lady walking through the foyer of a big hotel wearing a cocktail dress at one or two in the morning.

The days started to fly by. Money wasn't a problem any more, and we were enjoying life once again. I often hear people —usually do-gooders, hippies and born-again Christians — spouting the old cliché 'money isn't everything'. But when you don't have enough to feed your children, money *is* everything. Money releases the knot in your stomach, the sleepless nights and all the side effects that worry inflicts. To be able to live happily without money, one has to be without any responsibilities whatsoever. Sure, I could have sold the apartment, moved to south Auckland and worked in a nice little salon earning just enough to keep the mortgage paid and bread in our mouths. But it certainly would not have paid for Emma's school camps, extra tuition, or any of the other hundred-and-one things kids need for their complete education, without having to rely on charity and government handouts.

It took about a month to clear all the debts. Only a few hundred dollars remained owing on the car. I got to the stage where I was stashing money all over the apartment, and it was a real worry that someone would break in and rob us. So I took Clarkie's advice and started to invest. At least it was being kept somewhere other than in the house.

My only problem was the old question that people always ask when you are introduced to them — 'What do you do for a living?' I don't know why the general public are so obsessed with what people do.

'I work in a nightclub,' I'd say.

'Oh! Where?' they would ask.

'In the city,' I'd reply, and nine times out of ten they'd want to know which club it was so they could pop in for a drink one evening to see me.

Emma solved the problem. 'You should say you do something boring. Tracy's mum cleans offices and she works at night. Nobody would want to see you cleaning an office would they?' So, suddenly I lost my job as a barmaid and started a new career in office cleaning.

My mother was not pleased. 'There! What did I tell you? I knew that club job wouldn't last. All that money and training to do hairdressing, and you end up cleaning offices. It's a wicked waste.'

I told my neighbour Carol the truth, because she would notice I was going to a cleaning job in a cocktail dress and would want to know why. Also, she kept an eye on Emma for me while I worked, so I felt she had a right to know. And she was absolutely trustworthy. Her reaction was as I expected. 'Why not? I can't see there's any difference between me selling my brain in an accountant' s office, to you selling your body in a massage parlour, can you?'

I got in to work one Saturday night, about six weeks after starting at The Harem, and Sally greeted me at the door. 'Can you lend me sixty dollars before ten o'clock this evening, if I haven't done a job by then? I'll pay you back as soon as I've got the money.' I said yes. Within an hour I had it, and I gave it to her. 'Oh thanks,' she said. 'I owe it to somebody and he's coming to pick it up at ten.'

About half an hour later Mandy warned me that if Sally asked for a loan, to say no, because she wanted it to pay for drugs. I did not tell her it was too late.

At eight-thirty, R+on booked in with me. We went through to the room where I massaged him and we talked about the property boom. Sex with Ron was as boring as dry bread; always the same routine, which finished with him humping away on top of me. This night nothing had changed. There I was, lying on the table, legs in the air, with Ron pounding away in between them. I was just wishing he would hurry up and finish, when suddenly I heard the door rattle. I opened my eyes and there stood a man in a suit waving a police ID at me.

'You! Get off, get dressed and get out. You!' He pointed at me. 'Put a towel around you, get your handbag and go to the office.'

I got down off the table and stood there unable to move a muscle, seeing visions of the *Truth* headlines — 'Waikato Woman Arrested in Massage Parlour'. I was petrified!

In the office, the man said he was Detective Sergeant Mark Layton. He searched my handbag, and found my defensive driver's licence. 'Been in trouble with our transport boys, eh?' I told him my driving record was clean, and that I did the defensive driving course voluntarily. He said that although I had been caught red-handed indulging in sexual activities in a licensed massage parlour, and it was against the law, he was not going to charge me. 'You will no longer be able to work in this establishment, though. I shall inform the owner,' he said.

Of course Mel, who was also in a lot of trouble, being the licence holder, was nowhere to be found. By this time I was shaking like a leaf and crying so hard that I could not make myself understood. 'Look,' he said, 'if you must do this kind of work, try one of Don Springfield's parlours. At least they're run properly.'

Detective Sergeant Layton left and I got dressed and went into the bar, where Mandy was waiting for me.

'Where's Sally?' I asked.

'She took off when the vice arrived. She managed to flash the lights before she went. Didn't they work?'

'I had my eyes closed,' I said. 'I didn't see anything.'

Mandy took a deep draw on her cigarette and said thoughtfully, 'It was odd there was only one detective. The vice usually arrive in twos, and they are not allowed to search your bag unless they charge you. There's something very fishy going on here.' She suggested I stay and wait for Mel to come back.

Mel came in about two hours later, and — surprise, surprise — he walked in the door with Karen on his arm, who was drunk out of her brain. Mandy put her hands over her eyes. 'Oh no!' she said. 'Karen's been drinking.'

Karen was all over Mel like a rash. She could hardly stand up, and the language she was using would have made Sally blush. She staggered to the bar and tried to pour a drink.

'Don't you think you've had enough, love,' said a very concerned Mandy.

'Oh, mind your own fucking business you mother-fucking cunt!'

drawled Karen loudly. A client came to the door, and Mel, carrying Karen's drink, tried to lead her out the back to his room.

'The vice have been!' said Mandy, so loudly that her words echoed through the building and the man at the door turned on his heels and left.

That stopped Mel in his tracks. 'What they wan'?' he asked.

'You, for a start. You're supposed to be here, Mel, all the time. Angie's been busted, and Sally's gone.'

Karen staggered sideways and fell to her knees, and Mel, who was also quite drunk, helped her up and led her to his room out the back. 'I talk to you soon,' he mumbled.

'I thought Karen didn't drink. She gave me a hell of a lecture about drinking when I first started,' I said.

'She's an alcoholic, but she hasn't had a drink for years. I bet this is Mel's fault!' I could tell Mandy was angry.

'Mandy, I'm going home. Mel is too drunk to think straight tonight, so I'll call in the morning.' I was too upset to work any more that night anyway.

Mandy agreed. I left The Harem, and she closed the place up for the night.

At home, I found Emma in bed and sleeping soundly. I sat in the lounge with the television on, but I couldn't concentrate on the programme, and after Kiwi and his cat closed the station down, I went to bed and cried myself to sleep.

CHAPTER 9

Mel fired me the next morning. He said Detective Sergeant Layton had instructed him to do so, and he was sorry. I was devastated. Not having been fired from a job before, it was like a blot on my copy book, and the thought of having to go for an interview in another parlour filled me with dread.

Later in the day I telephoned Mandy. She once again advised me strongly not to work for Don Springfield, this time telling me he had his fingers in all sorts of unsavoury little pies and that rumour had it that any girl who worked for him would be sure to come to a very sticky end. But she'd heard that Total Escape, just off Queen Street, were looking for staff. 'My friend Sue works there. She does quite well, I think,' she said.

I telephoned Total Escape and made an appointment to see a man called Archie at two o'clock that afternoon.

I found the parlour tucked away on the first floor of a shabby little building in Durham Lane. Archie, the owner, looked to be in his middle fifties, a lovely smiling man who resembled the actor Ernest Borgnine. The parlour was dingy to the max — yellow nicotine-stained walls throughout, and high ceilings festooned with black cobwebs. There was a lounge at the top of the stairs. It had an old suite that looked as though it had seen generations of better days, its stuffing and springs bulging from the faded autumn-toned fabric. An ancient black and white television flickered from a dark corner, and at the far end, a kind of breakfast bar divided off a small space that contained a fridge, sink bench and tea-making facilities. On the bar stood the telephone and appointment book. The parlour was lit with red light bulbs set in dusty tiffany shades, and the whole place had a sleazy atmosphere about it. Two of the working rooms were really tiny with just enough space for a massage table and a walkway around it. The walls were nothing more than flimsy dividers, and you could hear a pin drop in the next cubicle. The third room was a fraction bigger and on the other side of the narrow passage, so the noise problem wasn't as bad. This room had a proper door rather than the thin sliders on the others. Archie said his top lady, Sue, always used that room, and when she wasn't at work the first girl to arrive in on shift could use it. Next to this was an alcove with a row of lockers set in the wall. On a shelf nearby, a pile of black draw-string bags were neatly laid. Archie told me the men would put their valuables in a bag and secure them in one of the lockers. The showers and sauna were situated down a steep flight of narrow stairs. Everything was much cleaner down there, and although the showers were a little mildewed in some places, they were basically clean and fresh smelling.

Most of the parlour's business was providing escorts, which was just as well when you took the state of the place into account. All the girls had to do a mixture of days and nights, and took it in turns to answer the phones and book clients in when Archie wasn't there, which didn't happen very often. He paid a small weekly wage, from which PAYE was deducted. He told me the house supplied everything but condoms.

The place was awful, but Archie was so nice I took the job, and was to start the following morning at eleven o'clock. I arrived at ten-fifty. The place was open, and I went upstairs to find Archie making some coffee.

'Sue is here today, so you will have to use one of the small rooms,' he said.

I chose the far one. At Total Escape, instead of using which-ever room the client requested, you chose one and used it for the whole shift.

About eleven o'clock, Nicky arrived. She was a pretty girl with the most beautiful thick blonde hair, which came almost to her waist. She wore it tied back with a black velvet ribbon. Her face was cute, with a pert little nose and high cheekbones lightly scattered with freckles. She was tall, with a generous bosom and long, slender legs. Archie introduced us and asked her to 'have a little chat' with me. She took me to the room I'd chosen to work in.

'The prices are fifty-five for sex and oral, fifty for sex, forty for oral and twenty-five for hand. Don't let the bastards kiss or maul you, get your money first. If you do anal, charge for it! Rubbers go down the pan. And don't put up with any shit! Got that?' I nodded, and she turned on her heels, went back into the lounge and sat down with her coffee. 'Yours is by the phone,' she said.

Archie was kept busy with phone calls about escorts and charges. Sue arrived in at midday to a couple of bookings. Nicky and I sat doing nothing, until a man came up the stairs at three o'clock. He looked to be the type of man I'd always imagined frequented massage parlours. He was thin, weedy and in his sixties. His clothes looked as though they'd been shoplifted from the Salvation Army op shop.

'This is Sid,' said Nicky behind her hand. 'He's a cheap bastard and you have to watch him. Make sure you count your money. He's been known to short-change some of the girls five or ten dollars.'

Archie came over and asked me to take Sid through to my room. 'Don't forget his valuables,' he whispered.

When we got to the room, I asked Sid to lock his valuables away, popped his wallet and watch into a bag, put it in a locker secured with a small padlock supplied by the house, and went back to the room with the key. A smell of stale perspiration wafted across the small room as he removed his clothes. He threw them on the floor, wrapped a towel around his waist and wandered down the stairs to the shower. I opened the sliding door, hoping for some fresh air to get rid of the body odour that was starting to make me feel sick, but only the smell of nicotine took its place.

Sid ambled back into the room and lay on the table. 'You've got nice tits,' he said, trying to slide his hand between my legs, 'let me see your fanny.' He grinned, showing a row of rotten teeth.

'When I've finished the massage,' I said.

He turned over onto his back. 'Come here and give me a kiss.'

I really did not want to give Sid a kiss. I would rather have kissed a camel, I think. From nowhere, his arm wrapped around my neck and was pulling my face down to his.

'I'm sorry, I don't kiss,' I said, pulling away from him.

'Aw! Trying to play hard to get, eh?'

'Look, Sid, do you want a massage or not?' I was starting to get angry.

80

He smacked my bottom. 'Just massage around here.' He pointed to his scrotal area.

'Sid, is there anything else I can do for you?' I figured he hadn't come in for a massage at all.

'Don't you try to cut me short of my time, I've paid for an hour. You girls are all the same, only after the money.' Now he was getting angry.

I looked at my watch. We'd only been in the room for fifteen minutes. 'Look, Sid, we have plenty of time. Now, why don't you let me give you a good massage, then we can play.'

'Okay,' he said. 'Massage me down there.' He was pointing at his penis again.

'Right, that will cost you twenty-five dollars. If you will get it from the locker now, we can get started.' I was getting nowhere, that was obvious.

He got down from the table and wrapped his towel around his waist. 'You're all the same, just a pack of money-hungry bitches.' He padded out of the room and was soon back, handing me a thin wad of money. 'Hand relief,' he ordered.

I remembered Nicky's advice and counted it. 'Sid, it's ten dollars short.' He didn't argue, just padded back out to the lockers and came back, handing me two five-dollar bills. 'And I want a good one,' he said, clambering on to the table, 'none of this "get it over with quickly" stuff. You get up here with me!'

'There isn't room for two of us, Sid.' I liberally coated my hands with oil and started to stroke his penis.

'You could lie on top of me and do that with your fanny,' he suggested.

'You've only paid for hand relief.' I was trying very hard not to sound irritable.

'Give it a little lick.' He was leering at me like something out of a horror movie. I ignored the request and went on stroking his penis, which was starting to show some interest. 'Go on, give it a tickle with that pretty pink tongue.' I ignored that one too. It was really amazing how big Sid's penis grew. It was huge, very long, and I could hardly get my hand around it. You wouldn't imagine that such a weedy little man would have one so big. I couldn't help glancing at his feet. Not overly large, I thought!

'Let me shove it in your fanny, just once.' Sid was trying to pull me onto the table. I fended him off with one hand, while the other was aching with the constant movement up and down his humungous penis.

'Please let it be over soon,' I said to myself.

'Play with my balls, give 'em a nice squeeze.' The sound of his nasal voice was getting on my nerves. I changed hands to give the aching one a rest.

'Come up here and sit on my face, and rub yer tits on me cock.' Again he tried to haul me onto the table.

'Will you shut up and leave me alone!' I all but shouted at him. There and then, Sid's penis did a little shudder, and a stream of semen spurted from the end, and lay in a pool on his stomach. I mopped it up with some tissues and said nothing. Sid, on the other hand, was as happy as Larry.

'That was all right, wasn't it?' he said, pinching my left nipple. I smacked his hand away, gave him a towel and told him to have a shower. 'Oh no, I'll have one at home,' he said, grinning.

Sid got dressed and went, and I was pleased to see the back of him. I went downstairs, where I had a long shower and breathed in some fresh air.

Back in the lounge, I sat talking to Sue. She was a quiet girl and not overly attractive, but there was something about her manner that made her nice to be with. She had a softness in her voice, and I could well imagine she was popular with the men. She told me that Nicky had gone to an escort at the South Pacific Hotel in Customs Street.

'The girls call the place Colditz Castle, because the security's so tough. There is one guard they call Hawk-eye. He can spot a working girl before her taxi has stopped outside, so half the time they don't even get through the front doors.' She also told me that the Sheraton had a back door, and up till midnight it was easy to get to the elevators without being noticed. I wish I'd known that at The Harem.

Sue had also worked with Mandy at Hostess, but preferred to be at Total Escape because it was out of the way, and as she lived in fear of being found out, it suited her. She was aware that more money was to be made at some of the upmarket parlours, but she had enough regulars to keep her comfortably off. We talked at some length about the job in general, and I asked her about anal sex, as Nicky had mentioned it earlier.

'I have no problem about girls doing anal,' she said. 'I don't do it because it's painful, but I believe if someone can do it without the pain and charges well for it, why not?' I agreed with her, but decided it was not for me, no matter how much a man was prepared to pay.

I asked her what she thought of Don Springfield's parlours. 'Oh, you hear these rumours about him, but I've known girls to stay with him for years. He's a hard man all right, but fair if you stick by his rules.'

Just before five, Nicky returned from the South Pacific Hotel. 'How did it go?' asked Sue.

'Oh, I got in all right. It's easier in the day because you're wearing street clothes, and Hawk-eye's only there at night.'

Nicky paid Archie the money she'd brought back with her, then strolled over to us and emptied out the contents of her large bag. Bottles of wine, cans of beer and soft drinks, plus tiny bottles of spirits, rolled out all over the floor. 'Help yourselves,' she said.

'If Archie knows you've stripped the mini-bar of a client's hotel room, you will be fired on the spot!' said Sue.

'They expect it,' replied Nicky, surprised that anyone would think it wrong. 'Anyway, they are hardly going to complain, are they?'

'It's thieving, and it will give the parlour a bad name.' Sue's argument was cut short when a client of hers arrived at the top of the stairs.

'Did you really steal these?' I asked, not sure if I believed it.

'Oh yes,' said Nicky, putting them back in her bag. 'Want some?' I shook my head. 'Look, it's that easy. After you've fucked him, you make sure you have your shower first. Then, when he goes in for his shower, you empty everything in the fridge into your bag. But never touch the crisps and things on display, that's a dead give-away. I always do it, it's like "perks".' I was amazed at how open she was about it all, and how she couldn't understand why we were so shocked.

'I learned to do it in Sydney when I was working in the Cross. Some of the girls I knew there emptied the guys' wallets as well. Do you think a man would go to the cops and say, "Please, Constable, I hired a prostitute and she pinched the contents of my mini-bar"? No, it would cause him more trouble than it was worth, and anyway, they expect it.'

The time dragged on until it was time to go home at six-thirty, and I left Total Escape with only twenty-five dollars in my purse.

My next shift was the following evening and things were a little busier. I did three clients, all of which were escorts. But although I enjoyed doing them, I felt it was a waste of time travelling to them, especially out to the airport hotels. By the time the booking was made and the taxi arrived, then twenty minutes to half an hour to get there, an hour in the hotel and twenty minutes to half an hour back, it took a good two hours. At the end of it we had eighty dollars for two hours' work, definitely not as profitable as 'in-house' work in a busy parlour. However, I was quite satisfied with the two hundred and forty dollars I arrived home with.

The next day and night I had off, and I started work on the day following. Once again I sat around most of the time doing nothing. Just before five, another grubby little old man booked in with me. He only had twenty dollars and wanted everything for it. I said no, so he had his shower and left. When I went to have my shower, I noticed what looked like semen running down the wall, just below the shower hose. I guess he must have done it himself. This day I arrived home with no money at all.

The moment I arrived at work the next evening, Archie called me into his office.

'One of our top clients wants a dinner escort for this evening,' he said. 'He's a businessman from Wellington and comes to Auckland regularly. He will be here to pick you up at seven-thirty.'

I looked down at my shiny red cocktail dress. 'Archie, I cannot go out to dinner in a cocktail dress. The poor guy will be a laughing stock.'

'You look beautiful, he'll love you. Don't worry about it. They tell me he pays well.'

'You wear a dinner dress to dinner, and a cocktail dress to a cocktail party. I wouldn't feel comfortable sitting down to dinner in this. Can't you send one of the other girls?'

But Archie wouldn't hear of it, and at seven-thirty on the dot Dennis arrived, impeccably dressed in a beautifully cut business suit. He paid the house fee with a gold Amex card, and off we went to the New Orient restaurant in Elliott Street.

Dennis ordered pre-dinner drinks, a gin sling for me and a Scotch on the rocks for him. I apologised for my appearance. 'Think nothing of it,' he said. 'The last girl I got from Archie's establishment wore stretchy tight leopardskin trousers with a matching top that nearly wasn't there, and she had the most appalling table manners imaginable. Archie's quite proud of you. Said you were a lady.'

I wondered why an upmarket businessman like Dennis would bother hiring girls from a downmarket place like Total Escape. We had a wonderful dinner, during which Dennis told me he was in property development and, like the rest of New Zealand before the '87 crash, was living life to the fullest. After dinner, we went back to his hotel room in the Sheraton, where we drank champagne.

Because of all the whisky, wine and liqueurs at dinner, then half a bottle of Moët, the extras were a lot of hard work for me. For, although Dennis had all the desires and his penis was ready for action, he could not achieve a satisfactory conclusion. I had to fake about four orgasms before Dennis gave it up as a bad job. There was no blaming, whinging or moaning on his part. He quite happily paid me a huge amount of money and gave me a bottle of extremely expensive French perfume. He asked if he could see me next time he was in Auckland. 'Why not,' I said.

It had been a slow evening back at work, and Archie had gone home. The girls were all sitting around talking. Nicky was telling them of an experience she'd had on a recent escort. It was to a car salesyard on Great North Road. Two girls were ordered, and she'd gone with Candy — a new girl who said she was nineteen, but Nicky thought she was no more than seventeen.

'She knows nothing. She's as green as. Anyway, we get there and seven men are waiting for us. We had to use the floor of a back office. Candy cracked up after her first, and left me to deal with six of them in one hour. It was hard going, I can tell you. One guy just couldn't get his rocks off, no matter what I did or said. I think

Candy would have been okay if we'd had an office each, but we had to do it on each side of the desk. I got four hundred and a gold pen out of it. That kid's far too young to be working. It'll mess her up for the rest of her life.'

'Is she on junk?' asked Cathy.

'If she isn't now she will be soon, you can bet your life on that. Her father's been screwing her for years, and she left home because of it. Sad, eh? Oh, Ange, by the way, a guy called Ron came up to see you. Said he was a regular of yours from The Harem. Anyway, he's coming back another time.'

Ron didn't come back; he must have taken one look at the place and run.

As I enjoyed going out as an escort, I became good at them very quickly. Some hotels were easy to enter, others, like the South Pacific, were not. The secret was to look as though you had every right to be there, which is not easy in the early hours of the morning. I always wore a full-length, businesslike coat over my dress, and low-heeled sensible-looking shoes. I carried my stilettos in a brief-case, and once in the elevator I would change my shoes and, if there was time, bundle the coat into the briefcase. Not once was I stopped by security.

On one occasion, while entering the Airport Travelodge, I was challenged by the receptionist. The hotel was just new, and I was not familiar with its layout. Unlike your average Sheraton, where room 635 is room 35 on the sixth floor, the Airport Travelodge had a different layout and the room numbers were confusing. On this occasion I was lost, and it was twenty-past-one in the morning. The only thing for it was to ask at Reception.

'What do you want with Mr So and So?' the receptionist wanted to know.

I held up my briefcase for her to see. 'I have some very important legal documents that must be signed by Mr So and So before my employer, Mr Thingamybob, can leave the country. I have been working on them all evening, and he is waiting for them now at the airport. Mr So and So is expecting me.' I was so convincing the receptionist actually called someone to show me the way!

The men we escorted and the men we massaged at Total Escape

were like chalk and cheese. One minute you could be fighting off a dirty old man like Sid, and the next minute drinking champagne with a millionaire in the penthouse suite of the Hyatt.

The day shifts were a waste of time. I expect that is why we were given no choice but to do them. The night shifts, on the other hand, could be quite lucrative. But as we only ever got two nights a week, the money worked out the same as doing four shifts at a place like The Harem. I couldn't see myself working very long at Total Escape. I liked Archie because he didn't hit on us for sex, he was always there, and he was pleasant, but the place was a mess, and frequently men would come to book in, take one look at it and make some excuse to leave. The only 'in-house' clients we did were grotty old ones like Sid, who only came into the place because it was cheap. And this in turn made us cheap!

Total Escape also encouraged another sort of ratbag — the rip-off merchant. I got ripped off more often at that place than anywhere else. They seemed to come from far and wide, sometimes passing five-dollar notes for fifties (under the low red lights you could not tell the difference), or writing a cheque with full ID, then cancelling it the next day. These guys knew damned well that their cheques were more likely to be accepted in a parlour like Total Escape, because it was not busy and the girls were desperate enough to take a chance. I figured it was worth it for a while, but when I had three cheques in two weeks cancelled, I stopped accepting them.

CHAPTER 10

There was no dress code at Total Escape. Anything went, and I wondered how the girls were able to get into any of the hotels with what they were wearing. Spandex trousers were popular, even with some of the larger girls, and I could see why Hawk-eye at the South Pacific Hotel was thought to be good at his job. The hotel was not called Colditz Castle at The Harem, because the girls didn't have any difficulty getting in. But Cathy at Total Escape had a good size-fourteen bottom and large thighs topped with a thirty-eight double-D bosom, and wore shiny purple spandex trousers and a low-slung halter-necked top, so when she went teetering into the lobby on high stilettos with a face that looked as though it was about to dance *Swan Lake*, she told the world she was up to no good without even opening her mouth. She would then complain bitterly that Hawk-eye was a bastard. I single out Cathy, but most of the girls were the same, though perhaps not so large!

Some of the stories the girls told were enough to frighten the life from an SAS agent. I think Nicky's were the most colourful. She had once been sent to a hotel where her escort made her do everything at gunpoint. She wasn't sure if it was a real pistol or not, but thought it might be because her escort said he was just out of prison, and he looked as though he was. She was more pissed off because he didn't pay her. On another occasion, she had to leave a hotel without any clothes on and, wearing only a towel, she ran out the back entrance to find a cab.

The most awful story of all, and it had happened to most of the girls at some time or other, was arriving in a room to find between ten and fourteen drunk men waiting, and not being able to leave until each one had been satisfied. Knowing the problems drunk men have with sex, and how nasty and belligerent they can get because of it, I felt sickened at the thought of having to cope with ten or fourteen. No matter how careful the parlour was, there was no way to avoid this. The girl would arrive in a hotel room with one man to take care of. She would be paid in advance and would phone the parlour to say all was well. Then suddenly the guy would have visitors and it was all on. The girls treated this as an occupational hazard.

Early in March, there was a mass escape from Mount Eden Prison. The newspapers and television were full of it. All the girls were extremely pleased.

'It keeps the "pigs" busy,' said Nicky. 'While those guys are running loose, every pig available will be on the case. We won't be having any visits from the vice for a while.'

A day or so after the escape, a man came to the top of the stairs to organise an escort. Archie said this man was a friend of his who was in advertising. The man said the escort was for his friend in a private house out at Titirangi. It was my turn for a job, and I made ready to leave. The man introduced himself as Bob and told me I was a surprise for his friend, who was from the South Island.

We went down to his car. I sat in the back seat, and Bob's girlfriend sat in the front. Bob said that he didn't know the actual address of his friend, but he knew how to get there. Once we got to Titirangi, Bob seemed to get terribly lost. We went around in circles for what seemed like an age, and after a while my gut feeling told me all was not well. Bob and his girlfriend didn't appear to be at all worried at not knowing where they were, in fact they seemed to be going around in circles on purpose. We eventually stopped outside a derelict house which sat back from the road on a rise.

'This is it,' said Bob, and as we approached the front door with its broken panes of glass, my uneasiness changed to fear. The door was opened by a man in his late twenties. He had a beauty spot type of tattoo on his right cheekbone. He was quite obviously stoned, as he grinned more than a straight person might and his eyes were marijuana red. 'Oh God,' I thought, 'he's one of the escaped convicts from Mount Eden Prison.' I figured my best course of action was to play the dumb blonde, notice nothing, giggle a lot and get on with what needed doing.

Bob suggested a drink first. He had brought some in from the car with him. I sat on an old couch next to my client. They offered me a joint, which I refused, but I did accept a rum and coke. As time went on, the three of them got quite stoned, and started talking about guns and bank robberies. I refused another drink, because I felt that I needed my wits about me. Before long Bob suggested the client and I go to the bedroom. There were no curtains or blinds over the window, and an unmade double bed standing on bare boards took up most of the room. In a corner on the floor was a pile of blue denim clothes, which to me was more proof that this man was an escaped convict. With the lights out, I disrobed and got down to business. Condom on, into the missionary position, wham, bam, and it was all over. I got dressed, not daring to ask for a shower, and went back into the lounge, where Bob gave me eighty dollars in crisp new twenty-dollar bills; he had paid Archie before picking me up. I thanked him and asked to use the phone to call a taxi.

Bob stood deliberately between me and the phone. 'It isn't working,' he said.

It was working perfectly earlier, because I'd used it to call the parlour to tell them I had arrived okay. 'But I need to call a cab,' I replied, trying to look calm.

Still standing by the phone, and eyeing me suspiciously, he said, 'S'okay. We already called one. It's on its way.'

I sat down to wait, while they drank, smoked and talked more about guns and robberies. I don't think that I have ever been so frightened in my whole life as I was that night. When the taxi arrived, I walked as calmly as I was able out of the place, and once outside I ran like a rabbit and climbed in the back. I then burst into tears. Heaven knows what the driver thought.

Back at work, I went straight to Archie and told him what had happened. 'There was something really strange going on,' I said. 'I reckon that man was an escaped convict from that break-out.'

He sat me down, made a cup of tea and pulled out the *New Zealand Herald* from the pile of magazines and rubbish in his office. He found a picture of the escapees. 'Which one was it?' he said. I looked hard at the mug shots. My client did not remotely resemble any of them. 'You must be tired and imagined it,' Archie said kindly.

'You go home now, get a good night's sleep and I'll see you tomorrow.'

I did not go back to work at Total Escape. There was something mighty peculiar about that last escort. Something deep down inside told me to get out of that establishment quickly. I don't believe Archie knew Bob at all, and even if he did, he should not have sent anyone out to an unknown destination. The whole set-up at Total Escape was too flimsy for my liking, and although I enjoyed going on escorts to hotels, I did not like sitting about for days on end in the squalor of the parlour itself.

Once again I was out of a job. I bought a *Truth* from the dairy and scrutinised the adult entertainment pages. The huge Fleure's advertisement kept hitting me in the eye. Should I or shouldn't I? Why not, I thought, and dialled the number.

'Have you worked before?' a well-spoken female voice enquired.

'Yes,' I answered. She wanted to know where, and I told her.

'Don will be interviewing tomorrow afternoon at two o'clock at the Executive House in Lyle Street.' She took my name and said to be there around two-thirty as he had a couple of girls to see before me.

That night Emma and I went out for dinner, and I told her I'd quit my job and was going for another one. It was all very serious to start with, but as usual Emma made some crack about if I couldn't even hold down a job as a prostitute, was there any hope for us. I started to laugh while trying to swallow some wine and choked on it. The evening turned out to be hilarious, and I'm sure the waitress thought we were crazy.

I found Executive House easily, and parked my car on the forecourt out front, next to a large brown Rolls Royce. It was a huge, gracious two-storeyed home right next to a church. I wondered who did the better attendance on a Sunday, the church or the parlour. I could well imagine that they would have disastrous effects on each other's business, being at opposite ends of the ladder, so to speak.

The inside was lavishly decorated in red and gold, with a crystal chandelier hanging in the main hall. The hall was at the bottom of a beautiful sweeping staircase. On close inspection, I noticed the place was a bit worn. The odd piece of flocked wallpaper was peeling away from a corner, there was a faint sign of wear on the stair carpet, and the long burgundy velvet drapes faded where they touched. But over all it had the look of an American bordello of the eighteen-hundreds.

I met Don Springfield in a small snug-type lounge off the main hall. He smiled a big broad smile as he shook my hand. He was of medium height and stocky build, his shirt buttoned low enough to expose a gold-bedecked chest. His clothes were expensive and he owned the Rolls Royce on the forecourt. Don spoke with a Cockney accent, which I always found fascinating. He told me to sit down opposite him on a plush sofa.

'There's one fing I got to tell you, Angie,' he said. 'That is, I ain't got no friends!' He grinned at me.

'Haven't you, Mr Springfield?' I said. 'I am sorry.'

'Na, na. You got it wrong, darlin'. When I say I ain't got no friends, I mean I don't send me friends in on special deals, and I don't touch me girls neither. Know what I mean?' He winked. 'Got me?' I nodded.

Don said he'd like me at Fleure's, but at that time it was being renovated and four extra rooms added, so meanwhile I'd be at Executive House. He then introduced me to the receptionist, Jennifer, who took me under her wing. She told me I'd be working with a redhead called Chrissy and a young brunette by the name of Vicci. She asked me what name I'd be using. I'd been thinking about that, and I chose Diana. It was a good-quality ordinary name, a contrast to the Jades, Ambers, Topazes, Tiffanys and Chanels that were so popular at that time.

'Don's put you on days. You can start tomorrow at ten o'clock sharp. And bring some ID.'

'ID?'

'For the police book. Didn't they have one at the last place you worked at?'

'No. I've worked at two places, and neither of them had a police book that I know of, nor was I asked to give any ID.'

'Well, they could be in big trouble if the vice did a check. All licensed parlours have to have the names, addresses, telephone numbers and ID's of all their girls. It's the law.'

I wondered if after I was busted Mel had got into trouble over not having a police book at The Harem. He wouldn't have a clue who worked for him most of the time.

The ID thing caused a bit of a problem for me. I had told both Don Springfield and Jennifer that I was thirty-five. My birth certificate and driver's licence both said I had just turned forty. If I turned up in the morning with either of these documents, I would have proved myself to be a liar before I even started work. Because of the very nature of the industry, with its heavy underworld reputation, I was frightened to admit I'd lied.

A few years earlier, while in the US, I had lost my driving licence. Back in New Zealand I had applied for another and received it. Two months later, my old licence had arrived in the post from the US; someone had found it down the back seat of a car I'd been travelling in. So I had two current licences.

Back home, after Emma had gone to bed, I gathered together all the pens in the apartment and carefully matched each one to the ink on the old licence until I had a perfect match. Then, though I know it seems ridiculous, I looked furtively around to make sure no one was watching! I changed the three to an eight, to read 1948 on the birth-date line. It was a brilliant piece of skulduggery, and the licence was to serve its purpose for years.

I then phoned my mother and told her that I didn't like the cleaning job and had gone back to hairdressing at a salon in the city. She was very pleased to hear it. 'It's for the best,' she said.

The next day I had to park the car miles away from the parlour because the forecourt was unavailable to staff, and anyway, quite frankly, you wouldn't want your car parked out there all day in case someone you knew saw it. All the other parks in the area were for two-hours only, and became Clearways during peak traffic time. I arrived on the dot of ten o'clock to find Jennifer unlocking the door. The narrow walkway down the side of the house was the main entrance and it was patrolled by a security camera. All comings (no pun intended!) and goings were shown on a television monitor in the office. The door was opened to clients by activating a switch under the desk, which unlocked it automatically.

Jennifer took me on a guided tour of Executive House. It was divided into five suites, two downstairs and three up. Each suite consisted of a large spa room, surrounded by mirrors and tall imitation palms and ferns. The floors were black and white tiles. The massage room contained a double bed totally surrounded by mirrors; there was even one on the ceiling. The room was carpeted in red and, in contrast, the black vinyl mattress on the bed was liberally decorated with colour-coordinated towels. There was a two-seater sofa in one corner and an armchair in another and, of course, low intimate lighting which could be controlled by dimmers. Each massage room was fitted with what the girls called 'panic buttons'. When pressed they sounded an alarm in the office, which was handy if an abusive client started throwing his weight around and the girl needed assistance.

All the dirty towels went into large bags and were taken to The Tokyo, Don's inner-city parlour, where they were washed and dried in the laundry by the girls who worked there.

Jennifer explained the working system to me. The first girl in had the choice of the room she wanted to use for the day, except that Chrissy always had room one and it wasn't wise to upset the apple-cart by taking it. Also, the first girl in took the first client, unless he requested a particular girl. From then on the 'turn' system carried on as each girl arrived.

'Now, the first thing we do is the cleaning. The upstairs and downstairs are to be vacuumed, then the bathrooms and spa rooms cleaned, all plants dusted, and the spa pools tested and chlorinated,' said Jennifer. 'The sooner we get it done, the sooner we can have some coffee.'

I looked down at my freshly laundered and ironed dress. 'But my clothes will get filthy!' I said.

'Take your dress off and wrap a towel over your undies,' suggested Chrissy, who had just arrived. 'I always do. You'll get in an awful mess if you don't.'

She took me up to room three, the one I'd chosen to work in, to have a wee chat about prices and such. I took my frock off and hung it up. Chrissy was busy hanging a towel over a mirrored panel set in a cupboard door.

'That's a two-way mirror, and there's a rumour that Don keeps a video camera rolling behind it!' She grinned at me. 'I'm only telling you what I heard, that's all. It could be a load of crap, but it's better to be safe than sorry I always think.'

'Perhaps I'd better choose another room,' I said.

'All the rooms have them. Mine's the only one that doesn't. Just keep the mirror covered with a towel.' She left me to clean the upstairs, and it took forever.

When the cleaning was finished we sat down in the lounge with a cup of coffee, and Jennifer and Chrissy went through the rules and regulations:

No fraternising with clients outside working hours.

No wearing jeans to work.

No phoning in sick. Even if you are.

No boozing on shift.

No leaving condoms or wrappers lying about.

No asking for time off unless you have your shift covered by someone else.

No being late out of your room.

No being early out of your room.

No asking to leave early.

No arriving on shift late.

No drugs.

And you were to do as you were told without question at all times. Punishment for breaking any one of the rules was to be 'struck off the roster'.

When we had all finished our coffee, Chrissy told me to go to her room and she would teach me to massage. 'Most girls who come from other parlours haven't a clue how to massage,' she said, 'and, after all, that is what massage parlours are about.'

I was told to take off all my clothes except my knickers, and lie tummy down on the bed. Then she proceeded to pummel and chop my body until I thought I'd die. The pain was excruciating, and I was extremely pleased when it was over. It was a therapeutic sports massage she did, and once the shock wore off I felt pretty good, but I didn't ask her to do it again. It was then my turn to give her a massage, and after a few tips about certain muscles and where to put my hands, I had it just about right. But I had to wonder if what Wally had taught me at The Harem wasn't a better way of doing it; I couldn't see any man getting turned on with all that violent pummelling and chopping.

The first client of the day requested Chrissy. All the details of each massage — time, Christian name of client, whether he was new or a regular, if he requested a particular girl and who, how he paid, how much he paid, how long he was going to stay and the receptionist's name — were recorded. The money, credit-card slip or cheque was then posted into a slit in the desk that dropped into a locked box below. This was to stop any pilfering, and if the book did not balance when Don came to empty the box, the receptionist had to make recompense from her wages.

While Chrissy was dealing with her client, Jennifer explained the dreaded request system to me. It was quite simple: if after a month of working at Executive House you did not get enough requests to keep management happy, you were struck off the roster!

'Most girls offer clients a little incentive,' she said. 'Tell them if they ask for you at the desk next time, you will reduce the price.'

My first client of the day was called John. The name John has to be either the most popular name for a man, or men called John need more sex than the average Jim or Peter, or more men, to remain anonymous, use the name John in the sex industry because they have no imagination to think up a more exotic one.

This man told me he was in the construction business, which sounded very grand, but you could tell by his clothes he was your average builder. He had a shower and then we sat in the spa pool for a few minutes, and I found it to be very enjoyable. In the massage room I gave him one of Chrissy's specials. 'Chrissy's been teaching you some of her tricks of the trade,' he said. 'Do you know, the last time she massaged me she ruined my golf swing for a month; but my God, when the pain wore off, I near got a hole in one. Did me a power of good in the long run.'

When the massage was finished, I asked the usual question. 'What do you charge?' he asked.

I told him the house prices told to me by Chrissy earlier. 'Hmm! Sixty dollars, eh? Chrissy only charges me fifty.'

'I expect that's because you request her,' I said.

'If you will do it for fifty now, I'll request you next time. I come in once a week. You and Chrissy can share me, how's that?' I reluctantly agreed. John's needs were simple, and in a flash it was all over.

When John had gone, I told Chrissy about the money problem. She laughed, 'He goes to The Tokyo and Fleure's telling the same story. He knows we rely on requests to keep our jobs and he plays on it. He will request you next time, and would have done today if he had known you.'

The clientèle at Executive House was more upmarket than at Total Escape, but not as upmarket as The Harem. They were mostly unskilled workmen, tradesmen and the odd accountant. They talked about themselves a lot more than I'd noticed at the other places, and because most of them were regulars, they paid us after the job was done rather than before, which sometimes had its drawbacks.

Peter, an immigrant from Europe who'd been in New Zealand for twenty-six years, booked in with me. He said he'd been to the parlour once before, so he went down in the book as a regular.

After he'd had his shower and massage, I asked, 'Is there anything else I can do for you?'

'Umm, I don't know,' he said. 'Let me give you a massage and I'll see.'

I must point out that at this stage he had a good erection. I agreed, and lay down on my stomach. He had a lovely soft touch, which was welcome after Chrissy's effort earlier. I turned over and he did the same to my front, taking extra care not to miss even a minute part of my breasts and inner thigh area. He was obviously wanting sex, and thinking he was a regular, I let him go for it. He went on for ever, stopping every so often to prevent himself from ejaculating. I was underneath and he was a big man, so I couldn't do anything abut it. He must have been pumping away there for a good twenty minutes before he eventually ejaculated.

When he was showered and dressed, I asked for my money. This was one part of the job I always hated.

'Oh, I didn't want sex, I only came in for a massage. You led me on. And anyway, I don't have any money!'

Ripped off on my first day! I couldn't believe I could have been that stupid. All I could do was to put it down to experience.

My next client was a request, Wally from The Harem. He gave me a big hug and looked genuinely pleased to see me.

'I went to see you at that awful place in Durham Lane. Mandy told me you were there. But it looked filthy, so I didn't check in. I've been here once or twice before, and I phoned to see who was on today. The receptionist said there was Chrissy, Vicci and a new girl, Diana, and when she described you, I thought, that sounds like my little Angie.'

It was so nice to see Wally and to get a request on my first day.

CHAPTER 11

Two days after I started at Executive House, Vicci was struck off the roster. I never did find out which of the seven deadly sins she had committed, but one day she was working away happily, seemingly without a care in the world, and the next day she was gone. That's the way it went in Don's parlours.

The request system kept you on your toes; we could not pick and choose who to be nice to, because every request counted. So the slightest hint of rejection could mean that a client would not request you next time, or worse, would complain to management and cost you your job. When working at The Harem and Total Escape, I would shrink from men I found repulsive to me and not let them get too intimate. I would let one man kiss me because he was attractive, but say no to another because he had a wart on his nose, or was extremely obese. This was because I was taking the job personally, when I should have had a more professional approach to it. I was now learning that the obese man's and the warty-nosed man's requests were very important, as was their money, and behind the warts and fat there were usually hearts of gold.

Of course, there was always the exception. At that time there were a troop of Chinese cooks who frequented Executive House. They spoke no English, except when it came to money, and they were really rough during sex. Of course, it was useless to complain, although Jennifer knew well how we felt about them.

My first experience was on the third day. Wong checked in about four-thirty in the afternoon for half an hour. He wanted a spa, and demanded in sign language that I get in with him. You could be struck off the roster for not getting into the spa with a client.

Wong lunged across the pool at me, and squeezed my breasts until I squealed with pain. I covered them with my arms and a hand shot between my legs with a finger trying to screw its way into my vagina, which was also painful. Suddenly a full-scale fight was on. He was standing on the seat, pushing his penis into my mouth. Although very small, his penis was as ridged as a piece of doweling, and I had to clench my teeth to stop it from going in. There was water splashing everywhere, and I was desperately trying to get out, but was unable to move because of Wong's thighs against my shoulders, forcing them back into the wooden surround. The fight went on for some time before he got bored with it and got out of the pool. My hair was absolutely saturated. I remember looking at him and wondering how such a little fellow could be so strong.

From the spa room to the massage room, Wong was acting like a randy terrier. He was walking behind me, his hands mauling my breasts and his little bottom trembling with pelvic thrusts. It was fearfully difficult to walk while trying to push him off.

In the massage room I checked the time. We were fifteen minutes through the half hour Wong had paid for, and to avoid being late out, I thought it best to skip the massage.

'Is there anything else I can do for you?' I said, looking in the mirror at my dripping hair and mascara-streaked face.

'Massa! Massa!' he replied, flopping down on the bed.

Massage? I dealt to him a Chrissy special with as much speed as I could, then asked him the question again.

'How mu' hextra?' he said.

'Pardon?'

'How mu' se'? Fir'y dorra?' He wanted sex for thirty dollars.

'No way! Sixty,' I said.

'Fir'y dorra, no mo'.' He was shaking his head.

We settled on forty, which he gave me then and there.

'No lubba,' he said as I was tearing the packet open.

'You wear it or you get nothing!' I snapped at him. I won that round.

He wanted doggy, me on top, him on top, then doggy again. When he finally ejaculated, I was exhausted. I stood up to get the tissues to find semen running down my legs and the condom on the floor. Whether it fell off because it was too big for his penis or he took it off without me noticing, I never knew.

Wong went, and Jennifer gave me a warning for being over the half hour, and told me to do something with my hair and face. I felt like crying.

Just before it was time to go home, I told Chrissy about finding Wong's condom on the floor. 'It makes me feel dirty inside doing it without one,' I said.

'You must get yourself a douche.' She went into her room and showed me what looked like a medium-sized rubber ball with a spout sticking out of it. On closer inspection, I saw that the spout was punctured with tiny holes two-thirds of the way down. She filled it with water and squeezed the ball until it cascaded from the spout like a fountain.

'You stick it up your fanny,' she said simply, 'give it a good squeeze, and it washes out all the nasties. I do quite a few regulars without a condom, and after each one I douche in the shower and abracadabra! All squeaky clean. You'd stink like a pole cat if you didn't.'

'Have you ever had VD?' I asked.

'No I haven't, but I do go for a test every fortnight, and sexually transmitted diseases are curable — with the exception of herpes, of course; all the condoms in the world won't stop that. Look, we have twenty minutes before the night girls arrive. You go and sit in the lounge and I'll get us a juice.'

I didn't like the juice they had at Executive House, it was made up from a packet and tasted awful, but I agreed anyway.

The clients were offered a complimentary tea, coffee, orange juice or a glass of wine when booking in. The wine came in crates, and was kept stacked in a cupboard, of which Jennifer was in sole charge. We were not allowed to drink any of the wine, and everyone said that Don could smell alcohol on your breath at a hundred paces. On the other hand, we were allowed to drink as much tea, coffee or orange juice as we could get down. I drank coffee; Jennifer and Chrissy drank orange juice . . . by the gallon! I could never understand how they could stomach it, but no sooner had they finished one than Jennifer would take their glasses and replenish them.

Chrissy came in and handed me a juice, and I sipped it. 'All right for you?' she said, grinning. The 'juice' was half juice and half wine.

Chrissy put her forefinger over her mouth and puckered her lips. 'Shh! Just between us. Not a word to anybody or we'll all be fired.'

'Do you always drink this?'

'Oh, all day. Jenny does too. She's got the key to the wine cupboard. Sometimes I'm so pissed when I get home I can't cook dinner.'

'Does Don keep account of it?'

'Not really. There are crates and crates of wine in that cupboard, a couple of bottles every day wouldn't be noticeable. When Don's here, we chew mints. We've been drinking his wine for years and he hasn't sussed us.'

When Don arrived to take the towels to The Tokyo, I made myself very scarce.

The next day was Friday. I was looking forward to the weekend. I had been doing an average of four clients a day, and although over an eight-hour stretch it doesn't sound much like hard work, I had been used to only four shifts a week previously and hadn't had to put much effort into the clients I saw. I used to arrive home after a shift at The Harem or Total Escape with heaps of energy, but this job was far more taxing to the system. Jennifer told me Executive House was a breeze compared with Fleure's. There they were kept busy all day, and Kelly, the top lady, was usually booked out every day she worked. All the requests at Fleure's were counted up every month, and a list was put up on the wall at the same time the rosters were made up. The names of those who didn't have the required amount of requests did not appear on the roster, and those girls knew they'd been struck off.

My first client of the day was Kevin, a man in his early thirties whose wife had left him. He was a regular to the parlour. He was so nice I couldn't imagine why anyone would leave him.

'Don't bother getting in the spa with me,' he said. 'I know the chlorine screws up your skin; all the girls complain about it.' He was right there, in one week my skin had dried out like a bad case of dandruff, and I had to apply huge quantities of moisturiser, which cost a fortune. 'Don't bother giving me a massage. How about I give you one?' said Kevin. He gave me the most wonderful massage imaginable, and I nearly fell asleep.

Then it was time for the extras. 'Is there anything else I can do for you?' I asked, not even bothering to get off the bed.

'I would like a foot relief,' he said with a face as straight as a die.

That woke me up! 'I beg your pardon?' I replied.

'A foot relief, with your foot,' he repeated, 'and a stocking on it!'

'A stocking on it! How is that done?' I couldn't imagine how anyone could hold a penis of about five inches in circumference with a size four-and-a-half foot!

He lay on his back with his legs open wide. 'Put your stockings and suspenders on, stand between my legs and run your toes over my cock,' he said.

This was easier said than done! Standing on the bed on one leg while rubbing Kevin's penis with the other foot made me fall over so often my right ankle became painful. His penis was flaccid to start with and kept rolling away from my foot. I could see myself from every angle in the mirrored walls, and the sight was so comical that I had an irresistible urge to roar with laughter, which in turn upset my balance and over I'd fall again. Kevin ejaculated twenty minutes later, and as I hobbled into the shower I understood full well why his wife had left him!

Massaging on a bed rather than a table had its drawbacks. The table method had the client waist high to the masseuse, who was standing on the floor. The masseuse was in full control and was able to fight off any amorous advances made by her client before the extras deal was finalised. The bed situation was different. The masseuse had to kneel beside her client, which left her open to all sorts of fiddling and poking from him before any arrangement had been made for extras. Then, when the question was put to him, it was quite likely he'd say no, because he would have already had a nice time which hadn't cost him a cent, and of course the masseuse would get nothing. The Australian girls who came across the Tasman to work could not believe how stupid the New Zealand girls were to massage nude not knowing if they were going to be paid anything. Taller girls were able to sit on their clients' backs to massage them, and this kept fiddling and poking to a minimum, but I was too short for that method and could not reach far enough forward to massage a client's shoulders properly.

Right after Kevin left, Peter booked in.

'He's new, so look after him well,' said Jennifer.

A man in his sixties, Peter looked as though butter wouldn't melt in his mouth. He had a mop of white hair, bright blue eyes and a smiling face that reminded me of Dr Who. He had his shower, while chatting on about his grandchildren, and how he was helping his daughter and son-in-law renovate their kitchen. Peter was a cabinet maker, who had sold his business to retire. He lay down on the bed with his arms by his sides and head turned away from me on the pillow. I was facing his feet and massaging his legs, when his right hand crept up between my buttocks and a finger was trying to push its way into my anus. I quickly sat back on my heels, and he stopped. Once again I leant forward to finish his legs. The finger once more crept up to my anus.

'Do you like it up your arse?' His voice had a sleazy drawl to it, nothing like his normal one.

'Just you lie back and enjoy the massage,' I said. 'There will be plenty of time for playing later.'

I turned around to face his head and started on his back. A couple of minutes went by and the hand crept between my legs, with the finger pushing its way into my vagina. I stopped massaging, picked up his arm and laid it alongside his body.

'Behave yourself!' I said, and gave him a playful slap on his bottom. He laughed and a hand shot up, grabbing my left breast.

'That's a nice handful. I like big tits. I'd like to fuck your tits!' His hand was back between my legs with his forefinger prodding away at my vagina.

I figured the only way to get any control over the situation was to turn him over and forget the massage. But when he got up, a large wet patch on the towel told me he'd ejaculated, and of course he was now not interested in anything he had to pay for. We were only halfway through an hour's session, and because you could get struck off the roster for short-changing a client with time, I had to keep Peter happy for another thirty minutes. He didn't want another massage, he didn't want a spa, but he did want to go home. I eventually got Peter talking about the old days, and then I couldn't shut him up. He left the parlour ten minutes over the hour, so I got another warning from Jennifer and not a penny to show for it.

Back in the lounge I did a bit of a grizzle to Chrissy.

'There used to be a girl called Francy at Fleure's,' she said. 'She was so popular with the clients that she was able to encourage all top-dollar jobs and discourage idiots like that Peter. You never heard her whinging about getting a "straight" because she was always booked up with the cream of the crop. They used to book a week in advance so they wouldn't miss out. It's an ideal working situation if you can get it. She retired a few weeks ago and broke the hearts of quite a few men in Auckland.'

I wondered what Francy did to get into that situation, and if I could do it!

That afternoon about three o'clock, Percy arrived from Whangarei. He had tracked me down from The Harem to Total Escape to Executive House, and was very pleased to have found me. He booked in for an hour, and we went through the same routine as before — I massage him, he massages me, and sex without bending his knees! But at least it was a lot easier on the bed than on the mattress at The Harem. In the lounge afterwards, Percy sat with a cup of tea and told everyone who would listen how I'd trusted him with sixty dollars worth of extras, and how he paid me the next day at his motel. When he had gone, Chrissy said, 'I don't believe anyone could be stupid enough to trust a client that far, most of them are rip-off artists. You could have lost the money and your life.'

But I didn't, did I?

Then Chrissy asked me to do her a favour. 'I get migraines really bad, and the only thing that gets rid of them is Codcomol. My doctor will only let me have a few at a time, and sometimes I've run out when I really need them. I was wondering if you would go to your nearest chemist and buy some for me.' She handed me ten dollars. 'You will have to sign the book. Tell them it's for toothache or something like that.'

'Of course I will,' I said, and tucked the money into my purse, thinking how awful it was for Chrissy to suffer with such an affliction. I could remember my mother getting migraines so badly she would vomit and have to be in a darkened room for at least twenty-four hours.

'You can bring them in tomorrow,' Chrissy added.

'No, Monday,' I said. 'I'm off tomorrow.'

'You are here tomorrow. Has no one told you we have to work six days a week here?'

'No! You're kidding me!' I couldn't believe it, six days a week. I looked at the roster in the office. Yes, six days a week!

'We choose to work six days because it is not busy enough here to earn big money in four shifts. If we don't agree on this, Don will hire more staff and our income will drop drastically, which I can't afford. Think about it!'

I didn't have to think about it. 'Okay, I understand.'

I must admit I didn't feel okay about it. I spent precious little time with Emma as it was. Six days a week was a bit over the top, I thought. However, there wasn't a lot I could do about it.

'Anyway,' said Chrissy, 'my friend Cat will be in tomorrow. She sells clothes and she's got some lovely stuff, so bring some money with you in case she gets here before we do a job.'

It was late-night shopping, so on the way home I stopped at our local pharmacy to buy some Codcomol for Chrissy. And what a palaver it was, too. The shop assistant had to get the dispensing chemist to deal with it, and he was dispensing at the time so I had to wait. A few minutes later he came out from the back, eyeing me suspiciously. 'Codcomol?' he said. I nodded. 'What do you want them for?'

'I have toothache,' I said, adopting a pained look for good measure.

'You will have to sign the book.' He pushed an exercise book in front of me, and I filled in the columns with my name, address, telephone number and the reason for buying them. He then gave me the pills. What a to-do for a packet of headache pills, I thought.

At home that night I told Emma I'd have to work on Saturdays as well. She didn't say much, but I could see she was disappointed.

'Tell you what,' I said, 'why don't you learn to drive? I'll organise some lessons on Monday, then we'll get you a small car. At least you will be able to get out and spend some time with your friends.'

That cheered her up. 'Oh, yes please, Mum. I could drive over to see Nana and Grandad then.'

'And tomorrow night we'll go out for dinner. Where would you like to go?'

I knew exactly where she would choose. 'The Jade Garden,' she said.

It was with bad grace that I went to work the next day. I was tired, grumpy and hoped like anything the day would not be a busy one. But Saturday was the one day in the week that Executive House was busy. Parking problems, a bus stop outside, Auckland University around the corner and a church next door dampened business from Sunday to Friday, but Saturday was a different story. There was all-day parking, because Clearway rules did not apply weekends. Buses did not run very often, and the streets in the vicinity were quiet because there were no lectures at the university and there was nothing doing at the church. I arrived on the dot of ten-thirty to find two men waiting in the lounge. One was a regular of Chrissy's, the other I took up to my room. An hour later I said good-bye to that client and found two more men waiting in the lounge. And so it went on all day without a break. At six o'clock, feeling absolutely exhausted, but with four hundred dollars in my purse, I said good-bye to my last client and was pleased to find the lounge empty.

'Cat will be here any minute,' said Jennifer. 'She always has beautiful top-quality stuff at a fraction of the retail price.'

'Where does she get them from?' I asked.

Jennifer gave me a knowing wink and said, 'She goes "shopping", if you know what I mean.'

I didn't know what on earth she was talking about. It seemed crazy that someone would go shopping for clothes to on-sell at a cheaper price. It didn't make a lick of sense to me.

'What does she get out of it?'

'Oh, she makes a very good living from it. She shops in Hamilton, Tauranga, all over the place; and she doesn't only get clothes, she gets perfume, accessories, manchester . . . You can put in an order if you know what you want.'

It all became clear when Cat arrived with her two suitcases full of shopping. All the clothes were top labels — Peppertree, Thornton Hall, Zambezi, Patrick Steel, the list went on and on. They were up-to the-minute fashions in the most exquisite fabrics. Out of the suitcases tumbled sets of satin sheets, lingerie, French perfume, make-up and a whole host of goodies.

Chrissy joined us, having said good-bye to her client. 'Fuck! You've been busy,' she said, holding a beautiful Thornton Hall creation against her body. 'Did you have any problems?'

'No,' said Cat, 'but those security tags are becoming a problem. All the best shops are installing them, and it makes it difficult to get the stuff out. I'm going to have to get my own release gun!'

I then realised what sort of 'shopping' Cat did. All the stuff was stolen; she was a shoplifter! I looked more closely at her, because it isn't often one comes into close contact with a real live shoplifter, and I was very interested in what they looked like. Cat was about five foot seven, slim and looked as though she had just graduated from St Cuthbert's College. She sounded very well educated, and I thought she was very nice — the sort of girl you could take home and introduce to the family.

To start with I was apprehensive about buying anything that was stolen, but then, among the piles of garments a flash of vibrant colour caught my eye. Just a look couldn't hurt, I thought. While sorting through the pile, I found an off-the-shoulder dress in hand-dyed silk georgette. It was the most beautiful dress I had ever seen.

'Go and try it on,' said Cat, opening a bottle of Moët she'd also pinched.

The dress looked stunning. 'How much?' I asked.

'Fifty bucks,' said Cat. 'It was over two hundred in the shop and I was asking one hundred, but I'm letting it go cheap because it's a very small size and I've had it hanging around for zonks.'

I sipped my champagne and said I'd take it, along with a Levis denim skirt for Emma and a bottle of Arpège, all for a hundred dollars. The fact that these items were stolen didn't really worry me, even when Cat said, pointing to the silk georgette number, 'That's a one-off, another reason I let it go cheap. So if anyone asks where you got it, say the Cook Street Markets. A lot of hot stuff was sold there, and as it has just closed, it would be difficult to prove otherwise.'

About this time the night staff started to arrive, and the piles of clothes diminished in size as the girls took out what they wanted to try on.

'I have to keep a good eye on them,' said Cat seriously. 'Last time I was here three garments were stolen from me. Those night girls are nothing but a pack of thieves!'

At home that evening, I showed Emma the silk dress and gave her the denim skirt. 'Go and try it on,' I said.

I could tell by the way she put the skirt on that she didn't like it. 'Go and look in the mirror,' I said. Perhaps when she saw it on she'd change her mind. I followed her into the hall to look in the full-length mirror. It fitted like a glove, and the pale blue denim showed off her long tanned legs. 'Well?'

'Oh, it's okay I suppose,' she smiled pathetically at me.

'You don't like it, do you.'

'Oh, Mum! It's okay. I could wear it to the beach!' She took it off and replaced it with the long grey dirndl skirt I'd bought her at Hullabaloo, and topped it with a huge red jumper that came to her knees. Her feet were clad in red ankle-socks and black sandshoes and she looked like a refugee from some war-torn country in Europe. 'Mini skirts are not in fashion,' she said.

CHAPTER 12

Before work on Monday morning, I booked some driving lessons for Emma and phoned a close friend in the motor trade for some advice on buying a car. The mung-bean jar was absolutely full of money, easily enough to pay cash for a nice solid little runabout for Emma.

It was a slow day at Executive House and Chrissy, Jennifer and I sat around talking through most of it. I was interested to learn that Chrissy came from a very wealthy family down the line. She went to a top New Zealand boarding school, hating every minute of it, and had worked in a variety of jobs, most of which she became bored with very quickly.

'This is about the only job I've stuck with and like doing,' she said. 'My parents would have heart attacks if they knew.'

Chrissy had a good clientèle, and they all adored her. Even when she treated them like dirt, they came back for more, time and time again.

One of her clients, Stanley, was from the north of England and spoke like an actor from *Coronation Street*. Every other Friday at ten-past-five he would be found in the lounge patiently waiting for Chrissy, more often than not clutching a bunch of flowers he'd obviously bought at a garage. She always kept the poor man waiting, and sometimes I felt she did it on purpose. As soon as Stan saw Chrissy, his chubby little face would light up. 'By! She's an 'ansome lass,' he'd say to anyone who would listen. Chrissy nicknamed him 'Two-stroke Stan'. She said it described his sexual performance.

Mike, a plumber from South Auckland, came in weekly to see Chrissy. She told me that always, while she was on top bouncing up and down, he would tell her how much he loved her, and she, still bouncing up and down, would tell him not to be so fucking stupid.

It didn't put him off, though. He came back to see her for years, to hear the same thing over and over again.

At two o'clock in the afternoon, Chrissy and I were talking to Jennifer in the office when a figure appeared on the television monitor.

'Oh no!' Chrissy exclaimed, and she ran into her room and closed the door.

'What was all that about?' I asked.

'Oh, you'll find out soon enough,' said Jennifer, activating the automatic button to open the door.

A man in his mid to late sixties carrying a small attaché case shuffled in.

'Hello, Cess, how are you?' said Jennifer. 'How long would you like today?'

'Oh, I don't know. Let me sit down and catch my breath first,' he replied, trying to push past her.

'Come on now, Cess, you know the rules. You can't come in until you've paid.'

He handed over thirty dollars. 'Is Chrissy here today?'

'She's busy, Cess, but we do have a new lady.' She pointed to me. 'This is Diana. She will be pleased to take care of you. Diana, if you would like to take Cess up to your room. Cess, tea, coffee, juice or a glass of wine?' He chose the wine, and I took him upstairs.

In the massage room, he sat down on the bed. 'I missed the twelve o'clock bus,' he said. 'I saw Mrs Bennett at the bus stop and she said that she'd been waiting for ten minutes. I don't think the twelve o'clock bus came at all. They sometimes don't, and they're not as punctual as they used to be, you know. I can remember the trams down Queen Street. Now they were always punctual, and lots of them.'

'Cess, if you would like to take your clothes off, I'll get the shower going for you, okay,' I said, wishing he'd get a move on. When I came back from the bathroom, Cess was still sitting on the bed. He had taken one shoe off.

'I bought these shoes in 1952,' he said, waving it in front of me. 'They cost me nineteen and elevenpence ha'penny.' He looked up at the ceiling thoughtfully. 'No! No! I tell a lie! They were

111

twenty-nine and elevenpence ha'penny. That was a lot of money in 1952.'

'Cess, the shower's ready for you. You will have to hurry or we'll run out of time.'

He took off his other shoe and socks. 'This shirt cost ten and six. It's nylon. I bought it from McKenzies in Queen Street. I had some socks to match, Ming blue they were.'

I thought it best to undress him myself, as he was getting nowhere fast, and I got the story of every garment, where he bought it, when he bought it and how much it cost. Cess talked constantly, in the shower, in the spa, while being massaged and even during sex. While we were doing it doggy style, Cess told me how, in 1961, he had a letter from the city council demanding fifteen pounds of unpaid rates. When I was on top, he told me how much it cost to pay the solicitor to sort the council out. When he was on top, he told me how State Insurance had done the dirty on him in 1975. 'They'll walk all over you if they can,' he said, getting off and removing the condom with a tissue. I hadn't realised he'd ejaculated, as he had been talking non-stop. Back in the shower, Cess said he didn't think the soap they had today was as lathery as it was when he was a boy, and while dressing he gave me his theory on the bad weather we were experiencing — it was due to the Russian sputniks, he reckoned. The only time Cess was quiet was when he was counting out the money he owed me. He opened the attaché case and withdrew an oval-shaped leather purse. Inside were fifty dollars in two-dollar bills, each folded into a tidy square. He unfolded each one and laid them out neatly on the bed, where he counted them several times. I was fifteen minutes late out and was given another warning, while Cess sat in the lounge with a cup of tea.

'You've got Doug waiting, you had better rescue him from Cess before he does a runner,' said Jennifer.

'I bought these shoes in 1952,' Cess was telling Doug as I walked in, 'they cost nineteen and elevenpence ha'penny . . . No! No! I tell a lie . . .'

Doug shot out of that room like a demon was on his tail. 'What a boring old bastard,' he said, and I agreed with him.

Doug was a lovely man, a regular of the parlour, and didn't mind who he saw, which was useless as far as a request went. We had all asked him to perhaps request us in turn, and offered incentives, but somehow Doug always forgot. He was a delight to be with in the massage room, kind and considerate. Sex was quick, and he paid top dollar — almost the perfect client. He would often talk about his wife. She was unwell and not interested in sex, but in spite of this he loved her dearly.

'She's a good mother and loads of fun to be with,' he told me. 'But a man has his needs, and I think coming in here to see you girls is the best way of relieving the need without hurting anyone.'

Chrissy, Jennifer and I sat about doing nothing from four-thirty onward. Only the odd telephone call broke the monotony. The night girls were all on time, and we were just about to leave when Don arrived, his face set in a grimace of thunderous fury. He swept through the parlour, bellowing at the night receptionist to get all the girls together in the lounge.

'Something's up!' Chrissy whispered, while cramming a couple of mints into her mouth. 'Heads are going to roll, I can tell.'

'Perhaps we'd better go!' I suggested.

'We won't be allowed,' she replied.

Because it was busier than the days, five girls were rostered on at night, and they came running into the lounge from all directions.

The end of a joint had been found by the night receptionist after everyone had gone the previous evening. It was found in the lounge, on the floor by one of the armchairs, and Don wanted to know who the culprit was. The night girls all looked as innocent as new-born babes, shaking their heads, not knowing what on earth Don was rabbiting on about, and after a minute or two it became obvious no one was going to own up. I could see Don was seething with anger, and standing there, arms akimbo, he let forth: 'You fucking molls are all fired! Now fuck off.' Turning to Chrissy and me, he said, 'You two will have to stay until we can round up some girls from Fleure's and The Tokyo.' And with that he swept out.

Don's language was always very colourful, he had a wonderful grasp of Anglo-Saxon, and astounded everyone by using it frequently, no matter who he was speaking to, prince or pauper.

'How long will that take?' I asked, thinking I ought to phone Emma and tell her I'd be in late and to keep my dinner hot.

'Oh, it could take all bloody night,' said Chrissy, who wasn't pleased either.

Now, if someone had fired me the way Don did those night girls, I would have been an emotional wreck. Just being called a 'moll' would be enough to reduce me to tears. But they all took it in their stride. Amber was angry that it was going to cost her eight dollars for a taxi home, but the others all decided it would be a good night to have dinner out and go clubbing, and left quite happily.

Chrissy explained, while fixing us one of her 'special juices' that it was the way things went in the sex industry.

'It's nothing like working in a straight job. If you decide you don't want to work for Don any longer, you wouldn't give a fortnight's notice. If you did, he'd fire you on the spot, because in two weeks you could have told all your clients where you were going to be working next and lose Don the custom. So you either phone and say you won't be back, or just don't turn up for your next shift, having quietly told your clients a month before that you were leaving.

'And those girls knew who dropped that joint. If the vice had done an inspection and found it, the whole parlour could have been closed, and none of us would have a job. What I want to know is, why the night receptionist didn't smell the stuff? Anyway, they'll all have jobs elsewhere by this time tomorrow.'

She was interrupted by the receptionist showing two Chinese into the lounge. They looked us up and down, then nodded.

'For half an hour,' she said.

My client was called Lum, and he was not as bad as Wong. He didn't want a spa or a massage, but he did want sex and plenty of it.

After his shower, he said, 'How mu' hextra? Fir'y dorra?'

'Sixty dollars.'

'Fir'y dorra! No mo!' We settled on forty.

'No lubba. No lubba!' I wondered if these guys learned their lines from a script! I insisted on a condom, but when it was time to put it on, I realised it was far too big for his tiny penis and would have been no protection at all. I had bought myself a douche, and his penis looked healthy, so I took a chance.

Lum started by sniffing all over my face and down over my breasts with his little flat nose. It tickled unbearably, and I started to laugh. This had a disastrous effect on Lum's ardour. 'No raughing!' he pleaded, and we had to start again.

Lum had obviously read the *Kama Sutra* from cover to cover and remembered every position in detail. At the end of the session, I was tired, hot, wet with his perspiration and he still hadn't ejaculated. I was worried about being over time, so decided to take the initiative by finishing him off with a quick hand relief, and was out with three minutes to spare.

Chrissy wasn't. Her man was another Wong, and had practically drowned her by trying to have sex in the spa. 'I kept telling the little bastard, you can't do the missionary position without someone getting drowned. Fuck, they're thick!' she said, and went off to dry her hair.

We were quite busy from then on, and when our replacements arrived at eleven-thirty, the receptionist said she had had to turn away nine men. I had done four clients since six-thirty and Chrissy had done five, so although we were tired, the evening had been profitable and had more than made up for the slow day. But the clients I had, apart from Lum, had all been drinking, and it reminded me of The Harem and Total Escape — constantly having to wrestle with belligerent drunks. It made me grateful for having a permanent day shift.

At home I found Emma had kept me some dinner. She was sound asleep, but had left a note on the dining room table:

'Dear Mum,

'Nana phoned. She and Grandad will be in Auckland on Friday. They will pick me up from home, you up from work (!!!) and shout us dinner.

'Luv Emm'

That was all I needed, my mother turning up at Executive House. That night I dreamed Mum had walked in on me and a client having sex, and Don was calling her a 'fucking moll' while bodily throwing her out. The nightmare woke me up and I could not get back to sleep.

The next morning I dragged myself out of bed. Emma had been up for ages. She was to have her first driving lesson after school, and was full of excitement and enthusiasm.

115

'Did you see the note?' she said, stuffing a *Road Code* into her school bag. 'What are you going to do?'

'I really don't know, and I'm too tired to think about it,' I growled.

The only thing for it was to tell another lie. So many had been told over the past months that one more wasn't going to make the situation any better or any worse. So when I got back from taking Emma to school, I phoned Mum and told her they could pick me up from home the same time as Emma. I said I was attending a colouring demonstration that day, it finished at three-thirty and I planned to go straight home. Mum fell for it.

But Jennifer didn't! 'There is no such thing as time off,' she said. 'You will have to get someone to fill in for you. Ask one of the night girls. And remember, if she doesn't show up on time, you will have to stay until she does.'

Of course, nobody wanted to be at work three hours early knowing full well they wouldn't make any money, but in the end I did a deal with someone who wanted to come in late on Sunday. The Sunday shift was from midday to midnight. Neither of us had anything to lose, as Sunday was also very quiet.

Once I learned to live with the rules, the job became enjoyable, and my clientèle grew. Most of them were darlings, but every now and then someone would be waiting in the lounge for me, and I'd think, Oh no! Not him again. Or a new guy would turn out to be a ratbag. But then, all jobs have their downsides. The one thing that surprised me was that, up to this point, I'd had no problems with the moral side of things. I felt that I gave a lot of pleasure to a lot of people, and surely it could not be wrong. The law against soliciting, and the stigma attached to prostitution, originated from Christian ethics, which in my opinion are wrong. The sooner they are changed, the better.

On the Friday, Mum and Dad were coming to take Emma and I out for dinner, I was sent to The Tokyo to work. They were very busy, to the point of turning clients away, and we had been sitting about all morning doing nothing.

'How long will I be there?' I asked Jennifer.

'As long as they need you,' she said.

'But Cindy's coming to fill in for me this afternoon. Will I be able to go early from The Tokyo?'

'As long as you're not busy. If you happen to be working it's tough luck. Look, what time do you want to leave?' I told her three-thirty. 'I'll see what I can do, but don't count on it, okay?' I thanked her and left.

The Tokyo was on the first floor of a building that was almost on the waterfront in Auckland city. On arrival I was bustled into a room and the receptionist quickly explained where everything was. The room was small, with an odd wedge-shaped bed along the wall, a large shallow bath with a shower hose over it, a spa pool in one corner and an enormous fan hanging from the low ceiling. The air was hot and damp with the steam from the spa pool, the fan managing only to move it around the room without actually cooling it. The room surfaces were liberally decorated with coloured towels, the walls with mirror tiles. A huge mirror was suspended on the ceiling above the bed, and plastic plants were crammed into various corners. It was a far cry from the spaciousness of Executive House.

The Tokyo was busy. They had six girls working that day, and they were all in their rooms when I arrived. The small lounge seemed to be packed with men, all intently reading and, I suspect, hoping no one would recognise them. The receptionist introduced me to a man called Phil, and told me to take him through to my room. Once inside, I didn't know quite what to do next. At Executive House I had a routine. The man and I would take off our clothes, which I hung up, and I would then give him a towel and take him into the bathroom for a shower. From there, we went into the spa, and after ten minutes or so we would go to the massage room for a twenty-minute massage, which left around twenty-five minutes for extras and a final shower. At The Tokyo, everything was in one cramped little room, and I found myself tripping over piles of towels and splashing water onto the carpet. And once the spa was turned on, all the mirrors steamed up and, no matter how fast I had the fan going, the room became unbearably hot. There was a hook and a hanger on the door for his clothes; mine had to be folded in a pile on the floor. The bed wasn't really big enough for me to kneel comfortably next to him for his massage, and it was too low to stand alongside. Luckily, Phil only wanted a hand relief, for which he paid thirty dollars. When I checked the time, there was still ten minutes to go. I tried to delay Phil from going, but he insisted. So I took him out and said good-bye, hoping there was no one else waiting for me and I could go back to Executive House.

There was someone waiting.

'Diana, this is Jack. He has booked in for three-quarters of an hour,' said the receptionist.

Jack looked to be in his late seventies, a lean, stringy man who reeked of cigarette smoke. His long, lined face had a sallow appearance and he talked with a raspy voice. In the room, he took off his clothes, threw them on the floor, put out his cigarette and turned on the shower.

'Going to get in with me?' he said, grinning. I took off my clothes and joined him. 'You can wash my back if you like.' I washed his back and he turned around. 'What about my front? Make sure it's clean enough for you.' He pointed to his penis, 'Go on, it won't bite you.' What the hell, I thought, lathered up my hands and gave it a good wash.

'Oh! You girls really make an old man happy!' Jack took the soap from me. 'Let me wash your tits.' He gently washed me from neck to knees, taking particular care of my breasts and inner thighs.

'There,' he said, 'we're both clean now.' Jack dried himself and lay on his stomach and I started to massage him. 'Only my bum,' he said, lighting a cigarette. 'I only like my bum massaged, and you can tickle it a bit with your fingernails.' I massaged and tickled, tickled and massaged for what seemed like an age. 'You can tickle my balls while you're at it,' he said, lighting another cigarette and blowing a huge puff of smoke into the already steamy and smoke-laden room. I could feel beads of perspiration trickling down between my breasts. When he finished that cigarette, he turned over and lit another one. 'I'd like a nice long hand relief with plenty of oil, and you can play with my balls at the same time.' He piled up some towels and lay back on them, inhaling deeply and blowing the smoke into puffy rings. Jack managed to smoke his cigarette and play with my breasts with more ease than I was able to give him hand relief and play with his testicles. My arms seemed to be at an unnatural angle, which would not allow my elbow to bend, and any motion with my hands was restricted to my wrists. At the same time I was keeping clear of Jack's cigarette, which was dangling from his mouth with a long piece of ash ready to fall off the end. I was perilously close to it, because Jack had his free arm around my back, pulling me in towards him. When he ejaculated, every muscle in my body had seized up. My left hand had a vice grip on the poor man's penis, my fingers had gone numb and I could not let go. However, as soon as his erection went down, the penis slid out and my fingers regained their circulation.

'Would you like a smoke?' said Jack, offering me a wrinkled packet of Pall Mall plain. I felt my contribution of smoke into the room could possibly cause a visibility hazard, and said no, but Jack lit up yet again. 'I've been smoking for fifty years, and never been crook in me life,' he said, and flexed his muscles at me through a wall of smoke. 'Not bad for sixty-four, you reckon?'

'Not bad at all, Jack,' I replied.

When Jack left, I checked the lounge to find it full of men. Time was getting on, and I was worried about not being at home when my parents arrived and them insisting on picking me up. Although Emma was very good when it came to covering up for me, I felt guilty when she had to do it, especially when her grandparents were involved. I had thought of telling them the truth earlier in the year, but I knew the pain and worry it would cause them and so decided against the idea.

'Diana!' the receptionist called from the office. My hopes of leaving on time vanished. 'Call a taxi and get back to the Exec quickly. They have a booking waiting for you.' That was all I needed. It meant I would finish work even later than if I stayed where I was by the time I'd waited around for a taxi.

However, the taxi arrived in no time at all, and back at Executive House Jennifer said, 'Tidy your room and get ready to go as soon as Cindy gets here. She's on her way.'

'What about my booking?' I asked.

'Oh him! He cancelled at the last minute, some meeting or something. Shame, eh?' she said, all wide-eyed. 'Now get your things and piss off. I'll see you tomorrow morning.'

'Oh, thanks, Jen,' I said, knowing full well she'd rigged the booking, and could get into trouble if Don found out.

'Don't thank me, it was the luck of the draw,' she said.

CHAPTER 13

The renovations at Fleure's were finished, and Don said I could start working there the following Monday.

'Phone Celia and ask her what days you're rostered on,' he said.

'Oh! That's all I need, a new girl to break in,' said Chrissy when I told her. 'It happens every time I'm working with someone I get on with, Don sends her to Fleure's, and I end up with some flibbertigibbet like that stupid Vicci. It pisses me off.'

I felt flattered she didn't want me to leave, and when I thought about it, I didn't want to go to Fleure's. It was nice working at Executive House with all its space and grandeur, and I enjoyed being with Chrissy and Jennifer. They were a laugh a minute.

'I think I'd rather stay here,' I said.

Chrissy looked pleased. 'You can tell Don when he comes to pick up the towels later. You wouldn't like it there. Fleure's girls are all up their own bums!'

Time seemed to pass extraordinarily fast. Winter closed in, and the old stately home started to get extremely cold. Icy drafts came whistling through gaps in the old sash-cord windows, making their way into every nook and cranny, and the massage rooms were freezing. We had one heater per room, which was situated halfway up the wall, but we were not allowed to have it on when the room was not in use. So, because the heat just disappeared up into the high ceiling, a client would have to undress standing directly under it or freeze, then lie on the bed, shoulders shaking with the cold. These undesirable conditions took their toll on our pockets by dampening the ardour of many of the punters. Even the fittest and hardiest of men would cringe at the thought of taking even a sock off, and by the time the room was anywhere near warm, the hour

121

would be up, the client would go, and it was time to turn the heater off. Not many men stayed their full time.

We wore as many clothes as possible without appearing to be sexless. The warmest room in the whole house was the lounge, where we sat huddled up in coats. As soon as the buzzer heralded the arrival of a client, or Don arrived unexpectedly, we would brace ourselves, toss our coats over the back of an armchair, and sit there looking gorgeous, trying desperately to stop our teeth from chattering. Jennifer was worse off, because she spent a good deal of her time in the office answering the phone and booking in clients. The wind funnelled along the alleyway leading in, under the door, over her feet, up the wall and down her neck! Well, that's what she told us when we complained about having to walk around our rooms in the nude.

Chrissy came to work one morning with her man friend in tow, who was carrying a large box. She and Jennifer had been doing a lot of whispering behind their hands recently, and were obviously up to something I wasn't to know about. Even a fool could tell that the box contained a video machine, and a new one by the look of it. I played dumb all day, and eventually Jennifer could not contain herself a moment longer.

'Look what I've got,' she said, opening the box for me to see. 'Chrissy gets them from a friend really cheap. Fallen off the back of a truck. If you want one, I'm sure she can get it for you.'

I had recently hired a television and video from a rental company, which I was more than happy with, and had no interest in a hot one. It seemed that Chrissy was able to get any appliances, cameras and all manner of things that had fallen off the back of a truck. In fact, her house was totally furnished from stem to stern with them. I was absolutely dumbfounded. Chrissy was such a nice person I could not believe she was involved in fencing stolen goods.

'Don't you tell a soul,' said Jennifer, wishing she hadn't told me. I assured her I wouldn't.

'Mum! Telephone,' called Emma, one Saturday morning.

I was in the shower. 'Who is it?'

'It's Chrissy, shall I tell her to call back?'

'Yes, in about five minutes.' I knew exactly what Chrissy wanted.

Five minutes later on the dot, the phone rang again. I answered it. 'Hi!' said Chrissy in her usual chirpy fashion. 'Do me a favour, love, call into the urgent dispensary and buy me some Codcomol, I'll pay you later, okay? Oh, and have I got some gossip for you! See you at work. Bye!'

At least twice a month, Chrissy asked me to buy her Codcomol for her migraines, and I was going from chemist to chemist in the area with excuses of toothache to buy them. Having once filled in the book that recorded the sale of certain drugs at one particular chemist, you were treated with suspicion when returning to the same chemist to buy the same drug for the same toothache. I was now driving over to Panmure and surrounding areas, and felt really sorry for Chrissy, who depended on the things for some relief.

At work, Jennifer and Chrissy were so deep in conversation they didn't hear me come in.

'What's up?' I asked.

'Don's selling Executive House,' said Jennifer. 'Chrissy heard it from one of The Tokyo girls.'

'Could be just a rumour,' I suggested.

'No such luck. Tiffany said she heard Don talking to someone on the phone at The Tokyo. It sounds pretty final to me,' said Chrissy.

'What will happen to us I wonder?' I asked, beginning to wish I hadn't turned down the opportunity to work at Fleure's.

'Fuck knows!' Chrissy lit a cigarette and passed the packet around. 'I'm hoping Don will take us with him or we could find ourselves working for some wanker we have to screw to keep our jobs. There's plenty around, believe me.' Didn't I know it.

Jennifer suggested we didn't mention it to any of the clients before it became official. 'You know Don has his spies coming in from time to time; if it isn't true and Don thinks we've been spreading rumours, we'll all be fired,' she said.

This piece of news really put a damper on the day. Even the clients noticed it.

'You aren't your usual bubbly self,' said Wally, my first job. 'Are you feeling crook?'

I told him I was fine and tried to cheer up, but in the back of my mind I kept telling myself there was no way I'd ever again work for a boss with whom I was forced to have sex.

Being Saturday, it was busy, and the day passed by quickly. At four-thirty Don arrived to pick up the towels. We all kept our ears pricked for any snippet of information about selling the business, but none was forthcoming, and I think that made us feel a little happier. Maybe it was just a rumour after all.

On Sunday, Emma and I went to the Victoria Park Market for lunch. We did this often, sorting through the different stalls and buying a whole heap of rubbish we would never wear or use, but for some reason we could not help ourselves.

'We should do something a little more cultural,' said Emma, 'the art gallery or museum.' I agreed wholeheartedly, but still we ended up at the market with a bag full of useless junk we'd bought.

By this time Emma had her driving licence and a smart little VW beetle. She would chauffeur me around, showing off her driving ability, and I thoroughly enjoyed it. In those days it was possible for a fifteen-year-old to get a driving licence. Looking back, I think it was perhaps a bit foolhardy, but Emma proved to be a good responsible driver and didn't give me a moment's worry.

We finished the day by going out for dinner. 'Mum, I've met this boy,' Emma said, looking over her orange juice at me.

Whenever I mentioned this subject to my own mother, her first question without fail was, 'What does his father do?' I was not going to follow suit.

'That's nice, dear, tell me about him.' I'd had that line rehearsed for years.

'Well, his name is Gareth, and he's a student and part-time camera assistant for a photographer. He's about the same height as Grandad and . . .'

'Yes dear, but what does his father do?' I could not help myself, it just popped out of my mouth!

'He's a businessman in Wellington,' she replied. 'They are very well off, but not snobby. Anyway, Gareth would like to take me to the pictures on Tuesday night . . . Mum! Before you say anything, I know it's a school day, but if I get my homework done early? We'll be home by ten. Please?'

'What about Friday or Saturday nights. You could stay out later then,' I said.

'We are going to the film festival. It's a very special movie Gareth wants me to see. It's an art film. Mum, please!'

'Oh! All right,' I said, against my better judgement.

At work on Monday morning, Chrissy told us that one of her friends, who worked in a parlour on the North Shore, had heard through the grapevine that Executive House had been sold and that the new owner was to take over in a month. Half an hour later, Don arrived with a man he introduced to Jennifer as Peter, and they closeted themselves in the small lounge along the hall. After about an hour they both left, with Don grinning from ear to ear, but not a word was said to us.

Chrissy and I sat in the lounge until just after one o'clock, contemplating what we would do if the new owner turned out to be a wanker.

'I don't think we'd get in at Fleure's; they're fully staffed at the moment. My friend Kelly works there,' said Chrissy. 'I'll give her a ring tonight and ask her to tell me when anyone gets fired or leaves. You never know.'

We were interrupted when Jennifer ushered in Dennis, my lovely escort from Total Escape.

'So this is where you're hiding! It's a damn sight better than the last place,' he said. 'How long have you been here?' He gave me a hug and sat down next to me on the couch.

It seemed Dennis had bribed Cathy at Total Escape to tell him where I'd gone. 'She told me quite happily,' he said. 'I booked her for a dinner escort last night, and she was dressed in some outrageous shiny outfit that made her look like an Easter egg. So I scrapped that idea and offered to pay her the full escort fee if she would tell me where you were, then took her back to the parlour.'

Dennis booked in for an hour, and we went up to the massage room. Because it was so cold, we sat most of the time in the spa talking.

'Can I take you out for dinner this evening,' he asked. I explained about the 'not fraternising with clients' rule, the business being sold and not wanting to spoil my chances of getting a job at Fleure's.

'Surely if I come to see you at the House as well, no questions would be asked,' he said. 'It isn't as if I'm doing them out of any money, is it?' That made a lot of sense, so I agreed and told Dennis where to pick me up.

The afternoon was another quiet one, and we spent the time wondering what our fate would be when and if the new man took over. Jennifer was kept busy because the buzzer seemed to be going continually, but as soon as she reached the office whoever it was had gone. However, during a long telephone conversation in the office, she noticed what looked like a student on the television monitor, and he proceeded to unzip his trousers.

'Come and get a load of this!' she called. Chrissy and I ran into the office just in time to see the young man flash his bottom at us, with much crouching and wiggling. We all hooted with laughter. Then he turned around, almost bending over backwards to expose a very undersized but erect penis. This brought the house down! 'I bet he's a law student!' said Chrissy, and we all roared with laughter again.

At four-thirty or thereabouts, Wong booked in with me. I groaned inwardly and took him up to my rooms. In a trice he had his clothes off, leapt into the shower, then made for the spa pool, beckoning me to join him. I got in and sat opposite, with my feet up on the seat.

'You here!' he demanded, pointing at the seat beside him.

'No!' I said firmly. I was past caring. If they struck me off the roster for being rude to a client, so be it. But Wong was not going to take that sort of defiance. He grabbed my feet and lifted them up in the air, which caused me to slip off the seat and slide under the water. I struggled as hard as I could, but he was too strong for me. Only a body-building contortionist could have lifted her head high enough out of the water to breathe. I really thought I was going to drown, but after what seemed like an age, Wong let me surface. Coughing and spluttering, I dragged myself out of the pool, with the little man hot on my heels doing his 'randy terrier' act. I grabbed a towel, wrapped it around myself, ran down the stairs and straight into Don, who was carrying a large bag of towels.

This is it! I thought. I'll be struck off the roster for sure, and I was running out of parlours to work in.

But Don took one look at me and ran hell for leather up the stairs. The next minute, Wong was being ushered out, still doing up his trousers. 'Now fuck off and don't come back,' Don snarled at him. Jennifer activated the door opener, and Don all but pushed Wong out into the street. We didn't see him again after that.

Jennifer made me a cup of tea, and Don told me to go home.

'You look fuckin' awful,' he said, but he was smiling at me when he said it!

At home, Emma was sorting out what she should wear on her date. She tried on everything in her wardrobe, and finally decided on her 'sloppy sweater floppy skirt look'. She tried them on with a new pair of heavy-soled black sneakers. 'How do I look?' she asked.

'Well, Emm,' I replied. 'I will not have to worry about you being molested in that outfit. You would frighten the hell out of any rapist within miles.' She pulled a face at me and flounced off into her bedroom.

At seven-thirty, Dennis arrived to take me out to dinner. We went to Number 5 in City Road, right next to the Sheraton, where he was staying. We started with champagne in front of the fire in the bar. Huge oil paintings of personalities from a bygone era lined the walls, and as I sipped my glass of Dom, soaking in the ambience of leather and old silver, I thought to myself, 'This is the life for me!' The meal, served with a bottle of Châteauneuf du Pape, was delightful.

We finished with cognac and some delicious mints, then went to Dennis's hotel room for more champagne. Of course, Dennis wanted sex, and we went through the same performance as last time, but this time I was able to get him to ejaculate. He paid me a hundred dollars, and gave me a gold pen and propelling pencil, beautifully wrapped in expensive embossed paper.

The next day, Tuesday, was the day of Emma's date. That morning she was a bundle of nerves. She bit and snapped at me, and I was pleased when I heard her car leave for school. What on earth will she be like tonight? I wondered.

*

At work, it became official that Don had sold Executive House, with Chrissy and I as a part of the goodwill. Jennifer had to find other employment, because the new owner's wife would be working the desk. They were taking over in two weeks. Although we had guessed as much, it came as a shock when we were actually told. 'At least the new boss won't be screwing us with his wife here,' said Chrissy, who always looked on the bright side.

'You never know!' said Jennifer. 'His wife could be a lesbian!' Jennifer did not always look on the bright side.

I felt extremely insecure. Don could be an out-and-out bastard, but he was reliable and dependable when it came to business. You knew you were safe when working in one of his parlours. No way would a policeman get into a room as easily as the one did in The Harem episode, nor would one of Don's girls have been sent out on an escort like the one at Total Escape. Don told us that Peter was new to the massage parlour business, and that he would be popping in now and then to see that everything was running smoothly.

When Chrissy and I were alone later that day, she told me to start telling my clients there was a good chance I might be leaving, and that I would put an advertisement in the *Star* newspaper as to where I'd gone.

'You never know,' she said, 'we might have to make a quick exit if this Peter turns out to be a bastard.'

At that time, the parlour bosses in Auckland were boycotting *Truth* because of the article they ran that originally attracted me to the business. Apparently *Truth* had sent an undercover journalist around several parlours recording every word the girls said, and this could have led to 'living off immoral earnings' charges for the bosses.

Chrissy said we could get a job at Hostess or Connoisseur temporarily.

'Don won't be able to employ us for a while, because that would be poaching, and parlours have been burned down for less,' she added.

The day was quite a busy one for Executive House, so I didn't have time to dwell on the future too much. Jennifer was extremely subdued. She was worrying about finding other employment. 'I don't want to get a straight job. I couldn't go back into a law office, I'd get bored stiff,' she said.

I found Emma all ready to go out when I arrived home. She was wearing make-up, and had applied it beautifully.

'Who taught you how to do that?' I asked, thinking how pretty she looked.

'Nobody,' she said. 'I've watched you, that's all. Anyway, a kid could do it, it's that easy.'

'Have you got any condoms?' I asked.

She blushed and said, 'Oh, Mum! I'm not doing stuff like that. I'm only fifteen.'

'Look Emm, being only fifteen does not mean you don't have any feelings or sexual needs. Plenty of girls your age and younger get pregnant all the time, and you can bet they didn't go out with the intention of having sex. It kind of evolves to a point where your hormones won't let you say no. Believe me, I've been there.' I took two Featherlite from my purse. 'Here, put these in your bag just in case. It won't do any harm.'

She reluctantly put them in a zip pocket in her handbag. 'None of my friends' mothers would do this,' she said, with a giggle in her voice.

At seven o'clock sharp there was a knock at the door. 'That'll be Gareth. Quick, Mum, you answer it! And don't call me "poppet" in front of him, and don't kiss me good-bye, okay?'

I opened the door and was confronted by a young man in his late teens. He had fair hair that stuck out in all directions and a chubby face with a flawless complexion. He was wearing a cream shirt and red trousers. I was so preoccupied with his appearance that I forgot my manners altogether and just stood staring at him. He smiled and offered his hand. 'Hi, you must be Emma's mum. I'm Gareth Wilson.' He had a lovely humorous smile and a gentle voice.

'Hello Gareth,' I said, pulling myself together. 'Emma's here somewhere. Come on in.' Emma came out of her room, self-consciously smoothing her skirt. 'Well, you two have a good time, and don't be too late, Gareth. Emma has school tomorrow.' He nodded, she glared at me, and they disappeared into the darkness.

When Emma had first told me about her date with Gareth, I planned to have an early night and read. But as soon as I heard Emma's car take off up the road, I started to worry. What if he takes drugs and talks her into taking them too? I thought. What if he takes her drinking and she has an accident? What if they're late home? Then I started to worry because I hadn't asked which movie theatre they were going to, or where he lived, in case she didn't arrive home at all. At ten minutes to ten, I was standing by the window looking down the street for her headlights and thinking, what if she's broken down and there is no one around to help? I made a mental note to join her up with the Automobile Association first thing in the morning.

At five to ten, Emma drove up the driveway and parked the car. She burst through the door. 'Hi! I thought you were going to have an early night,' she said.

'Oh, I wasn't tired. How was your evening? Did you enjoy the film?'

'Oh, yes,' she said. 'It was made by a small New Zealand film company, all in black and white.'

'That's nice. What was it about?'

'It wasn't about anything, Mum. It was an alternative art-house film.' She sighed with frustration at my lack of knowledge.

'Come on, Emm! It must have been about something,' I argued.

'Mum, if I were to explain, you would never understand it!' she said, and went into the bathroom and closed the door.

CHAPTER 14

The two weeks went by very quickly, and before we knew it our last shift working for Don was upon us. He arrived with Peter around midday and introduced him to Chrissy and I. They spent a lot of time in the office, which was obviously irritating Jennifer, and scaring the clients away — most men prefer a woman to book them in. Chrissy said Peter made her feel uncomfortable and she was going to leave Executive House, no matter what. I felt extremely insecure and let down.

Just after midday, a man whom I'd not been with before booked in, and requested me.

'A friend recommended I see you. He said you were very good,' he told me. I thought no more about it. After having a shower, he said to me he didn't want a spa, just a jolly good massage. He lay on the bed quietly while I massaged his back, and obediently turned over when I asked him to, without the usual fiddling and prodding. He had a simple but unusual preference for sex. 'Put your high heels on, and bend over the chair,' he said. I popped a condom on his large erection and bent over. I felt his penis slide into me and thrust slowly and firmly, while he cupped my breasts with his hands.

After a minute or two he gave a loud sigh, and it was over. 'That was exquisite,' he said, patting my bottom. 'My friend was right, you are good.' I could not see, for the life of me, how the man thought I was good! All I'd done was bend over a chair wearing a pair of stilettos. How good do you have to be to do a simple thing like that? He gave me sixty dollars and left.

'He's one of Don's spies,' whispered Chrissy, as the door closed behind him. 'He sends his spies to see if the girls are doing their job properly. Did he seem happy?'

'Oh yes,' I replied, thinking that it was a bit late for Don to check on my working ability; in a few hours I would no longer be employed by him.

Don and Peter left about three-thirty, and Jennifer brought us a special juice each. 'May as well drink the stuff while we can.' She raised her glass and said, 'Fuck Don Springfield!' and swigged her drink down in one go.

The only job Jennifer could find was as a receptionist in a sleazy parlour in the city, on the night shift, and she was feeling very bitter towards Don because of it. I felt sorry for her, as she was to take a cut in wages and had two kids to support.

We drank quite a few special juices between us, and when it was time to go home I was extremely tiddly and so were the others, especially Jennifer, who must have been drinking two to our one. Chrissy and I left together, and were just about to cross the road when Don's Rolls pulled up on the forecourt. He wound down the window and beckoned us over. I was aware that my breath must have smelt like a vineyard; we didn't think for a minute we'd ever see him again and had forgotten completely about the precautionary mint. I took a deep breath and held it.

'Yer didn't fink I'd leave you two be'ind, did yer?' He grinned at our surprised faces. 'You both start at Fleure's on Monday. Now piss off home and get some rest. You'll need it!'

Chrissy, who had also been holding her breath, and I both let out a cheer, nearly suffocating the man in a fog of breath that would have put a wino on the wagon. But if he noticed, he didn't say a word.

I arrived at Fleure's twenty minutes early on Monday morning to find it closed. The main entrance was situated next to a set of traffic lights, and I noticed that the occupants of every car that stopped at the lights would gaze at the doorway. I really did not want to be seen outside Fleure's obviously waiting for the place to open, so I went into the small lunch bar below for a fruit juice and to while away the time. Three girls were sitting at one of the tables smoking and drinking coffee.

'Hi! Are you Diana?' asked a short, dumpy woman in her mid-thirties. I nodded. 'Come over and sit down. This is Jill,' she pointed to a tall, serious-looking girl with big green eyes, 'this is Amber, and I'm Linda.' Amber was young, petite and extremely shy. I wondered how she managed to do the job successfully, as quite obviously her shyness was a problem for her. Linda was not shy, and what she lacked in looks she made up for in personality. Her quick-witted sense of humour had me screaming with laughter in minutes. Even Jill's serious countenance fluttered a weak smile every now and again. We were joined by Carol, a girl in her late twenties with sparkling blue eyes. She was also a barrel of laughs, and between her and Linda, the whole lunch bar was in stitches. The owner, his wife and several customers could not control themselves. What a good start to the day!

Celia, our receptionist, arrived on the dot of ten-thirty, and we all filed out and waited for her to open the door. The lights turned red, cars queued up, and what entertainment the drivers and their passengers had watching a line of prostitutes waiting to get into a massage parlour! Every eye was on us. Celia found the right key at last, and we all tumbled in, falling over one another trying to get off the street. I climbed the stairs behind the others and waited on a small landing at the top for Celia to turn on the lights, as it was so dark you couldn't see a hand in front of you. We went into what they called the day room, and Celia, holding an exercise book and pen, asked, 'Who was in first?'

'Me,' said Linda.

'Room one?' Linda nodded, and Celia made a note in the book. 'And who was next?'

'Me, room two please, and Amber came in after me,' said Jill.

'Amber, room six as usual? Next?'

'Diana,' said Linda.

'Right, Diana, I'll put you in room four today, because it's close to the lounge. The rest of the place is a bit of a rabbit warren, and it'll take a while to get used to it, but usually it's first in, first served. Once you get to know the place, you can decide which room you like the best,' said Celia.

The rest of the girls arrived in dribs and drabs; last of all was Chrissy.

'This is a bit flash!' she said. She was given room five.

Linda showed me to room four. It was in the new part of the parlour and very modern. A large bed sat on a black and white tiled floor, just like Executive House, the black vinyl-covered mattress festooned with colour-coordinated towels, artistically draped in flower shapes. The bed was surrounded by mirrors and plastic plants. A couple of metres away from the bottom of the bed, four steps ran the width of the room, leading up to a wooden platform where a large spa pool stood majestically crowned with a bright-blue plastic cover. In the corner, the bottom step widened and there was a large round shallow bath, with a shower hose protruding from the wall and sunk into it.

Linda showed me where the panic button was, and pointed to a single light bulb on the wall above the door. 'That's the squad light,' she said. 'If it comes on while you're working, it means the vice squad have arrived. Now, because we don't want to corrupt their morals, cover yourself and your client with a towel and carry on. Of course, if you're having sex, don't carry on!'

'I thought warning lights were illegal?' I said.

'They are. But these aren't warning lights, these are inspection lights to help the vice squad,' she said, tongue in cheek. 'Don had special bright-white lights fitted in every room including the lounge, so that the vice squad can see what they are looking for. I mean, with the soft low romantic kind of lighting we work in, the poor buggers can see fuck all. Condom packets, joints, syringes and needles would all go undetected and the country would sink in a wave of sex and debauchery. As soon as they arrive at the office, the receptionist throws the switch and the whole place lights up like a Christmas tree before they even get through the door. So little old ladies can sleep peacefully in their beds at night knowing full well the vice squad will not break a leg falling over in the dark!' I was laughing so much that my jaw ached. 'True!' she added.

'What's this?' I asked, picking up a squeeze bottle from the side of the bath.

'Bubble bath,' she said. 'When you've finished the "rumpty doo", you run a bath, squeeze some of that in, and have a bath with your client. They love it.'

Linda also showed me the rest of the parlour. The new part was certainly a rabbit warren, with rooms running off small corridors that didn't seem to go anywhere in particular. We went into the old part, which consisted of a smallish lounge lavishly decorated in red and black. The walls were textured white plaster and had long black iron pikestaffs and spears hanging on them and, of course, the ever-present plastic plants. Inside the door to the right was the sauna, not used very often apparently. At the other end were three doors leading off at angles.

We went in the first one. 'This is room one,' said Linda. 'I always work in here, that's why I'm so early in the morning.' It was a larger room than the newer ones, with an enormous round bed covered with a black vinyl mattress. A wooden spa sat on a raised platform alongside the bed, and a huge round bath and shower hose on another platform opposite. An old-fashioned wash basin set in an equally old vanity stood between the bath and the door. Every available space on the wall was covered in mirror tiles, and an enormous mirror hung horizontally on the ceiling. The floor was carpeted in 'massage-parlour red'.

'That's the intercom,' said Linda, pointing to a loudspeaker near the ceiling. 'They usually pipe music through it, and can let you know if there is someone waiting for you, or to hurry you up. Kelly swears they listen in to what's being said in the rooms. She says she can hear it being turned on and off.' Although this room was older than the one I was using, it was much cosier.

We went back into the day room, where Celia gave me a guided tour of the stock room, and Linda went to do her share of the cleaning. The stock room was nothing more than a very long walk-in cupboard with shelves that ran its whole length. Just inside the door, clean towels were stacked neatly in piles, and further along the cleaning products, soap, containers of talcum powder and boxes of tissues were stored. 'In here,' said Celia, patting the top of a large ten-gallon drum, 'we keep the massage oil. Every room has a plastic bottle for oil, and it's up to you girls to keep them full.' She pointed out a tap on the lower part of the container. I found it quite amusing that the oil drum had 'SHELL OIL' in huge letters on the top in red and yellow.

'Every morning the cleaning has to be done before anything else. I test the water in the spa pools for chlorine and pH levels. You girls make sure the floors are vacuumed, surfaces and plants are dusted, and baths and mirrors cleaned. The towel bags must be moved downstairs, ready to be picked up and taken to The Tokyo.

At the end of the shift, you must thoroughly clean your bath, wipe your mattress with disinfectant, empty your rubbish bin and make quite sure you have left *nothing* behind. You may not leave the premises until I have checked your room. Now, do you understand all that? Did you think to bring some ID for the police book?' I nodded. 'And please fill in this declaration form.' She handed me a form to say I hadn't had any prostitution or drug convictions. I signed it and gave it back to her.

I got the job of cleaning the mirrors. Armed with two clean pieces of towelling and some blue creamy stuff called 'Glint Heavy Duty Glass Cleaner' I set about the glass in room seven, which was a very poky little room. The bed was a bit bigger than a single, and was surrounded on three sides with mirrored walls which, unlike the other rooms I'd seen, were not tiled but fitted sheets of glass. It had the appearance of a large shoe box. The glass was smudged with oil so badly that the image was distorted. No matter how much glass cleaner I applied, I could not get rid of the smudges. When I thought of all the other mirrors in the place that had to be cleaned I started to get a bit panicky, because at the rate I was going there would not be enough hours in the day to finish them before it was time to start on them again tomorrow. Linda popped in to see how I was doing.

'It's the cleaning rags,' she said, when I complained about the stubborn smudges. 'Even when they're just washed, they're full of oil. Everything in the place is. We could solve the world oil crisis in here. You can only do your best, and it will be okay, unless Celia is in a mood and gets picky. Even then it doesn't last long; she soon forgets what she was getting picky about.'

Suddenly a piercing voice called through the intercom, 'Linda! Massage.'

'Oh bugger!' said Linda. 'I wanted a coffee before I started. See you later.'

The last mirrors to clean were in my own room. I had smeared the Glint over the mirror behind the bed and was having a breather while it dried, when the piercing voice called 'Diana! Massage' over the intercom.

As quickly as was humanly possible, I polished the stuff off and proceeded to get dressed. I became very aware that after all that vigorous cleaning, I was in desperate need of a shower, and was contemplating whether or not to jump in for a quick one when over the intercom came 'Diana! Massage! *Now!*'

'Where have you been?' Celia wanted to know when I hurried into the day room, hoping like hell she wouldn't notice the heavy-duty Glint embedded in my fingernails. I tried to explain about the mirrors and my need for a shower.

'You must come when I call,' she said, not taking any heed of my explanation. 'Some men do not like to be kept waiting, and we could have lost him.'

My first client at Fleure's was Ray, an older gentleman wearing a suit and carrying a briefcase.

'I usually see Kelly, but she isn't here today and I'm off to Wellington for the rest of the week,' he said in a very cultured British accent.

The floor in room four was cold and uncomfortable underfoot, and soon my toes had gone numb. 'Would you like a spa after your shower, Ray?' I asked, hoping like anything he'd say yes.

'No thank you, I hate the things, but I would like you to come in the shower with me! Kelly always does.' A hot shower was just what I needed, and I was in like a flash. I gave his back a wash, and he gave my back a wash. I handed him a towel and we got out. He lay down on his tummy. I dried myself, then started to massage him.

Ray had a smelly bottom! Over the few months I'd been working as a masseuse, I had noticed that quite a few men had smelly bottoms. They don't wash them properly in the shower at home, or in the parlour. When it was time for him to turn over, I noticed Ray had a smelly penis as well. Everywhere else on his body was as sweet as a nut except these two places. It wasn't pleasant working under those circumstances, and I made myself a promise to personally shower every man that came to me from then on. The huge bath and shower hose would make it quite easy, and I knew the men would love it.

When I had finished the massage, I asked the usual question. 'Is there anything else I can do for you, Ray?'

'Yes please,' he said. 'I'll have a spanking and hand relief.'

I'd heard about men like this. 'A spanking and hand relief,' I repeated.

'Yes, that's right, over your knee. I pay fifty. I like a good spanking, as hard as you can.' He smiled at me.

There was a wooden chair in the corner of the room, but not a lot of space to put it that would give him enough room to bend over my lap. However, I dragged it out and he clambered over me, thrusting his smelly little bottom in the air. But, every time I got into spanking mode, Ray began to slip off.

'Kelly always puts a towel over her lap first,' he said, all red in the face. We started again, and it made my hands really sore. I had to stop once or twice to rub them together to stop the stinging.

'I should spank you with a hairbrush,' I said.

'Oh! Yes please!' he was quick to answer.

I got my hairbrush from my bag. It was perfect, with a large, flat area just made for smacking naughty smelly bottoms. Before Ray got back on my lap, I noticed he had an erection already. A good start, I thought. The hairbrush was a brilliant idea, and within seconds Ray's little buttocks clenched together, quivered for a second or so and relaxed. He had ejaculated, and I hadn't even touched his penis! At this point I caught sight of myself in the mirror tiles opposite, and what a sight reflected back at me!

Ray scrambled off my lap, stood up and stretched. His bottom was bright pink and looked extremely painful. I was about to ask him if it was when he said, feeling his left buttock, 'Every time I sit down today, I shall think of you.'

I said good-bye to Ray, and Celia said I had someone else waiting in the lounge. It was a man in his late fifties with spare white hair and piercing brown eyes. He called himself Colin. He told me he was a teacher of life skills and travelled quite a bit with his job. Colin was a real pain in the neck. He was constantly whinging about the door fee being too much, and in the shower he insisted on washing my breasts and inner thighs.

'Are you clean, Diana? I only like clean girls,' he said.

He didn't want a spa in case it wasn't clean, and even when I assured him there was enough chlorine in it to clean the Pacific Ocean, he refused to get in. He wouldn't have his back massaged, because he wanted to look at me the whole time.

'I intend to have my money's worth, Diana,' he said, and kept fiddling with my breasts and pubic area. I tried to spin the massage out to the usual time, but found it impossible because of his hands constantly fondling me. In the end I gave it up as a bad job.

'Is there anything else I can do for you?' I asked, trying hard to smile.

'Open your legs and let me see if you're clean, Diana,' he said. I did as he asked, and he peered in.

'I'll have hand relief please, and I would like you to enjoy it too, so lie down beside me. And don't do it too quickly, because I'm entitled to my money's worth.'

'That will be thirty dollars, Colin,' I said, knowing full well that if the man was a cheapskate I'd very likely get ripped off.

'Oh no, Diana! I only ever pay twenty-five dollars,' he said, smiling sweetly at me. 'You girls always do it too quickly and I don't get my money's worth!' The sound of his voice started to aggravate me.

Against my better judgement I agreed on the twenty-five dollars and got started, planning to get it over as quickly as possible — he would indeed get his 'money's worth'! Colin wanted to make me orgasm, and had read several books on the subject. He stuck his forefinger into my vagina and started poking at it vigorously, then onto my clitoris, and rubbed it with a circular motion which was extremely painful. 'Do you like that, Diana? Does it make you feel good?'

I wanted to yell, 'No, you stupid, irritating man, I hate it. It makes me want to scream! And shut up! Shut up! Shut up!' But instead I smiled as sweetly as I could and got on with the job in hand (as it were). But every time I got him close to ejaculation, he stopped my hand from moving. 'Not yet, Diana, not yet,' he said, smiling that stupid condescending smile of his. Colin kept his hand relief going for the rest of the hour, and I was so angry I could have hit him.

He had a shower that took forever, saying, 'We must always be clean, Diana.' My shower was a quick one, because I did not want to be late out on my first day. Colin gave me a disapproving look. 'That was a very short shower, I hope you're clean, Diana?'

Against all odds, I got Colin out on time. If I never saw him again, I'd be delighted. Still smiling a false smile, I saw him to the door and said good-bye through clenched teeth.

'Thank you for a lovely hour, Diana. I'll see you next time. Good-bye.' Oh no, please no! I thought, as he walked down the stairs. I was never more pleased to see the back of anyone in my life.

Fleure's had a back entrance which was unmarked, and most of the men used it. Both entrances were monitored with a video camera, and all arrivals were heralded by a buzzer and the doors were automatically opened from the office. The monitor itself was situated in the day room and could be seen by us all, and every time a buzzer sounded, all eyes went to the screen. The whole system gave one a sense of security that made working a lot easier.

On my first day at Fleure's, I did six clients and went home with three hundred and fifteen dollars in my purse. I felt I'd earned every cent of it.

Leaving Fleure's was a problem. After your last client of a very busy day — even on my first day I'd not had a break since setting foot in the place that morning — you had to clean the bath and surrounding mirrors, wipe the bed over with disinfectant, empty the rubbish bin and reset the bed with decorative towels, then wait around for the receptionist to inspect it. Once told to leave, it wasn't just a matter of walking out of the place, because of the traffic lights out front. We were not allowed to use the back entrance. I used to wait halfway up the stairs for the traffic to clear away from the lights, then make a run from the building and, once on the street, walk nonchalantly away.

When I first started working at Fleure's our shifts were not set, so you could not make plans for any longer than a week ahead. This was a hassle for us, and also for Celia, who had to make up the shift roster every week. As she could not please the whole staff, someone's nose was always going to be out of joint because her rostered days on did not suit. In the end Celia's decision was upheld, and if you made too much of a fuss the likely outcome was to be struck off.

Even when the system was changed and we were given set rosters, nobody wanted to work weekends, especially Sundays because it was a twelve-hour shift and not very busy at that. I copped

Saturdays, but Celia promised she would get me off them as soon as someone else joined the staff. New girls had to take what was offered.

There was one good thing about a Saturday shift; I got to work with Chrissy. As it wasn't as busy as the weekdays and there were only three of us rostered on, we were able to have a good old natter.

The routine for booking in clients was exactly the same as Executive House. The client paid at the door, and was offered tea, coffee, fruit juice or a glass of wine. It was not long before Chrissy had the wine cupboard sussed and was back to her special juices.

The receptionist on Saturday was a young lass who used to be a working girl herself, then quit when she got married. It was unusual for Don to employ ex-working girls as receptionists, because he thought they were too soft on the staff. But there was nothing soft about Laura! She was as hard as nails and treated everyone like dirt, even the clients. But she never did catch on to Chrissy's special juices.

On Saturday mornings, not only was the usual cleaning done, but the spa pools had to be emptied and scrubbed, refilled, then tested for pH balance and chlorine. To scrub the inside of a spa pool you had to take all your clothes off and put a towel around you. It was an awful job and took a long time to do, and you could bet as soon as you started a voice would boom over the intercom, 'Diana, massage!' Then it was a marathon to get your clothes on, face fixed, hair done and into the lounge before someone grizzled at you. And, of course, when you had finished with your client, back you got into the spa pool to scrub away until the next one came in. I can remember one particularly busy Saturday we didn't finish scrubbing till about four-thirty in the afternoon, and when the night shift came in, the water in the spas was still cold. I would have preferred to come in earlier and get the job done before starting work, but as the receptionists had nothing to gain by that arrangement they were not keen on coming to work any earlier than necessary. However, we usually had the lot finished by one o'clock and could sit down to relax.

CHAPTER 15

Three weeks after starting at Fleure's, the first request list was put up on the wall. Chrissy and I were at the bottom, and even though we were a week behind the others, I knew I'd have to do better. Kelly, the top girl at the time, was always busy with her regulars and complained that she didn't have time to meet any new clients. Sixty-seven requests were marked next to her name, and I was told it wasn't one of her best months.

Kelly was a very attractive brunette with large brown eyes and a wicked sense of humour. Her method was to give them what they wanted and be cheerful about it. I knew a lot of what we did was acting out a part, but I found it difficult at the end of the day if I was stuck in my room with a man who had a problem with not being able to ejaculate, as I would often be extremely tired, having had half a dozen others that day with similar problems. But to have this man leave my room feeling dissatisfied and grumpy would not lead to a request next time he called in. This situation was likely to happen on four shifts a week, which added up to sixteen requests lost in a month. I realised my performance had to be increased by one hundred percent or I would lose my job. The money I was making was extremely good, and that was without really trying. The mind boggled at the potential if I put my mind to it. The problem was, there were no opportunities for extra training as in, say, hairdressing, where one could attend seminars and demonstrations to improve one's ability. In the sex industry you made it up as you went along. Sometimes the others would give you a couple of tips, but a lot of the time they were the wrong ones.

At home, on the evening of the dreaded request results, I made a list of all the things I needed to do to improve my working ability.

'Lingerie' headed the list. I knew Kelly wore some beautiful lingerie because some of her clients had told me. The following day

I went into town to buy some sexy undies — three boned corselettes in red, black and white with matching G-strings and slips; two black bras with matching French knickers, suspender belts and slips and, of course, half a dozen pairs of stockings.

Second on the list was 'Ways to improve my working environment'. We all decorated our black vinyl mattresses with the coloured towels provided by the house; usually one in a sort of swirl in the middle, then several others arranged around it in an attractive pattern, and jolly nice they looked too. But, when a client came in, you had to fold and pile them up somewhere else to make room for him on the bed or you would have them falling all over the floor while you were working. This took up the man's time, and I had noticed that men didn't really care if the bed looked attractive or not; their eyes were for you only, and they would far rather spend the time having a bit more 'rumpty doo', as Linda put it. So from then on my mattress had only a single clean towel for him to lie on, plus one for his head. The rest of the towels were in a neat pile by the spa pool. Also, I would make more use of the mirrors. After all, that's what they were meant for.

Third on the list was 'Health'. I found that most days I would not have time for lunch, and sometimes not even for a coffee break — Fleure's would have been a real challenge for a union representative. By about four in the afternoon I'd start to feel super-tired and sometimes a bit faint. So vitamins were the order of the day, and I planned to have a healthy sandwich to eat in the lunch bar before work every morning.

Fourth on the list was 'Working Method'. From now on I was going to spoil my clients sick. Start by undressing them, showering them, and acting out a complete love scene, the way an actress would in a film. Until now I had always tried to get my clients to ejaculate as quickly as possible. This meant less work for me, but in the long run it would not lead to return business. I allotted five minutes for each shower, ten minutes for a spa, fifteen minutes for a massage, fifteen minutes for the rumpty doo and ten minutes for a bath. This sounded easier than it was to put into action. Many clients suffered from premature ejaculation, and, of course, you had no way of knowing about this before you started unless they told you, which they were usually too embarrassed to do. I would have to learn to spin these guys out so they were getting value for their money. On the other hand, with the ones having problems ejaculating at all, I'd have to learn to deal with them so they would leave my room happy and satisfied.

Fifth on the list was 'Give up smoking', which I didn't get round to for years, although I knew full well that more than half our clients were non-smokers and did not like the smell of smoke on a girl's breath. Some of them would actually ask for a non-smoker, but working girls who didn't smoke were few and far between, so the clients would have to put up with the smell. A few mints worked wonders.

Monday morning I took a taxi to work, figuring it would cut the hassle of parking miles away and having to walk back to the car after work. As far as exercise went, with all the positions we were obliged to take up and the energy we put in to the job, at the end of the day we had done enough exercise for two people.

I was the first person to arrive in the lunch bar that morning, which was unusual because Linda was rostered on, and she always arrived a good half an hour early to ensure she had room one. I bought a salad sandwich and some coffee, and sat down to enjoy it while waiting for the others. Linda had still not arrived when Celia unlocked the door at ten-thirty.

'There is a leak from the spa in room four. The man will be here early this afternoon to fix it. All the spas in the new rooms will be out of action for the rest of the day, because they are all connected to the same system,' Celia said, bustling around the day room. 'Diana, Linda has the flu and will not be in today, so I suggest you take room one. Jill, room two? Amber room three, and Carol room seven. If any of your clients insist on a spa, we will have to do a room shuffle. Sorry girls.'

We had the cleaning done quite quickly, as Carol said there wasn't much point cleaning room four until the spa man had finished.

My first client of the day booked in around ten-fifty. He called himself Roger. Celia took him through to my room, where I joined him, eagerly looking forward to trying my new working routine out on somebody.

I entered the room to find a tall, colourless man waiting for me. He had a pale, gaunt face and watery blue eyes.

'Hello, Roger,' I said. 'My name is Diana, and I am going to take care of you today.'

He seemed a bit nervous, so I decided to take my clothes off first, then help him off with his, as he hadn't even attempted to start undressing. He stood watching me intently as each garment came off. Once naked, I approached him and started to unbutton his shirt. He pushed me away and, clutching his shirt to him, said, 'This is a sin! God does not want you to do this, Diana!'

Oh no! A religious nut! 'My God doesn't mind,' I said. 'My God likes everyone to have a good time. He thinks I do a good job. Your God sounds like a boring old fart if you ask me.'

This took him back a bit, and he stood for a moment looking lost and confused. But then he got some strength from somewhere and started chanting some passages from the Bible that didn't have anything to do with prostitution whatsoever.

'Now come along, Roger, you must get undressed if you want a massage. Isn't that what you came for, a nice massage?' I asked, trying once more to unbutton his shirt. Again he shrank away from me.

'The people stoned Mary Magdalene, but Jesus forgave her. Jesus can forgive you too, Diana. Repent now, it isn't too late!' His pale, watery eyes kept flicking down to my breasts.

I could tell this was going to be a long and difficult hour, but I was not going to give up yet, and after some gentle persuasion and a promise that I wouldn't touch his 'private parts', he stripped down to his underpants and lay down on the bed for a massage. He lay on his tummy, his whole body rigid with fear, and when massaging his legs I had to prize them apart, promising not to do his inner thigh. I asked him to turn over, which he did, covering the front of his underpants with both hands. When I had finished, he saved me the bother of asking him the usual question by sitting bolt upright and chanting, while pointing and looking up to the heavens, 'WHAT ARE THE WAGES OF SIN, DIANA?'

'SIXTY DOLLARS FOR ORAL AND SEX, ROGER!' I chanted after him.

Roger did not like me saying that. He leapt to his feet, got dressed and left. So much for my new working routine. 'C'est la vie!' I said to myself, hoping I wouldn't get struck off the roster for being out of my room too early. But Celia was surprised I was there for as long as I was.

'He's a bit strange, isn't he?' she said.

I really didn't think that I'd ever see Roger again after making fun of him like that, but I was wrong. 'Religious Roger' came back fortnightly for the rest of my time at Fleure's, trying to make me repent, and not once did he stop me from taking *my* clothes off!

After my third client of the day left, I realised how much easier it was working in room one. It was warm and cosy as opposed to the stark modern layout of room four, with its cold tiled flooring. The clients seemed to feel at home in room one, and were more able to relax. The bath was in good proximity to the bed, and one wasn't obliged to climb four steep steps to reach the spa. This always caused a problem for our older gentlemen in room four, and it was my constant worry that one of them would slip and fall.

'Linda has a booking at three,' said Celia. 'I doubt he'll see anyone else, but if he does, I'll put him through with you, Diana, because the Japanese usually like blondes. Now, he is a very important and wealthy client, so give it everything you've got.'

Mr T arrived on time, and yes, he would go through with someone else, and yes, he liked the look of me. Celia took him through to room one and I joined him a moment later. Mr T was impeccably dressed in the most beautiful European suit. He was extremely polite and very quiet. I helped him off with his clothes, gave him a shower and settled him into the spa. He sat there not saying a word. I tried talking about the weather, the economy, even told a couple of harmless little jokes. Mr T sat looking at me, poker faced. I was pleased when the automatic timer stopped the spa from bubbling. I got out, handed him a towel and dried his back with another. He lay on the bed not uttering a sound while I massaged him. Whether he enjoyed it or not I couldn't tell, as his deadpan face told me nothing. Then it was time for 'the question'.

'Is there anything else I can do for you?'

'Sex and oral please, Diana,' he said in perfect English.

I felt like I was making love to a robot. Mr T made not a sound through the whole procedure. He just lay on his back, hands by his sides, and I did the rest.

Suddenly, after about five minutes of me bouncing up and down on top, he said, 'I've finished, thank you.' I got off, removed the condom and ran the bath. When it was time for him to leave, Mr T, still with the deadpan face, said, 'Thank you, Diana, that was very nice,' and he left.

'I don't believe that guy!' I said to Carol in the day room. 'I couldn't even get a smile out of him.'

'Do you know,' she said, 'Linda has him in stitches. You can hear him screaming with laughter and passion from one end of the parlour to the other. I don't know how she does it!' I found it difficult to believe.

Just before leaving for home that night, I heard that Linda had been struck off the roster.

'Why?' I asked, astounded.

'I telephoned her home to find out if she would still be away tomorrow, so I could cover her shift with someone else, and I was told by one of the household that Linda had gone to the pictures and would be home by five o'clock,' said Celia.

'But she's a good worker, doesn't that come into account?'

'No, definitely not. No one is indispensable. If you start giving girls privileges, they take advantage and become prima donnas overnight. If you buck the system, you get struck off the roster; it's as simple as that. We lost six clients because Linda wasn't here today; it would have been seven if Mr T hadn't stayed.'

'Yes, but it will add up to many more with her not being here at all. Linda has quite a following,' I argued.

'That's the rules, I'm afraid. And anyway, there's a rumour that Francy will be back in a couple of months.'

'Who said?' asked Carol, looking concerned.

'She phoned Don last night, apparently. She's leaving her boyfriend and is returning to work.'

I could tell by the looks on the girls' faces that they were not that pleased with the news.

'What's wrong with Francy?' I asked Carol, while we waited for Celia to check our rooms. 'She's famous in every massage parlour in Auckland.'

'Oh nothing. She's nice enough. But if you think Kelly is busy, Francy is even busier, and when she left a few months ago the clientèle of the rest of us went up noticeably. When she comes back it will be noticeably down, along with our money. But I suppose it keeps us on our toes,' she said.

Although I liked Linda very much, I was really glad she'd gone, because it meant I could take over her room. Jill used the room on Linda's days off, so I knew she would be keen to take it over, but the rules were 'first in, first served' and I was going to be first in.

The next day I walked into the lunch bar at five minutes past ten to find I was the first one there; room one was mine! Jill joined me not long after and she sat chatting away to me, obviously not knowing I was going to pinch the room she wanted.

Celia came a few minutes later. 'Who was in first?' she asked.

'Me, and I'd like room one,' I said.

Jill's face fell like a stone. 'I wanted that one,' she said, almost pleading.

'You know the rules, Jill. You should have been here earlier,' said Celia, scribbling away on her pad. 'I really can't see what difference it makes, all the rooms have the same things in them.'

For the rest of the day Jill walked around with a face as long as a fiddle, and to make things worse, one of her regular clients booked in with Carol, while Jill sat round waiting for a booking who didn't turn up.

Late in the afternoon Carol massaged one of Linda's regulars, and he told her that he had loaned Linda a large sum of money and wanted to know where she lived. He said he had waited in the building where she parked her car a couple of times, but Linda had avoided him. He was worried about losing the money, which was many thousands of dollars. We all talked about it and came to the conclusion that he had made it up to find out where she lived because he was upset at her leaving Fleure's. Celia divulged to us that Linda had reported to Don that she was being stalked by a client, and on one occasion Don had accompanied her to the carpark building because she was frightened. 'But it wasn't old John, the one who saw Carol today,' she said.

*

At home, I counted the money in the mung-bean jar. I had enough to put a deposit on a new car. At nine o'clock the next morning, I walked into one of Auckland's top European car salesyards and picked out a natty little sports model. Everything seemed quite straightforward until the salesman tried to organise finance for me. I could not prove that I had a job, let alone enough money to pay back the loan. I wanted that car more than anything else in the world, but how? I telephoned Mr Clarke for some advice. 'Try being honest with them, Mrs Blake. It worked with me, if you remember. Should they want a reference for your ability to pay, tell them to call me. I would be pleased to help. And tell me, how is your job going? Still enjoying it?'

'Oh yes, Mr Clarke, and I'm getting better at it every day!'

'Are you, indeed? Splendid, splendid! And are you still . . .' I could just see him rolling his forefinger around.

'Oh yes, Mr Clarke, all the time.' I loved these conversations with old Clarkie. We never actually got to talk about anything specific, just a whole heap of innuendoes going back and forth.

The car salesman was speechless, I suspect for the first time in his life, when I told him my true occupation. He asked me to give him twenty-four hours and said he would telephone Mr Clarke. The next day I was driving my beautiful sports car around Auckland, all paid for with Religious Roger's 'wages of sin'. It was a wonderful feeling.

On my next shift, I arrived to find Jill sitting in the lunch bar with a smug expression on her face. I looked at my watch, it was right on ten o'clock. Tomorrow I shall have to be here at a quarter to ten, I said to myself. No matter how long it took, I would be at work earlier and earlier, until Jill gave up.

One of my clients was a top New Zealand accountant, a very smart gentleman who sat on the board of several large companies and seemed to spend his time commuting from board meeting to board meeting all over the country. George took an interest in my affairs and gave me some very good advice.

'Diana, you must start paying tax or you will get yourself into a lot of trouble. An accumulation of wealth will not go unnoticed, and the Inland Revenue will eventually catch up with you.' He gave me the name and address of a small group of accountants who specialised in taxation. 'You are not obliged to tell them what you do for a living, but of course if you don't, you cannot claim for your condoms and the like. It would be in your best interest to tell them the truth, and will in the end save you a lot of money.' This made a lot of sense to me, but when I mentioned it to the others, they were horrified.

'I'm not giving anything to the government,' said Amber. 'When they legalise soliciting, then I'll think about it. If you got busted, paying your taxes wouldn't get you off the hook, you'd still get your name in the paper and be shunned by the neighbours.'

'On the other hand,' said Carol, 'if we all paid tax, it would make Mr Muldoon, the government, the police, and civil servants all guilty of living off immoral earnings. Think about it!' We all thought about it and screamed with laughter.

I decided to find my own tax accountant. I found one locally, but when I told him what I did for a living, he stared at me blankly and said, 'I don't think I can help you, Mrs Blake. I'll have my secretary show you out,' and that was that! His attitude made me angry, but I kept my cool and left his office with dignity.

The next day I made an appointment with the taxation specialists George had recommended, and went to see a Mr Edwards. 'I work in a massage parlour, and one of my clients advised me to pay tax and recommended I come to see you,' I said, waiting for his reaction.

'I see,' said Mr Edwards, without turning a hair, 'and how long have you been working, Mrs Blake?'

I knew if my earnings over the last months were taxed it would cost a fortune; and anyway, I'd spent most of it. So I decided, rightly or wrongly, to tell a white lie. 'A month,' I said, with my fingers crossed.

'Okay, now you won't have to pay any tax until next year, and what I want you to do is keep a daily record of your earnings and of things you would use in the job which may be tax deductible — condoms, etcetera. In fact, make a note of every little thing, no matter how insignificant.'

'Taxi fares?' I asked.

'I don't know about taxi fares,' he said, 'but get receipts for them, and we'll give it a go. The IRD will soon let us know if they don't agree.'

'Well, we should be able to claim on them. We couldn't possibly use public transport in what we wear to work,' I said. 'We have to work in evening wear on the night shift.' Who was to know I wasn't on the night shift!

'For every four hundred dollars you earn, I want you to pop one hundred into a savings account. That way, next year your tax money will be all ready to go and will have been earning interest for you in the meantime. In March next year, we will fill in a return for you, and your first payment will be in July.'

That all seemed pretty straightforward to me, and I felt more at ease having done it. I did not tell the girls that I had gone ahead with the tax, probably because they'd laugh at me, but when it was time for my first payment, while writing out the cheque, a little voice inside me said, 'Today, the New Zealand Government are guilty of living off immoral earnings from the wages of sin.'

A few months later I was to learn that quite a few working ladies were paying tax and that the New Zealand Government had been living off immoral earnings for years!

Jill was not rostered on Fridays, so there was no need to be at work early, for which I was very grateful because Fridays were always busy. Kelly was usually booked up from the time she came in, so we were short-handed with the cleaning, and it still had to be done even if it took all day. That was another reason I wanted to be a top lady. If you were always busy, you didn't have to do cleaning. We finished around eleven-thirty, and Celia told me I had Dennis in my room and that he'd just arrived.

'Boy! You move fast,' he said. 'I telephoned Executive House, and they made an appointment with Diana. But when I got there, it wasn't you. She looked a bit like you, but when she got her gear off . . . Yuk! Cellulite everywhere. Anyway, it cost me sixty dollars to find out where you were.'

Dennis told me he was in Auckland for two nights and was dining with a client that evening, but would like to take me out the following evening, to which I eagerly agreed. We spent a very pleasant hour together, for which he gave me eighty dollars and some perfume. Just before Dennis left Fleure's, he made another appointment with me for the following day.

151

The rest of the day was very busy, as predicted. I went home exhausted, counted my money, and stuffed it in the mung-bean jar until I had time to bank it.

CHAPTER 16

On Saturday morning Laura was already at work when I got there. That was one thing in her favour, she was always early, and as the lunch bar didn't open on Saturdays this saved us from the audience at the traffic lights. At the top of the stairs, I was brought to a halt by the most putrid smell. It was a cross between rotting fish and old tyres.

'The incinerator's too full, so I'll get you to clean it out before you get going on the spas,' said Laura, without actually looking at me.

The incinerator was a small electrically operated one, which was attached to a wall in a toilet just outside the day room. It was used for burning condoms, and jolly efficient it was too. But, no matter how many times the girls were told that the metal condom packets do not burn and are likely to short the electronics out, they still piled them in, even when it was obvious the thing wasn't working. I stood looking at the machine; it was full to overflowing and still warm from where the centre had been smouldering. The smell was from melted rubber and stale semen. I think that was one of the most awful jobs I have ever had to do in my life. After that, cleaning the spa pools didn't seem so bad.

Chrissy came in late, all flustered and angry. Her house had been burgled the day before and the thieves had taken just about everything that was precious to her, including several pieces of very nice furniture.

'Are you insured?' I asked.

'Fuck no! It was all hot,' she said. 'You can't insure stolen property!' I felt silly for asking.

That afternoon a man came in wanting a 'line up'. This was the first time I'd had to do this and I did not like it. I felt degraded and cheap. Chrissy, Amber and I stood in a line while he walked

153

along looking us up and down in turn. He felt one of Chrissy's breasts, and she slapped his hand away.

'Are you a natural blonde?' he said to me. I nodded. 'Show us your pussy then.'

I wanted to shout, 'I'll show you my knee in your groin!' But Laura was lurking in the passage, waiting for him to make his choice, and I knew she'd have me off the roster quicker than lightning if I said anything to upset him. So I smiled sweetly and said, 'Oh! You're a cheeky one, aren't you?'

He settled on Amber. 'I like 'em young,' he commented as he followed her through to room two.

Because Saturdays were not busy, we had time for lunch. Laura would phone a take-away bar close by, and organise a taxi to pick up our order. Anything from hamburgers and chips to Chinese food, we gorged the lot, Chrissy washing hers down with a special juice. She would often offer me one of her juices, but I always refused. Drinking alcohol in the afternoon always made me lethargic, and my work suffered because of it.

Dennis came for his appointment, paid me a further sixty dollars and made arrangements for dinner that evening. He had booked a table at Antoine's for seven-thirty.

He arrived on the dot of seven with a bottle of Bollinger, which Emma helped us drink, then we went by taxi to Parnell Road. The meal was superb, and I lingered over every succulent mouthful. Dennis ordered a bottle of Château Margaux, a beautiful French red wine, and as usual we finished with cognac, coffee and some truffles made on the premises by the chef, which melted in your mouth. We went back to the Sheraton for more champagne, and rumpty doo. But Dennis, who wasn't used to so much sex, had made a pig of himself twice in the last twenty-four hours, and was about to make a pig of himself again full of booze. Of course, the inevitable happened. Dennis couldn't get it up, let alone in, so we gave it up as a bad job, drank more champagne and talked about his wife and kids in Wellington. Just before I left to go home, he gave me a present, beautifully wrapped as usual. I opened it up to find a very expensive dress watch in the box. This man was something else.

*

Sitting for ten minutes in the spa pool six or seven times a day was having its usual effects on my skin, and I was beginning to look like an old prune. As it was compulsory to join all clients in the spa, unless they chose not to have one, I had to devise a way of getting around it before ending up with a serious skin condition. Old Arthur was my guinea pig. He loved his spa, and it was going to take a lot of manipulating for him to make the decision against having one without being conscious of any coercion from me.

I undressed him and myself, and showered him slowly and seductively. To keep the carpet from getting damp and mouldy, we liked the guys to dry off a bit before going to the spa. 'I'll get you a towel,' I said, and crawled across the large bed on my hands and knees to get one from a pile I'd placed on the other side of it. This left absolutely nothing to the imagination.

'Oh, that's a lovely sight!' said Arthur, almost drooling.

I stretched and sat on the bed with my legs apart, and he came over and sat next to me, rubbing his hand between my thighs.

'Oh, that's nice,' I said, running my hands between his legs. 'I'll have to get you to give me a massage one day, you have good hands.'

'I'll give you one today,' he said, his eyes gleaming.

'I'm sorry, Arthur, there won't be time.' I turned the spa on. 'Come along, in you get.'

'I don't think I'll have a spa today, massaging you sounds like more fun,' he said.

'It's okay, Arthur, I know how much you love your time in the spa,' I started to get in.

'Diana! I do not want a spa!' he said, and he really meant it. 'Please let me massage you?'

Well, that was that problem sorted out! That method worked nearly every time, and with all the oil on my skin from the massages I was having, the dryness disappeared in no time. Although some of the massages I got left a lot to be desired, it was far better than the spa. And the guys loved it. My requests improved dramatically from then on.

One morning I arrived at work to find Amber was no longer on the roster.

'What did she do?' I asked Celia. I could not believe she had broken any of the rules, she was far too shy to flout authority.

'She didn't do anything. She's met a really nice guy and is getting married soon,' said Celia. 'It happens a lot, but doesn't usually last very long. They can't live without the money constantly coming in.'

I found that easy to believe. Because you were paid after every job in cash and the parlour was so busy, you knew at the end of the day you would have a purse full of money. And it just kept on coming. I would often call in to Liquorland and buy a bottle of Moët to quaff, or take Emma out shopping and blow a couple of hundred dollars and not miss it. Of course, the money was all going into the bank, but my cheque account was very well used, and there was a never-ending supply of money to go into it. The morning after every shift, I would bank the previous day's takings, putting a quarter of it in a savings account. I knew full well it would be very difficult to go back to living on an ordinary wage paid out weekly.

My plan to work in the sex industry only until I was back on my feet had flown out the window. Who in their right mind would take on a hairdressing business and put up with the worry of PAYE, ACC and all the other hundred and one things one had to do to run it. When working in a parlour you only had to turn up for work four times a week and, once you knew your stuff, collect the money and pay someone to do the rest. I was very happy in my work, and was proving to be extremely good at it!

Two new girls started with us to take the place of Linda and Amber. Anna was a nineteen-year-old blonde with the most enormous bosom ever, and Sylvia was a delightful Maori woman in her late thirties. Sylvia and Chrissy were friends from way back. No one had heard any more about Francy starting back at Fleure's, and we forgot about it.

A week after Sylvia and Anna started, a notice appeared on the wall in the day room, alongside the usual lists of rules and requests: STAFF MEETING SIX O'CLOCK TUESDAY. ANYONE NOT ATTENDING WILL BE STRUCK OFF THE ROSTER.

Tuesday was one of my days off, and I had made plans to be somewhere else, so I asked Celia to be excused.

'You see where it says "Anyone not attending will be struck off the roster"?' she said. I nodded. 'Well, it means, if you are not there at six o'clock, you will be struck off the roster!'

'But I have made other plans,' I protested.

'I'm sorry, those are the rules and there are no exemptions.'

Of course there had been other staff meetings, but they had always occurred on my working days. They made me a bit late home, but this was nothing to get upset about. But this situation impinged on my leisure time, and I felt angry that I had to change my plans to suit the management, knowing full well it would be a total waste of time. Don would shout and bellow at us for some misdemeanour committed by an unknown person or persons, and tell us that if we didn't all shape up, we could ship out. Any input we had would be ignored, and we'd all be sent home.

I grizzled to Carol about it. 'At least you can change your plans,' she said. 'My friend Jade was away on holiday for three weeks. We had a staff meeting, and, of course, Jade didn't know anything about it. When she got back from Hawaii she found she didn't have a job.'

'You're joking!' I said, not believing even Don Springfield could be that hard on his staff. But I found out later that Jade was a hopeless worker, and she was to be struck off anyway.

No matter low long you worked in the sex industry, or how popular you were with the clients, or how many requests you managed to get in a month, you were never able to rest on your laurels. Things would go along swimmingly for a time, and life would seem to be a bowl of roses. Then, just when you thought you couldn't go wrong, a day would dawn that brought you down to earth with a sharp smack in the face! Such a day started with Emma's report. It was a good report, except she'd had seven days off that term and I'd only been aware of two. She had not only wagged five days, but had also forged my signature on notes she had written to excuse herself. I was more hurt than angry, and I felt I had to take part of the blame when I realised she had only been doing this since her car had arrived on the scene. She and several girlfriends were taking days off and cruising around town. Emma was truly sorry, and very embarrassed to have been found out so easily.

'Your teacher must be an idiot not to have realised the signature wasn't mine,' I said.

'Oh Mum! A five-year-old could forge your signature, it's so simple,' she said with no shame.

'Emm! If you try anything like this again, I shall take the car away. Do you understand?'

'Yes Mum! I'm sorry.' She gave me a hug, and it was forgotten.

At work, Celia told me I had a booking at ten forty-five. Great! I wouldn't have to do much in the way of cleaning. At ten forty-five my client had not arrived, and Celia suggested I start dusting down the plants until he did. At eleven o'clock, my booking telephoned to say he'd been delayed and would be in by eleven-thirty. The other girls started to get busy, and I was left with all the cleaning.

'I could have booked you in with old Bob if I'd known Dave was going to be late,' shouted Celia over the noise of the vacuum cleaner.

At eleven-twenty, Dave telephoned to say he was delayed yet again, and wouldn't be in till after lunch, and that he'd call back later. Meanwhile, Celia had turned away two guys because she had no one available to take care of them. Then a man came in and booked in with me for half an hour. He got out of the shower and made it quite plain that he was only in for a massage.

'I don't need to come into places like this for sex, because I've never had to pay for it,' he said. 'I've got loads of women in my life practically throwing it at me . . . Oh, I like my feet massaged well . . . One of my lady friends phones me at least three times a week for a quick one at lunchtime. She's a real goer.' I couldn't believe this man was so far up himself! 'The last time she called me,' he said, 'we had sex on the front seat of my car in the Domain. Anyone could have seen us.'

I finished his back. 'Would you like to turn over?' I said.

'Er, no, only my back please,' he said, and he proceeded to tell me about all his girlfriends and what their sexual preferences were. When I'd finished he thanked me, had his shower and left. I walked with him to the door, then went back to tidy my room and found he'd ejaculated on the towel he was laying on. I had been ripped off beautifully and should have known better. All the talk about his girlfriends was nothing more than a fantasy to get his rocks off without having to pay a cent, while a naked woman massaged him. It was one of the oldest tricks in the book, and I fell for it like a fool.

'You've just missed Ken, but he went through with Anna because he couldn't wait,' said Celia.

I thought an extremely rude word! Ken was a lovely man, who had been to see me on several occasions and always paid me ten dollars extra. And I'd missed him because of that last rip-off merchant. I lit a cigarette, made a coffee and sat in the day room whinging to myself. After about ten minutes or so, the buzzer went and a figure appeared on the television monitor. It was 'Clean Colin'.

'I've just dropped by on the off-chance Diana is free,' he said in that clipped way he had of speaking that irritated me so much. Celia booked him in and took him into my room. Now a situation like this is a test of how good your acting abilities are. Although I detested this man with every fibre of my being, I had to make him think he was the love of my life and that I was very pleased to see him.

He was as awful as ever. 'Hello Diana,' he said when I walked into the room. 'I know this is an unusual time for me to see you. I do so prefer to catch you first thing in the morning when you're clean. But I have to make an exception this week because I'm off to Australia for a few months, and this afternoon is the only free time I have before leaving.'

That was the best news I'd had all day. We had a shower together, he making doubly sure I was clean. He then had his 'money's worth' for the rest of the time, took far too long in the shower afterwards and got me into trouble for being late out of the room.

'You are a good ten minutes over time, Diana,' said Celia, when I went back to the day room. When I tried to explain how Colin had a 'clean fetish' and it was impossible to get him out of the shower, Celia said, 'Well, chop his massage short to compensate.' Of course I couldn't tell her about the 'money's worth' problem he had as well. Our arrangements with clients for extras were not allowed to be talked about with management. That could get me struck off the roster too!

Don arrived, and we were asked to vacate the day room for a while as he wanted to have a private conversation with Celia. So we all trooped into the lounge and talked about all the things we were not allowed to talk about in front of the management staff. The main topic was the problems one of the condom manufacturers were having at that time. They had recalled a whole batch because a flaw in the rubber was causing breakages. A couple of the girls said they'd had problems with this particular brand, and stopped using them long ago.

We could hear a male voice that was not Don's coming from the office and the next minute my lovely Wally walked into the lounge and sat down on the couch next to Anna, the only seat available. I had just taken care of him a few days previously, and as he usually came in to see me every fortnight, I felt flattered he had returned so soon.

'Hello, sweetheart!' I said, giving him a peck on the cheek. 'If you would like to go into my room, I'll get you some refreshment. What would you like?'

Wally sat there looking extremely embarrassed and didn't make a move. I couldn't understand what I'd said wrong. Then Celia came into the lounge and handed Wally a glass of wine. 'There you are Wally, I'll just pop you into Anna's room, and she will join you presently,' she said. Anna was sitting there looking extremely uncomfortable. So was everyone else. I could have bitten my tongue off. Why had I taken it for granted that Wally had come to see me? At that moment, I wished the ground would open up and swallow me then and there! All eyes were in my direction, even Celia's, although she didn't know what was going on, which was one thing to be thankful for! I could feel my face flushing from the neck up and I was desperately trying to think of something I could say to make it all right. There was nothing! So I beamed the biggest smile I could muster, mumbled, 'You guys have fun,' and went to the loo until Wally and Anna had gone through to Anna's room.

For the rest of the afternoon the others were steadily busy, while I sat doing nothing. One man arrived at the door and, when told I was the only lady available, said he'd come back another day. Celia couldn't give me away free that afternoon! The straw that broke the camel's back was when, at ten past six, a man actually paid some money at the desk to see me and was taken through to my room. When I went in, he took one look at me and said, 'Oh! I didn't want a lady quite so old. Do you know if anyone else is available to take care of me? I'd like someone a lot younger.' I told him there wasn't, and he would only be able to take a credit if he left Fleure's, as they never refunded. He agreed to the credit and left my room!

I reached home that evening with twenty-five dollars in my purse and an enormous inferiority complex. Maybe I was too old for the job, and I should stop kidding myself that I was a good hooker and quit! My thoughts were interrupted by the telephone. It was Chrissy wanting some more Codcomol. We talked for a while, and I told her about my dreadful day.

'Oh, everyone gets those days, no matter how old they are. The young girls are told that they're too young, the big girls are too big, the small girls are too small, the Maori girls are too dark and the Pakeha girls are too pale; you can't please everyone, and sometimes it happens that you can't please anyone. It will be someone else's turn tomorrow, you'll see.' I hoped so!

One Wednesday, around midday, Chrissy and Sylvia asked if they could go down to the lunch bar to buy something to eat and were told they could. At two thirty in the afternoon they had not returned. It was a busy day, and Celia had to turn away a lot of business. She was absolutely petrified that Don would find out she had let them go out during work time, as it was against the rules. They returned just after three so drunk they could hardly stand, and were having to hold one another up. I had never seen Celia so furious. They stood in the day room swaying back and forth with stupid grins on their faces, while she screamed abuse at them. Right in the middle of this, Don turned up unexpectedly and joined in! The result was that both Chrissy and Sylvia were fired on the spot and told to 'fuck off now'. Carol, Jill and I hurried about our business, pretending we hadn't noticed anything untoward was going on. 'I wonder if he'll fire Celia as well,' said Carol.

Sylvia was reinstated, and Chrissy was taken back at The Tokyo a week later, when Don was in a better mood. A new girl started with us called Jane. She was absolutely stunning, in her early twenties with long blonde hair and the figure of a super model. She reminded me of Nicky at Total Escape, except Jane was refined and well-spoken. For the first week, she proved to be very popular, and a couple of clients returned to see her within a day or so of their first appointment. On her second week, she failed to turn up for one of her shifts. Normally a girl, no matter·who she was, would be struck of the roster for this. But when she turned up bright and early for her next shift, Celia decided to give her the benefit of the doubt and let her off with a warning.

'I bet she's a junkie,' said Kelly, who'd been working longer than any of us and knew a thing or two about junkies. 'I can pick them a mile off!'

'Well, before she started I checked her for track marks and she was clean,' said Celia.

Jane worked well for a week or so, then blotted her copy book again and failed to turn up for a shift. We were quite pleased, as she was taking our clients one after another and this time she was sure to be fired. But when she arrived for her next shift, nothing was said, and she was not even given a warning.

One day, one of our regulars came out of Jane's room complaining she'd fallen asleep on him. Celia went into the room to find Jane, still in her underwear, sound asleep on the bed. This in itself was a fireable offence; but blow me down, she was given yet another warning and sent home. The next day Celia telephoned Jane's flat to ask what the story was, and told that Jane had 'man troubles' and was being stalked by an ex-lover. She needed a couple of days to get a non-molestation order put into effect. She was given five days off!

'She's a junkie,' insisted Kelly. 'Have you noticed our teaspoons? And she spends an awful lot of time in her room when not working.'

'What about the teaspoons?' we all wanted to know.

Kelly showed us one. It was bent at an odd angle and burnt underneath. 'Junkies use teaspoons to prepare the drug for injecting. They heat it up over a candle or lighter. See how the bowl of the spoon has gone nearly black? Stainless steel discolours like that when it's been overheated. Well, someone here is mainlining. I don't think it's any of us, and the night girls have been here a lot longer than the bent teaspoons!'

When Jane returned to work, she had dyed her hair jet black, telling us she was worried that her ex-lover would find her more easily with blonde hair, but he certainly wasn't looking for a brunette.

She became busier and busier, and we would sit in the day room watching her go in and out of her room with what we had thought were our regulars.

All but one of our teaspoons disappeared. 'The bowl of the spoon eventually falls off through being overheated,' said Kelly. 'I wonder what she'll do when the last one gives up the ghost?'

We didn't ever find out, because one day Jane just disappeared. Celia telephoned her flat when she didn't turn up for a shift, to find she'd done a moonlight flit. Not long after that we found that Kelly had been right, Jane was a junkie, and the reason she had pinched so many of our clients was that she spent most of her working time so spaced out she was incapable of controlling what she was doing, and the men were having a grand old time for anything from fifteen to twenty-five dollars a pop. One man said he'd had sex with her twice for fifteen dollars. I often wondered what had happened in Jane's life to get her into that state. She was well-educated, intelligent and beautiful. What a waste.

Celia was very surprised at the news about Jane's habit. 'Most junkies wear sleeves to cover the track marks,' she said. 'Her arms were clear of anything like that, and she always wore short sleeves.'

'She was injecting the stuff between her toes,' said Kelly. 'Didn't you notice? They were blue with bruises.' Not one of us had noticed.

Jane's place wasn't filled immediately, because Francy was definitely coming back to Fleure's and would start in two weeks. So whenever we became busy, a girl was sent from The Tokyo to fill in.

Since Linda had been struck off the roster, we learned that she had borrowed huge sums of money from different clients, using a non-existent farm she was supposed to have owned as collateral. Most of the men involved were really nice older guys, and some of them had lent her their life's savings. But Linda had disappeared off the face of the earth, and to my knowledge, none of them got their money back.

CHAPTER 17

Carol and Jill were quite concerned about Francy's return, and terrified their requests would go down because of it. Kelly was so busy it didn't matter to her. The rest of us wondered what this Francy had that the rest of womanhood missed out on. Word passed quickly around the clients, and a lot asked exactly when she would be starting; Celia had even taken some bookings for her. From what I could gather, Francy was tall and blonde with the most beautiful legs ever. According to one client, her countenance was that of an angel and she 'fucked like a rattlesnake'!

It was with some excitement that I walked into the lunch bar on the morning that Francy was due to start. I was a few minutes earlier than usual in case she had designs on my room. One by one the others arrived, but no Francy. Jill and Carol were noticeably subdued, but when Celia unlocked the door at ten-thirty and told us Francy had the flu and would not be starting until next week, they cheered up no end.

I expected a blonde version of Joan Collins to arrive on the Monday Francy actually started. But she was far from it. Indeed she was tall, blonde and beautiful with legs to die for, but unlike Joan Collins, Francy had a heart of gold, a cheery smile and a wonderful sense of humour. No wonder the clients loved her, I thought.

When last working at Fleure's, Francy had always used room three, but now there were four new ones to choose from. She took room five, the one Jill had settled on when she realised she wasn't going to get room one. A pathetic, hard-done-by look settled on Jill's normally serious face, and was to last for weeks, until she finally left to do a full-time course at Tech. I think she blamed Francy for her diminishing clientèle, although really it was her own lack of charisma that finished her off. But maybe if Francy hadn't returned to Fleure's, Jill would never have got around to doing the course she'd talked about so often in the past.

The lights were dim, my client was lying peacefully on his stomach while I slowly massaged his back, and soft music was wafting over the sound system. The atmosphere had a lazy, faraway feel about it, and all was right with the world.

FLASH! The whole room suddenly became an interrogation centre as the stark white light bulb above the door was activated, and shone into my eyes. The vice were on the premises!

'What's happened?' asked my client, trying to get up.

'Oh, it's only the inspection lights,' I said, pushing him back down and hoping I didn't sound as frightened as I felt.

'Inspection lights? For whom?' he wanted to know.

I didn't think it was a good idea to tell him the truth for two reasons. Firstly, if he ran out of the room with fright, he would run right into the arms of the vice squad, and who knows what would have happened. Secondly, I would lose any chance of making some money out of him. According to what I'd heard, the vice squad were very quiet with their inspections and did not linger; so I decided to tell a lie. 'It's okay, John, it's the Health Department. They are here to check on some work we were advised to do to the spa pools. It's a bit like a building inspector checking on work at a building site. This lighting system is all wired up to one switch, but they won't come in here. It's only the pump room they're interested in.' He seemed to believe my story, covered his eyes and settled down to enjoy his massage again. A few minutes later, I heard a faint rattle, and in the reflection in the mirror tiles I saw the door open. A head peered around it for a moment, then the door silently closed. John was almost asleep and absolutely unaware that a member of the Auckland Vice Squad had looked in and seen him on the bed, bare bum and all — in my panic, I had forgotten to cover it with a towel. It wasn't long before the inspection lights went out, and my client stayed to enjoy his sixty dollars worth.

'I've just had a call from The Tokyo,' said Celia, looking extremely concerned. 'Chrissy's been busted. Two police officers have just taken her down to Central.'

'Have they charged her?' asked Kelly.

'Yes, for soliciting! They sent in an undercover earlier this afternoon. The receptionist at The Tokyo will keep us informed.'

I couldn't believe it, not Chrissy! Rumours had circulated about odd girls getting busted, but they were just names, people you didn't know and were never likely to.

'I wonder what she'll do now?' said Carol. 'She won't be allowed to work in a parlour, not with a conviction.'

The phone rang. It was a receptionist from an inner city parlour to say that one of their girls had been busted and that the vice were doing the rounds. She warned us all to be very careful. It was a little before five in the afternoon, and I was praying no one would come in for the rest of the shift. When I left Fleure's for the day, it was with a very heavy heart.

The 'jungle drums' had been working overtime on the night shift, and in the morning there was a wealth of information waiting for us. Seven girls throughout Auckland had been arrested on soliciting charges in twenty-four hours. Rumour had it that the police had a large undercover operation underway, using policemen from Wellington dressed as everyday working men. The policeman who busted Chrissy had been dressed in a suit and had carried a briefcase; another one was dressed as a tradesman. All the arrested women said they picked up that something wasn't quite right about the men, and should have gone with their gut feelings. The undercovers had all only booked in for half an hour — to save the taxpayers' money, we thought — and after a brief massage had asked what the girl could do for twenty-five dollars. When told, they said they would think about it and come back another time, then they left the parlour. Later in the day, two detectives had returned to the parlour and arrested the girl concerned. Every account was almost identical. Rumour also had it that the police operation still had a couple of days to go, and that everyone should be extremely careful. We all decided to have sex only with regular clients until the heat was off.

My first client of the day booked in for half an hour and was a tall, muscly young man with a moustache, dressed in a green ARA bus-driver's uniform. I noticed his trousers were far too big for him, and were held up with a brown leather belt pulled in so tightly that huge tucks formed into sort of pleats all around his waist. Either he had lost one hell of a lot of weight, or the trousers were borrowed from a fat man. Very odd! I thought.

'You're a bus driver?'

'That's right,' he answered.

'What run are you on?'

'Otahuhu,' he said.

Now this man was a Pakeha, and these were the days before political correctness had been invented and everyone began to use the correct pronunciation for Maori words. So in Auckland, everyone, whether Pakeha *or* Maori, pronounced the name of this South Auckland suburb as 'Otahu'. Only someone from outside, perhaps from Wellington, would say 'Otahuhu', and not even then was it spoken with the proper Maori pronunciation. This was getting very suspicious, I thought.

After further conversation, I realised this young man didn't know Auckland very well at all, and I was able to catch him out on several things. I had a very large pit in my stomach, and my gut feeling told me something wasn't right.

'What can you do for twenty-five dollars?' he asked.

I nearly died! This guy had to be an undercover cop.

'I beg your pardon!' I said, trying to sound like my mother when she heard someone swear.

'What can you do for twenty-five dollars?' he repeated.

'I don't know what you mean! But I'll tell you something, young man, this is a decent establishment, and I'll have no hanky-panky going on in my room!' I threw a towel at him. 'I think you had better have your shower and go. Any more of that sort of talk and I will be obliged to call the management.' He was out of the door quicker than a robber's dog, and whether he was an undercover cop or not I never did find out. I hope he was, because if he was an ordinary man wanting a nice time with a nice lady, I would have put him off massage parlours for life.

We were all very worried about what had happened to Chrissy, and how she would make a living from then on with a soliciting charge behind her. But then Kelly said she'd heard from a girlfriend working in another parlour that Chrissy had done a deal with the police to do with a homebake operation, and the charge of soliciting had been dropped.

'What's homebake?' I honestly did not know what it was.

'It's a process where heroin is made from codeine-based tablets. They do it with test-tubes and things,' she said.

'You mean like Codcomol?'

'Yeah, that's right. Codcomol, Panadeine, there are heaps of them.'

'I was buying Codcomol for Chrissy for her migraines,' I said. 'You mean . . .?'

'So was I!' said Carol. 'I had to go over to Henderson for them, because the chemists in Avondale wouldn't let me have any more.'

'So did Celia, so did Jill, and anyone else she could sweet-talk into it,' said Kelly. 'Didn't you know she was into junk?'

'No,' I said. 'I knew she drank a lot, but not drugs!' I couldn't believe it.

Kelly had worked in the sex industry for so long and with so many different women with all sorts of problems, she was an expert in these matters. 'Like alcoholics, drug addicts are very crafty,' she said. 'They have to be to get what they need in a day. Look at Jane. No one picked up that she was an addict out here, but in the room she was spaced out so far she sometimes forgot to charge the guys at all. Only the teaspoons told the story. You cannot trust them as far as you can kick them. They're all charm and fun, while picking your pockets behind your back.'

'Chrissy wasn't a thief!' I argued.

'Wasn't she? Why couldn't she report to the police the fact that her house had been burgled? She may not have committed the actual crimes, but she sold the stuff, which makes her just as guilty as the thieves, and it was all done to keep up her habit.' Kelly grinned. 'I had to stifle a wee laugh when Chrissy told me how upset and shocked she and Keith were when they walked in that Friday night to find the ranchslider smashed and their house empty. It just goes to prove there is no honour among thieves.'

I really admired Kelly. She was married with two children, a son and a daughter, who were both at private schools. Her husband had a small business, while she worked in the sex industry, and between them they brought in a small fortune. They lived very well. They each drove a new car, and took holidays abroad regularly.

Her husband was to be admired too. Not many men could handle a wife working in a massage parlour and be able to look upon it as just a job. The fear of the children finding out was the only thing I could see that could possibly be an eventual threat to their relationship.

The cleaning was finished, and I sat down with my cup of coffee. My first booking was due to arrive in fifteen minutes. On the sofa next to me was the previous day's *Herald*, and I glanced down at it. Right on the front page was a photograph that made me freeze. I read the caption underneath: 'Have you seen this man?' It was a picture of the man I'd escorted in Titirangi when working at Total Escape. The article said the police thought he may have been murdered, and that he had robbed a bank to finance a drug deal prior to coming to Auckland from down the line. I showed it to Celia and told her the story.

'Have a word with Don,' she said. 'He'll know what to do.'

I telephoned The Tokyo, and was told Don was away with his wife for a few days and wouldn't be back until Tuesday.

'Wait till Tuesday,' advised Celia.

I tried to bury myself in work for the rest of the day, but it was difficult with the image of that man in my mind.

When I arrived home after work several days later, Emma said, 'A man called you. He said he'd phone back later.'

I couldn't eat my dinner.

'Mum! Why haven't you eaten anything? It's your favourite. I cooked it specially,' said Emma, like some suburban housewife. I was halfway through an apology when the phone rang.

'May I speak to Angela Blake please,' said a familiar voice I couldn't quite put a face to.

'Speaking,' I replied.

'This is Detective Sergeant Mark Layton. Do you remember me? I met you at The Harem?'

'Yes, Sergeant Layton. How could I forget an introduction like that. And what have I done now?'

He laughed. 'Nothing, we hope. I have been talking to Archie who runs Total Escape in Derby Lane. You worked for him some months ago, I believe?'

'Yes.'

'Angela, do you remember an escort you did to a house in Titirangi? Archie has a record of the escort. He remembers you were very upset, and left his establishment immediately afterwards.'

'Yes, I remember it well.' How on earth did they find me? I thought.

'Angela, the man you saw, we think he was murdered shortly after you left him. I wonder if you would mind coming down to Central first thing in the morning so we can piece together some of the details we think you can help us with.'

I could hardly say no, so I agreed to be at Central at nine o'clock in the morning.

For some strange reason, I felt relieved. Back at the dinner table I finished my food and had a second helping.

'What was that all about?' asked Emma. 'Why do you have to go to the police station tomorrow?'

I had told her about the escort when it first happened. 'The police think the man's been murdered, Emm, and I was one of the last people to see him alive. They want to talk to me about it.'

Emma didn't turn a hair at the news that her mother was mixed up in a murder. 'I expect you will have to make a statement. They'll keep you there for hours, so let me know if you're going to be late for dinner. I'm doing a casserole,' she said.

I was very nervous when I walked into Auckland Central Police Station next morning. The reception area was a hive of activity. I had to wait to see someone at the desk, then I was asked to take a seat for a few minutes. Almost immediately, Sergeant Layton appeared and took me through a security door, up several floors in the elevator and into a very busy office. Telephones were constantly ringing, people were coming and going, and I wondered how anyone got any work done among all the hustle and bustle. We went into a small adjacent room and Sergeant Layton asked me if I'd like some coffee. Good start! I thought.

'I have been in touch with the management of Fleure's, and have cleared it with them for you to be late in today.' He grinned at me. 'We don't want you being struck off the roster do we.' I was beginning to like this man.

Sergeant Layton explained that the murdered man had robbed a bank to finance a drug deal. He had then started to talk too much about it, so others in the gang had decided to eliminate him. They brought him to Auckland for a 'holiday'. They hired prostitutes to keep him happy, then shot him on the very sofa I'd been sitting on! The eighty dollars paid to me had been stolen money from the robbery.

'Just because the man was a bank robber doesn't mean he is any less important than any other murder victim. We have to find and punish whoever was responsible,' Sergeant Layton said.

For the next hour and a half we went over and over the events of that escort visit — who sat where in the room, what they all looked like, what the house looked like, what they all said, and what happened in detail from the minute I climbed into Bob's car. At that stage the body had not been found, but it was only a matter of time, Sergeant Layton said. Then he received an urgent call, and I was asked to sign the statement and told I could leave.

'There is a likelihood you will have to appear in court eventually, and we may need to speak to you again. So keep us informed about any change of address, as these things usually take time. Oh, and how come you have two driving licences?'

I started to tell him the story, then another urgent call came through for him, and I left.

On the front page of the *New Zealand Herald* the following day was a picture of the murdered man. Police had found the body buried under the garage floor at the house in Titirangi and arrests had been made, one of them being Bob, the man who took me to the house in his car! So, I had been picked up by a murderer, taken to have sex with a bank robber and paid with stolen notes from an armed robbery!

'What would Nana say?' said Emma when I told her. It didn't bear thinking about!

About this time, HIV and AIDS reared their ugly heads, and we all went for tests. The results took three weeks to come back to us, and those three weeks were hell. We had all done our share of sex without condoms, and although most girls were choosy about who they did without using them, there still lingered in the back of our minds the fear that perhaps we might have fallen prey to the dreaded syndrome. Overnight, all sex was done with a condom no matter what, which upset many clients. Some of them tried all sorts of tactics to get their own way.

'What do you mean I have to use a condom? Francy doesn't!' was a common ploy, but you knew damn well that Francy was as staunch as the rest of us. 'I'll pay you extra to do it without,' was another tactic. But we all stuck to our guns, and no one I knew was ever infected with HIV or AIDS.

This was mostly due to the hard work of the Prostitutes' Collective, which worked extremely hard to keep us all informed of the latest developments in the epidemic overseas. Although they didn't actually see us personally at Fleure's (management wouldn't let them in for some reason) we picked up the info from other establishments. They distributed pamphlets on safe and unsafe condoms, lubricants that actually ate through latex and caused all sorts of problems, and, of course, they encouraged us all to have 'The Test'.

Life goes on after bank robberies, murders and AIDS scares. Summer was on its way, and the money was still rolling in. My income and requests went down somewhat after Francy started, and for a while it was a little hurtful to see clients you thought were loyal scurrying through to Francy's room, hoping no one would notice. But this was short-lived. Once the novelty had worn off, they drifted back to me. Eventually, Francy, Kelly and I worked in with one another. If one of us was going on holiday, we would advise certain clients to see one of the other two, depending on their preference; for example, Francy was a soft, sensuous lover, where Kelly was a raunchy, 'sex hanging from the chandelier' kind of woman. You would not advise a little old gentleman who wanted lots of kisses and cuddles to see Kelly, nor would you recommend a man with the sexual performance of a pneumatic drill to see Francy.

'I have suggested Grant sees you while I'm away,' said Kelly one morning, before flying off to Fiji for two weeks. 'He has a wee problem with not being able to ejaculate, but talking dirty to him usually has the desired effect.'

Very often men would ask me to talk dirty to them, but for the life of me, I could not do it. I didn't know where to start.

'I'm not very good at talking dirty. Perhaps Francy would be his best bet,' I said.

'Grant can only come in on a Friday, one of Francy's days off. Why aren't you very good at it? Anyone can do it.'

'It just doesn't sound right when I try.'

'Well, what do you say,' she asked.

'Umm . . . dirty words, you know!' I felt embarrassed.

'What do you mean, "dirty words"? You don't just throw a barrage of dirty words at them, that's boring. You wouldn't get anyone off with that. If a man needs you to talk dirty to help him along a bit, make it good the first time or you'll have him humping away forever. I'll show you!' She half-closed her eyes and said in a dreamy voice, 'Oh! I can feel your big hard cock right up inside me, right up my juicy cunt. Fuck me with your big hard cock . . . harder, harder! Ooh . . .! Ahh . . .! I'm coming. Ohh! Ohh! Harder! Deeper! Ooh! Ooh!' She opened her eyes. 'He should have ejaculated by now. Okay, now you do it. Look as though you're in ecstasy . . . No! Not like that, you don't want to put him off for life!' Once again she half-closed her eyes and gave a wee moan. I tried again. 'Yes, that's it. Now, put some feeling into it . . . You've got it! Now, repeat after me, "I want to feel your big hard . . ." '

After many fits of laughter, and a whole heap of practice, I got the hang of it. I was to put my new skill into practice that very day.

'Is there anything else I can do for you?' I asked a new client.

'I beg your pardon,' he said. I repeated myself. 'You certainly can, sixty-dollars worth please.' We got down to business, and not long after settling into the missionary position, I realised he was having trouble ejaculating. He would work himself up into a crescendo of thrusts, only to wear himself out and not manage it.

'Talk dirty to me,' he said. 'It'll help if you talk dirty.'

His eyes were closed and his face screwed into a tense mask, so I didn't bother with the ecstatic expression. 'Oh! I can feel your big hard cock deep inside my juicy cunt!' I said dreamily, crossing my fingers and hoping God wasn't listening in. 'Fuck me hard!'

'Pardon?' he said. 'Speak up, I can't hear you!'

I repeated myself louder.

'You'll have to do better than that. I'm a bit deaf you know,' he shouted at me.

'HARDER, HARDER . . . OHH . . . AHH!' I yelled at the top of my voice, and looking up into the ceiling mirror, I thought, 'Is that me?'

Butcher, baker, candlestick-maker, once they had paid their door fee and were in the room with no clothes on, each had his own fantasy. Some wanted to believe they were having a love affair and would bring in bottles of wine and flowers. Others wanted to act out a blue movie. There were men who liked to wear women's clothing. One man had his nipples pierced, another his foreskin — and this was long before piercing was fashionable.

Some of them brought in strange clothes for us to wear. Richard had a raincoat fetish! He liked me to wear a white plastic raincoat throughout the massage and extras, because he loved to see my perspiration trickle down the inside of the plastic. The more perspiration, the quicker Richard ejaculated; no perspiration, no ejaculation. I would catch a glimpse of myself in the mirrors and have to stifle a laugh. To Richard this was serious stuff, and if I laughed out loud it could stop him from ejaculating altogether, and I might not get paid. The hour with Richard was usually a very long one!

Michael could only get sexual satisfaction if I moved with him, which was difficult when in the missionary position and pinned under a man twice my weight. One afternoon, I was trying very hard to move the way he wanted me to, and he was almost there, when his hairpiece fell off and hit me in the face. Of course, my first reaction was to move it away, but I couldn't without stopping the rhythm; so I left it there, hanging around my nose and chin like a big black beard. Michael grunted and had obviously ejaculated. Without a word, he grabbed the hairpiece from my face and flopped it back on his head sideways, then pulled himself to his knees between my legs.

'Oh! I needed that, nobody does it like you,' he said, grinning at me with the hairpiece now hanging over his right eye. He straightened it up, and I went to run the bath. When I turned around, the damn thing was hanging over his left eye.

'There is a mirror above the sink, if you would like to adjust it properly,' I suggested, hoping that I was not being too personal.

He pulled it off, exposing a totally bald head, and stuffed it into a brown paper bag he pulled from his jacket pocket. 'Oh! I only wear this when I come to see you. I know you couldn't get any satisfaction from a man with a head like a billiard ball, and I do want you to enjoy it too!'

CHAPTER 18

Barry came to see me for the first time early in November, 1985. Celia told me I had a man waiting in the lounge. 'Barry,' she said.

Barry? I didn't recall a regular named Barry, so I went to find out who this person was. I did not recognise him at all. 'Hello Barry, I'm Diana.'

'Yes, I know. I've been wanting to see you for some time. I actually made an appointment last week, not knowing your name. I described you to the receptionist and got another blonde lady.' He gave me a chirpy smile and followed me into my room.

Barry was in his early forties, not very tall, but slim. It was an hour session no different to any other, and at the end of it he asked me out to dinner. I gave my usual answer, and forgot about it.

The next week Barry was back. He told me he was separated from his wife, and was living in their beach house on the North Shore. He said he was a director of a company close to Fleure's, and had seen me leaving the building on several occasions. He found me attractive and wanted to get to know me better. He was very witty and humorous, and I enjoyed the time I spent with him. Before he left, he again asked me to go out to dinner with him, and I refused once more, saying it was against the rules. Barry said he was going to return each week and ask me until I changed my mind.

He kept coming back. I kept saying no.

I loved Christmas at Fleure's. Before the '87 crash, money and champagne were flowing like water, and expensive gifts of jewellery and wine poured into Fleure's over the pre-Christmas weeks. I would arrive home in the evenings laden with boxes, flowers, bottles and vast sums of money. The Christmas of 1985 was no exception.

As all our clients booked up days in advance to ensure they wouldn't miss out, the goodies kept pouring in. Of course, Christmas also brought in the drunks. Men you thought you knew, easy-going, well-mannered gentlemen, after a firm's Christmas lunch would turn into drunken belligerent bastards. I felt very sorry for their wives. We only had to deal with them for an hour; wives had them for as long as they were drunk.

Barry came in to see me on the last day before Christmas. He brought me a bottle of French red wine and asked me out for dinner. He said he was spending Christmas with his ex-wife, his daughter and his parents, and he was not looking forward to it. I told him I was going to my parents for Christmas, and would be back at work on the thirteenth of January. He said he'd be in on the thirteenth to see me.

With a carload of presents, Emma and I left Auckland on Christmas Eve, and drove to the Waikato. Mum had her hands full with family from all over New Zealand staying, but everyone pitched in, and a good time was had by all. Emma and I stayed until New Year's Eve, when we drove home and picked Minty up from the cattery. We had been invited to a party and were looking forward to it.

At the party we mingled with personalities of stage, screen and radio. It was a who's who of New Zealand celebrities. The time passed quickly, and in the early hours of the morning I found myself talking to a group of news media people.

'And what do you do for a crust?' asked a very prominent newsreader.

At this stage, I had quaffed several glasses of wine, and didn't care who knew what I did for a living. 'I work in a massage parlour,' I said.

There was a moment's silence, while each and every one of them looked me up and down. Then a red-haired woman started to laugh, and before long the whole group were shrieking with laughter. The newsreader said, 'Christ! You're a hard case, Angie! You really had us thinking it for a minute.' They didn't believe me! And the next day I was really pleased about that.

From after Christmas until the end of January was usually pretty slack as far as work went. I'd learned from Christmases gone by not to spend the abundance of money you made before the holidays, because you sure as hell needed it after. So I started back on the thirteenth of January knowing it would not be busy. But I did have one regular on that day — Barry.

'If you will come out to dinner with me, I will take you to any restaurant of your choice, anywhere! You just have to name it.'

'I have told you before, it is against the rules. We are not allowed to go out with clients. I could lose my job!' I protested, and quite frankly, I did not want to go out with him, I did not find him that attractive and I really couldn't be bothered getting ready to go out to dinner with someone I wasn't that keen on after a hard day's work. I just knew I'd be bored to tears. And, of course, I would have to pay for my meal 'in kind' afterwards.

'How are they to know? You're not telling me they follow you around to see where you eat and who with? Look, Diana, just come out with me once, anywhere you like. I promise not to touch you or expect sexual favours. Just a nice dinner, and I'll run you home straight after, no strings. I promise faithfully. Please?'

'Any restaurant I choose?' I'd put him off with the price.

'Any restaurant you choose.'

'Number 5?' I said and waited for the reaction.

There wasn't one. 'Number 5 it is! A very good choice.' We made arrangements for the following evening. He was to pick me up from home at seven-thirty.

Barry left looking very pleased with himself. I wished I'd stuck to my guns and said no, but he was so persuasive that I felt I'd been cajoled into it.

'Oh, Angie, what have you done?' I whispered under my breath while cleaning up my room.

At home I told Emma, and she said, 'Good, it's about time you had some fun. Go out and enjoy yourself.'

I went to bed that night still wishing I hadn't agreed to the dinner, and the next morning I wished even more I hadn't agreed to it. I racked my brains for the name of Barry's company. I thought I would telephone and cancel out, but for the life of me I could not remember. I decided to go through with it, then tell him not to see

178

me at work again. I had been stupid enough to tell him where I lived and my proper name. I could have kicked myself for it.

'You're quiet today,' said Kelly later in the morning. 'Everything all right?' I told Kelly about the dinner invitation with Barry, and how I regretted accepting it. 'You never know, you just might enjoy yourself,' she said.

On the dot of seven-thirty, a sleek, low-slung English sports car pulled up in the drive, and there was a knock at the door. Emma rushed to answer it and ushered in Barry, who was impeccably dressed in a very smart suit.

Barry was a gentleman. He opened the car door for me, and helped me on with the seatbelt.

'No hanky panky!' I reminded him.

'No hanky panky!' he repeated, started the car and backed down the drive.

We started the evening with a bottle of Moët and some canapés served in the bar, then went upstairs to the dining room, where we ate a meal fit for a king. Barry had exquisite taste when it came to wine, and a bottle of Châteauneuf du Pape accompanied our meal. Later in the evening we went downstairs for coffee, cognac and after-dinner mints.

The time went by so quickly that suddenly we were the only people left in the restaurant and it was twelve-thirty. Outside, the night air was warm and Barry held my hand as we crossed Symonds Street to where his car was parked. He drove me straight home, and just before I got out of the car he said, 'Will you have dinner with me tomorrow night as well?'

I didn't have to think about it. 'Yes please,' I said.

'Where would you like to eat?' he asked.

'I think it's your turn to choose. Surprise me.' Barry walked me to the front door and waited until I had it unlocked. 'Thank you for having dinner with me tonight; I'll see you tomorrow at seven-thirty. Good-night.' He turned on his heels and left.

Once inside my apartment, I went straight to the bathroom and started taking off my make-up.

'How did it go?' asked a little voice from behind, which made me jump a mile.

'Emm! What are you doing still up at this hour?'

'Mum, I'm nearly eighteen. Anyway, I couldn't sleep. How did it go, was it too boring?'

'No, not in the least. In fact I'm going out with him again tomorrow night.' I could see Emma's smile reflected back at me through the mirror. 'It's not like that! We had a lot of fun, and I like him. Now go to bed!'

'He's going bald, Mum!'

'Emma!! Will you please go to bed!'

'I'll put the jug on and make some tea, eh?' She was still grinning at me.

'Oh, okay. I'll be with you in a minute.'

The next evening we went to a little restaurant opposite the Sheraton Hotel. Barry parked in an office carpark belonging to an architect friend. The evening was even more enjoyable than the first. Barry was a very funny man, and sometimes he made me laugh so much I couldn't catch my breath. Once again the time went by so quickly that we were the last people left in the restaurant. It was well after midnight, and the staff were obviously waiting to go. When Barry saw me home, he asked if I'd see him again tomorrow, which was Saturday. He suggested we spend the day at his beach house, and then have dinner at a little restaurant nearby. It sounded like lots of fun, and I accepted.

That was the start of a whirlwind relationship. We laughed, drank and made merry in practically every trendy restaurant in Auckland. Life had become a social feast of fun.

'Love me, and I'll love you for ever,' Barry said to me one Saturday morning a couple of months later. He had brought me a dozen red roses and a beautiful solitaire diamond ring. 'Will you marry me?' he said.

This was the most romantic thing that had ever happened to me up till then. I was so overwhelmed, my eyes were brimming with tears. 'Could I live with this man for the rest of my life?' I asked myself, and the answer came back loud and clear, 'Of course you can!' So I accepted his proposal, knowing full well he could not marry me until his divorce came through in just under two years.

'Now, the first thing I want you to do is to telephone Fleure's and tell them you will not be back at work. From now on, I'm taking care of you.'

I dialled the number, 'Good morning. Fleure's, can I help you?' It was Patsy, our Saturday receptionist at the time.

'Hi, Patsy, it's Diana. Can you do me a favour love?'

'Anything for you, Di.'

'Strike my name off the roster, please.'

'Why?'

'Because I won't be working any more. I'm . . . I'm getting married!'

There was a brief silence, then a muffled, 'Guess what? Diana's getting married. She's finished work . . . for good! Are you still there Di? All the girls say congrats. Drop in and see us when you're in the neighbourhood.' I promised I would.

To start with, life was a ball. Holidays abroad, long weekends in the Bay of Islands, expensive dinners in exclusive restaurants. One of these dinners was at the Regent Hotel at one of their black-tie nights. We were dining with Barry's board of directors, who were from the Wellington, Hamilton and Christchurch offices. It was a silver-service dinner, and there seemed to be two waiters per person. One of the bottles of wine cost three hundred dollars, and it was the most beautiful wine I have ever tasted.

At that time, there was a meeting looming up in the company at which a new chairman was to be elected. Although Barry knew he was not in the running this time around, he had to play a game of politics for the next time. Having the right people on his side and being on side with the right people was very important. Our dinner guests were very wealthy, the ladies dripping in diamonds and wearing clothes that must have cost a fortune. But as the evening wore on and more wine was consumed, their manners began to fail them and their true colours started to show. One lady, who boasted recently attending an old girls' reunion at one of New Zealand's top girls' boarding schools (I noted it was the same one Chrissy had gone to) and spoke in obviously contrived Queen's English, stole one or two pieces of silver from the table. Her table manners deteriorated steadily throughout the evening, and she staggered uncontrollably while leaving the hotel and had to be helped into the car. This was my first introduction to how the rich minded their manners, and I was not impressed. The other women were little better, and I felt pleased that I was able to hold my own against them. I learned that business dinners were not to be enjoyed, more to be endured. One slip of a drunken tongue could easily put your partner on the wrong end of the corporate ladder.

Meanwhile, Barry's ex-wife started causing me some strife. Helen was obviously still hurting from the separation and made it quite clear she wasn't going to let me have her husband without a fight. She made phone calls in the dead of night, quite obviously drunk, demanding to know where her husband was. I dealt with this by hanging up on her, because experience told me it would be a total waste of time to argue with someone who was inebriated. One evening, however, Barry and I had gone away for the weekend and Emma, who was then flatting with friends, had come home to look after Minty. The phone rang very late and it was Helen demanding to know where Emma's slut of a mother was with her husband. Emm, as usual, took it all in her stride and said, 'Out having some fun, I should think.' It was Helen who hung up that time.

Then a box of Barry's old clothes appeared in my garage one morning. It concerned me that she had been roaming around the apartments late at night, as the box of garments had not been in the garage the day before.

When we moved to the North Shore, Helen would turn up at a neighbour's house opposite, and watch us for hours on end. She phoned early one evening during a barbecue we were having for some of Barry's work colleagues, threatening to jump off the harbour bridge. A fellow director answered the call, and became quite upset. It was all very nerve-racking, and while I can understand she was feeling grief-stricken, it would have been better for her to have taken some professional help. Nothing is ever gained with a negative attitude, no matter what the situation, and positivity will always win through.

One morning when I was in the middle of doing the ironing, the phone rang. It was a detective from Auckland Central.

'Detective Sergeant Layton spoke to you some months ago about the Titirangi murder,' he said. 'The case is due to come to court in a few weeks, and we need you to come in and have a chat with us beforehand. Sergeant Layton has been transferred to Wellington, and I will be dealing with the case from here in.'

'I can't go into court! Not now!' I said. 'My circumstances have changed, and there is no way I can stand up in court and tell the world how I came to be mixed up in a murder. It would ruin my life!'

'I see,' said the detective. 'Look, leave it with me for the time being and I will see if they will accept an affidavit. And, of course, there is always name suppression.'

I then learned that the defence counsel was a personal friend of one of the directors of Barry's firm, whom I had actually met at a cocktail party a month or so before.

The affidavit was not accepted, and there was no way I could get out of going to court. Name suppression meant nothing when I would be standing in court knowing the defence counsel would recognise me by sight and Barry's career could go down the gurgler.

'There are always things that can be done,' said the detective. 'You ladies are renowned for changing the colour of your hair, and a pair of glasses can make all the difference in the world. We will pick you up in a plain car, take you to court, and bring you back if you want.' I felt angry about the situation, but had to go along with it.

On the day of the court case, I was to be there by ten o'clock in the morning. I had made arrangements to get dressed in Emma's flat. All her flatmates would be at work during the day. I had hired a mousy brown wig from a fancy dress company, borrowed a pair of glasses from a friend, and bought a loose-fitting brown dress and a pair of low-heeled sensible shoes from an op-shop. When the police car drew up in the driveway at nine-thirty, as if by magic Angela Blake had changed into a matronly schoolmistress type of woman, who wouldn't be looked at twice in the street. The driver did a double-take, knowing he was picking up the prostitute witness in the case, and kept looking at me through the rear-vision mirror. I expect he was wondering who in their right mind would pay for my services. At the court, I was put into a small office on my own.

Mark Layton had a quick chat to me and made a crack about me looking good. I then had to wait until my turn came to give evidence.

When I had organised my disguise and had asked my friend if I could borrow her glasses, I hadn't taken into account the difference between reading glasses and long distance glasses, mainly because I didn't know there was much difference. The ones I had borrowed were reading glasses. When my name was called to go into court and I put them on, I found my sense of balance was altered to the point where I had to walk in a peculiar fashion to compensate for my distorted vision. By the time I entered the witness box, I was feeling sick and a bit woozy! I took the oath and swore I was who they said I was, then I was asked if I could identify a picture of the Titirangi house, and identify from those in the dock the man who took me there. I could see some men standing in the dock, but my glasses distorted the images to such an extent that I could not tell who was who. I was obliged to peer over the top of them. Yes, there was Bob, looking me straight in the eye, smirking at me. 'That's him, there.' I pointed to Bob, and prosecuting counsel said they had no further questions. Then came the tough bit. Defence counsel was asked if they had any questions. I had been looking at him over my glasses, and until this point he had not even looked in my direction.

'No questions, thank you milord,' he said, and still didn't look at me.

I was dismissed and left the court. No harm was done, and I had the police to thank for it. They were wonderful.

One evening, Barry came home with a video. 'We'll put it on before bedtime. It'll be a lot of fun.' It had a picture of a man and a woman naked on the front. This was the start of a constant stream of pornographic videos brought home by Barry. I said nothing and watched them dutifully. Barry had a bit of a problem with sex, due to the amount of rum he drank, I think. The videos certainly helped him achieve ejaculation, so I didn't complain. I had nothing against porn videos as long as they did not contain children or animals. I just found them boring. They did not turn me on one little bit, but Barry kept on bringing them home, night after night.

I was aware that Barry was a heavy drinker from the word go, but he never gave the impression of being drunk. After an afternoon and night of heavy drinking, he was still able to walk and talk straight. But sometimes, after being the life and soul of the party, he would turn into a tyrant when the last guest left. He would shout and bellow at me for no apparent reason, tell me he still loved his wife, say that he hated his parents, demand presents back that he'd given me, and sometimes cry. I learned later that a diamond bracelet he'd given me was actually bought for another woman — not his wife — then taken back from her and given to me. He eventually took it from me and gave it to someone else.

Just before Christmas 1986, Barry became very quiet and hardly spoke to me. In the New Year he told me to go, which I was going to do anyway. My apartment was rented out, and I had to wait six weeks for it to be vacated, so I moved in with a friend for that time. The experience was absolutely shattering. I became ill and my weight dropped to a little over six stone (thirty-eight kilos). However, life had to go on, and with the help of my doctor and friends I pulled myself together.

The day I moved back to my home was in some ways a relief. The first thing I did was to telephone Fleure's for a job. Celia had left, and a lovely lady called Ginny had taken over.

'Oh, yes, I've heard all about you. We still get clients phoning for you, after all that time,' she said.

I started back at work feeling just as nervous as my first day at The Harem. Fleure's had changed a lot. Don had gone to live in Australia, and life was easier. Ginny was a treasure, always making sure that bookings were made so you had time for lunch and coffee breaks. As long as you had a good excuse, time off was available. The cleaning was done in easy stages, without any of the 'rip, shit and bust' methods employed previously. Kelly was no longer working at Fleure's. She had been fired a year or so earlier because of a tiff she had with management over some time she wanted off at short notice. I could not believe Don would let a girl as popular as Kelly go. She must have brought him in a small fortune.

'You are aware that the house no longer pays wages?' said Ginny, on my first day back.

'No, why is that?'

'Business has gone down so much since the crash that they just can't afford it. There is talk of charging the girls a fee to work. You know, so much a day.'

It became very clear that the '87 stockmarket crash had taken its toll on business. Regular clients who used to come in weekly could now only afford to come fortnightly, some of them only monthly. One very regular client of mine told me he had lost nearly everything in the crash. His Rolls Royce had been replaced with a humble Honda Civic, and he was now on the unemployment benefit. He said he had been very close to suicide, and finding the money to come into Fleure's once every two months helped to keep his sanity intact.

Another dampener on business was the AIDS epidemic. The Health Department had issued pamphlets to every household in New Zealand, explaining how the disease was transmitted and listing the high-risk factors. Prostitutes came very close to the top of the list. 99.9 percent of the working ladies in New Zealand adhered to the 'safe sex' rule advised by the Prostitutes' Collective to stop the spread of AIDS and most of us had regular checks and used condoms. The odd junkie and non-English-speaking Asian girl did break the rules, but these nowhere near added up to the amount of 'one night standers' among straight women. The sex workers in New Zealand were very proud of this fact, not only at Fleure's.

A close friend of mine who was renowned for the amount of 'one night stands' she was able to pick up from the local pub, asked me one day, 'Aren't you scared of catching AIDS in your job?'

'No,' I replied. 'I've learned how to use condoms safely, and my last test was clear. How was your last test? Clear, was it?' She looked at me with a blank expression on her face. I knew damn well half the time she picked these men up she was so drunk she couldn't remember what she did with them, let alone whether she used a condom to do it with. And as for an AIDS test, why should she bother? She wasn't a prostitute after all!

CHAPTER 19

Barry and I had to talk about the property, so we decided on a civilised lunch at the Melba restaurant, behind High Street in the city.

A few days after the lunch, Barry telephoned and asked me out to dinner, and I accepted. At dinner, he told me he'd bought an apartment in Remuera, not far from me. It was the penthouse suite in a new block. After dinner he drove me around to see the outside of it. When he dropped me home he asked to see me again in the weekend.

On the Saturday morning he drove me to the North Shore property, where he told me he was sorry for all the trouble he'd caused, that he still loved me, and would I marry him. I believed every word he said, with not a thought to how he was going to finance the new apartment without his share of my property! I had wanted the relationship to work, and had pledged my part of it forever. I accepted. We moved into the new apartment together. My furniture was sold, and we let my apartment out to a lovely South African couple.

Barry bought me another engagement ring, a diamond cluster that cost a fortune. He took me out for lunch, then to a jeweller's shop in Shortland Street. I had my heart fixed on a large sapphire set in a ring of diamonds, but then I spied the cluster, and nothing else would do.

Over the previous few weeks I had spent a lot of time analysing what had gone wrong between Barry and me, and had come to the conclusion it was most probably my fault. If I hadn't argued back when I knew he'd been drinking, if I'd cooked more meals he liked instead of healthy ones, if I'd not complained about lugging the vacuum cleaner from the basement to the main house in the rain . . . If, if, if. But I was going to make no mistakes this time. Of course, I left Fleure's immediately, and I found a part-time job in a salon, as I thought staying at home all the time made me boring. This was the first straight job I'd had since starting in the sex industry. I found my workmates extremely narrow-minded and parochial, or 'up their own bums', as Chrissy would have said.

One day at morning-tea time, a senior technician told us about a friend of hers who had recently married. After a few weeks, it became known that his wife had at one time been a prostitute.

'Of course, I wouldn't have her in my house again!' she said. 'And the rest of our crowd don't speak to her. He'll end up with no friends. I mean, who would want a person like that hanging around? She's nothing but a slag.'

'Didn't you pick she was a prostitute before?' I asked, a little tongue in cheek. 'Aren't they all fish-nets and filthy language?'

'Well, no! She wasn't any different than me or you. But the fact is, once a hooker, always a hooker! She could have AIDS!'

I thought that was rough, when this particular girl picked up a different man several times a week from bars she frequented, and took them home and slept with them with no protection whatsoever.

Barry and I made plans to get married and honeymoon in Europe. We had a quiet wedding at home with only a few friends and family present. Our wedding night we spent at Huka Lodge in Taupo, and two weeks later we flew to London on the first leg of our six-week honeymoon. In London we stayed at the Hyde Park Hilton, shopped in Oxford Street, and dined and danced in the restaurant at the top of the Hilton, which overlooked Buckingham Palace. From there we went to Paris, where we stayed in a lovely old hotel where the plumbing rattled, but it was so romantic we didn't care. We dined and lunched in many famous Paris cafés, shopped in boutiques on the West Bank and sat on the steps of the Sacré Coeur. We laughed, drank, dined and danced our way south, and gambled in the casinos, revelling in all the sparkle and glamour only the south of France can offer. We dined in a restaurant perched up on the cliffs of Cap d'Antibes, which had panoramic views of the Côte d'Azur. We stayed in an old château stuck out in the middle of nowhere, surrounded by brown fields full of dead sunflowers, their bowed heads all looking in the same direction. We spent a day in a little artisans' village, way up in the Luberon hills, and wandered along the narrow cobbled streets with their ancient houses.

Italy, Switzerland, Germany, Austria — on and on we went, and the laughter and fun seemed endless. But all good things do come to an end, and in Hawaii Barry learned that because of the 1987 stock exchange crash, his company had lost a big contract they had signed up for just before we got married, and that things were going to be tight from now on.

At home, nothing really changed, and we knuckled down to day to day living. Barry fell out with the body corporate in our apartment block, and it became apparent that no one liked him. There was a lot of corporate politics going on in his company, and people were taking sides. Once again, Barry started drinking heavily and became very moody. Just before Christmas, he went quiet and stopped talking to me. On the third of January, he told me he wanted a divorce and that I was to get out. Up to this point, I had suggested some marriage guidance, and had tried all sort of ways to find out what I was doing to deserve this treatment. But now I'd had enough.

My apartment, or should I say my half apartment, was rented again, and I had to wait six weeks for it to become vacant. This time I did not move out. It was not easy living in the same house as a man I suddenly despised. However, I made good use of the six weeks I had to wait. Questions had to be answered, and I did all sorts of self-improvement classes and courses to find out what was wrong with me. When I explained my situation to a prominent psychologist, he said, 'I don't see that there is anything wrong with you, Angie. I feel it's your husband that needs help, and a lot of it!' All my classes and courses told me the same thing; I was not the one that needed help, and I rejoiced in the knowledge.

Those six weeks were interminable. I needed money to buy more furniture, as mine had all been sold, and Barry kindly let me have four thousand dollars. Which, of course, didn't go very far when I had all the whiteware to buy as well. I rested in the knowledge that the day I moved back home, I would start working again and be on my feet in no time. Towards the end of the six weeks, Barry started to get friendly, asking me out to dinner, and waiting for me to come home in the evenings with a stupid 'I'm sorry' smile he kept for such occasions. I ignored him, and in early March I moved into my apartment with eight small boxes of my possessions, all I had left in the world. Barry had hidden a lot of stuff he'd bought me. My ski gear, he said, was not bought for me but bought for me to use; it was not actually mine. I couldn't have given a toss for the ski gear. I hated skiing. So there was no need to hide it.

I had lunch one day with a friend I'd met through Barry. She was a single lady in her early thirties, and a career woman to boot. She said how sorry she was to hear that we had separated and asked if it had anything to do with his ex-wife.

'Why should it have anything to do with her?' I asked.

'You didn't know about the private investigator?'

'What private investigator?'

'She had you followed around for two days, some time back. They found out about where you worked. You know.' She mouthed some words that could have been anything, but I knew were 'massage parlour'.

I felt sick. 'How many people know?'

'Oh, just about everyone, darling. She told everyone, but I don't think many believed it. Did you . . . you know?' She started mouthing again.

'You mean, did I actually work in a massage parlour? Yes, I did! And I don't regret one second of it, but I do regret being involved with Barry, his ex-wife and his boozy lifestyle.' I was getting angry.

'Oh, how exciting. Tell me all about it,' she said, leaning across the table towards me. 'I mean, what was it like, with all those men? Have you worked out how many?' She was doing a good impression of old Clarkie, making rolling motions with her forefinger. I was amazed how people could not bring themselves to say 'having sex with all those men'.

'Around three thousand, I should say,' I said, exaggerating to shock her.

'Don't you get exhausted, having sex several times a day?'

'You don't have orgasms. You just act out a part, like in a movie. Think about it, Joanne! It would be impossible to have that many orgasms in one day, day after day — even if you wanted to, which you don't. Of course, on the odd occasion it does happen, but you don't plan it.'

'And is it very profitable?'

'I'd earn easily as much if not more than you. Of course, the tax man takes a good cut.'

'You pay tax?' I nodded. 'I thought prostitution was against the law?' she said.

'It's not prostitution but soliciting that's against the law. But the tax department are not interested in what you do, just that you pay tax on it, and I'd soon get caught if I didn't.'

We sat at the table until three in the afternoon talking about prostitution. Joanne was fascinated.

I was very concerned that I had been followed around Auckland for two days by a private investigator and hadn't noticed. He or she obviously did a very good job, and, I hope, charged Barry's ex heaps!

Phoning a couple of old contacts I found out that Ginny, the receptionist at Fleure's, now ran her own parlour in Newton and was looking for staff. I telephoned her, and she said I could start immediately.

Jezebel's was in an old stucco house wedged between two factories in a narrow back street. The small garden was neat and tidy, with a walkway along the right-hand side. At first glance, the place did not look like a parlour, but on closer inspection, the old boarded-up sash-cord windows gave it away. A doorbell heralded the arrival of a client, and once you were inside the house gave a welcoming, cosy feeling. The wallpaper, carpet and fittings told a story of a lot of use, and a smell of stale tobacco hung in the air. There were four rooms serviced by two showers in a block at the back. The sauna was the usual wooden type that reeked of eucalyptus. Ginny allowed men to come in for a sauna only, for a nominal fee of ten dollars. I felt this was false economy, because the saunas cost a lot of money to heat up each day and we would only have one or two clients in a week who used it. Most of the men who came in to use the sauna were only after a free 'perve', the girls said, and sometimes the evidence would be there for us to clean up!

The rooms were small and a trifle dingy, each sporting a double bed, its mattress covered with a coloured fitted sheet and pillow. We decorated the beds with colourful towels, which brightened the rooms up no end. I always used room two because the others didn't like being next to the shower block, which made it noisy. The wallpaper was once white with a blue sprig pattern over it, but had now gone yellow with age and nicotine, and in a couple of places it was stained where someone had ejaculated over it.

Through the back door of the parlour was a walled area with large decks and a sunken spa pool. Around the spa were outdoor chairs and tables, shaded with colourful brollies. In the summer the girls would go out and eat their lunch, sunbathe naked and sometimes sit out with a client under one of the umbrellas, sharing a bottle of wine. Being well sheltered from the wind, the situation was perfect.

Ginny told me of her plans to do the place up, and it certainly could have done with it.

Things had changed drastically in the sex industry. Instead of the twenty or so parlours in Auckland, there were now about sixty-five advertised in *Truth* and the *Auckland Star*. But there were only the same amount of 'punters', and because of the '87 crash, very little money. The prices for extras had gone up from sixty dollars for the works to one hundred dollars; hand relief was now forty to fifty dollars. I put an advertisement in *Truth* and the *Star* that Diana had returned to work and was now at Jezebel's.

I found several familiar faces from Fleure's working at Ginny's parlour. One of them was Francy.

'That wouldn't please Don,' I said to her.

'Oh, he isn't interested in Fleure's anymore, the place has gone to the pack. The lady that runs it for him doesn't pay the power bill, and it's always getting cut off. It's a real shame.'

It became apparent very quickly that getting back on my feet was not going to be as quick as I'd anticipated. Although the prices had gone up, the quantity had gone down, and I was earning a lot less than I was used to. The days of buying a bottle of Moët on the way home were over. Moët had almost doubled in price, and there was no money to buy it with anyway. Blowing a couple of hundred dollars on a spending spree without noticing it was totally out of the question.

One by one my old clients found me, some of them telling me they felt heartbroken when I left Fleure's.

Ginny was wonderful to work with, to the point of being a bit too easy-going. She'd lose money because of it. We had a washing machine and dryer out the back of the parlour, where we washed the towels as they became dirty. The drier, a domestic, could not keep up with the flow, and one wet weekend Ginny instructed us to put the towels in the sauna to dry. It was very efficient, but also very dangerous, and one night the inevitable happened and the place caught fire. Insurance polices for massage parlours are extremely expensive and difficult to come by, and we believed Ginny lost a lot of money with that episode.

Ginny's saving grace was her telephone manner. She had an amazing gift of being able to talk men into visiting Jezebel's. Some regulars wouldn't book in at all if Ginny didn't answer the phone, so if you were rostered on a day when Ginny was on the desk, you could guarantee it would be pretty busy. On the other hand, Ginny employed one of her daughters to manage reception in her absence, and she had a disastrous effect on business. Sheryl was a frail, watery-eyed lass with fair hair, and her monotone voice grated on the nerves. She sounded totally uninterested in whatever it was the client wanted to know. Most of her time was spent stretched out on a sofa in the office with a boyfriend draped over her. When the phone rang, it took a couple of minutes for them to untangle themselves, and many a caller hung up because no one got to answer it. But Ginny would not hear a word against the girl, even though it lost her a small fortune.

Ginny also employed working girls sometimes, because she felt sorry for them. Marina was in her mid-forties and was built like Mama Cass Elliot. She had the most unfortunate face, which wasn't helped by a tooth missing in the front. She dowsed herself in cheap perfume to cover the stench of body odour, which was very noticeable from six paces away, and her conversation was limited to what she was going to eat next. The occasional client, who was either cajoled into seeing her or was too drunk to worry about who he saw, would never stay the full time. One man ran from her room wearing only his undies. Ginny said she felt sorry for Marina, because she was broke and had nowhere to live.

Toni was an attractive lass in her twenties and very popular with the clients, but was obviously an addict. I often worked on a Saturday with her, and as we were without a receptionist, we relied on one another to make bookings accurately. Time and time again Toni managed to double-book me, and it was always when she had no work and would have to take my regular.

'We don't want to lose him,' she'd say, a thin smile stretched across her vacant face. We found out later that Toni was popular because she was working without condoms.

'It's my body!' she said, when challenged.

Toni eventually died from an overdose.

One morning a client came in, and on his heels followed a very thin and obviously hungry tortoiseshell cat. We started to feed her, and before long she appeared with a couple of half-grown kittens running along behind.

'If she's not spayed, there will be more on the way in no time,' said Kate, a real sucker for a sob story. 'How about we start a fund to have her spayed, and if we can befriend the kittens, the SPCA could find them homes.' Everyone thought it was a grand idea. Kate was put in charge of the 'cat spaying fund' and a large jar was kept on a shelf in the office. Of course, those who loved animals put heaps in the jar frequently without being asked, and those who didn't were shanghaied into it. But Josi the cat became sick before the fund had enough in it for the spaying, and as Kate and I were the only ones working that morning, we decided to get the mobile vet in to look at her and pay the fee between us, not touching the spaying jar.

Kate made the call, and carefully explained to the vet that our cat needed treatment and that she lived in a massage parlour. He didn't say anything for a long time. Kate then felt it necessary to say it was not a hoax, and the cat really needed help. The vet arrived within the hour. Meanwhile, we had cleared the reception desk and covered it with old clean towels for him to use as an examination table. He was extremely nervous when he walked into the office. He looked furtively about, hoping he wouldn't spy a naked body, we thought. Kate introduced herself and me, and we shook hands; his were moist and sweaty. I hoped Josi was not in need of an injection, because it would have been very painful the way the man's hands were shaking.

'I haven't been into one of these places before,' he confessed, as I picked Josi up out of her cage and popped her on the table.

'Would you like a cup of coffee while you're here?' asked Kate. The vet beamed us a lovely smile and nodded. Josi did need an injection, but our veterinary friend was over his nerves by that time, so it wasn't a problem.

'You don't look like . . . like . . .'

'Prostitutes,' prompted Kate.

'Umm . . . yes,' said the vet.

'I suppose it depends on what your idea of a prostitute is. We certainly are prostitutes, and this is what we look like. So anyone looking like us must look like a prostitute, don't you think?'

'I suppose you're right,' he said, and that was the end of that topic.

It turned out Josi had an infection. But what was worse, she was heavily pregnant again, which made the spaying operation very dangerous.

'You would be better to take her to a local vet with a surgery. We are only mobile and don't have the facilities to do major surgery like this, and you will have to do it within a week or two.'

The young vet left with a totally changed opinion of prostitutes and massage parlours. He had taken quite a shine to Kate, and she hoped he'd come back to see her. I don't know if he did or not.

Three months after leaving Barry, I learned he had another lady friend and she had moved into his apartment with her two children. Our neighbours downstairs disliked him intensely, and telephoned me regularly to keep me informed about his movements. I would have preferred not to have known. I felt very hurt, and I think, deep down inside, I had always thought there might be a chance for us to get back together if he took the time to get his head straight. Then the neighbours told me there had been a drunken brawl in the grounds of the apartment block, which involved Barry and a male visitor to Barry's apartment, and suddenly I realised I'd been spared a lifetime of misery with this man, and I felt truly sorry for his lady friend and her children.

Then a new girl called Billi started at Jezebel's. She was a little like me to look at, but a bit younger. She came from one of the city parlours and had quite a good clientèle. At the end of the first shift that she and I worked together, Ginny called me aside.

'Something I have to tell you, love,' she said. 'Billi, Francy and I were in the office talking while you were with your last client, and a man came to the door. He saw Francy and looked embarrassed. He then said he'd popped in to ask her if she knew where you worked, as he needed to talk to you. Francy told him she didn't know. When he had gone, Francy said it was your husband. But Billi said he was a very regular client of hers and had been for a few months. It is obvious to me he was here to book in with Billi, not for a moment thinking he'd see someone he knew. Thought you ought to know.'

I couldn't wait to question Billi about this episode.

'How long have you been seeing him?' I asked.

'Oh, about once a fortnight for three or so months,' she said.

I did a quick calculation. He must have started seeing her just after I left him, and was now running around behind his new lady's back, having sex in massage parlours again. She must have said no to the porn videos. I thought it was odd how much Billi resembled me!

At this point in time, I could have caused a lot of trouble for Barry if I'd wanted to get even. I could have telephoned his lady and told her about Barry's secret love at Jezebel's massage parlour. I could have sent an anonymous fax to all his companies' offices, telling anyone who would read them that Barry T was knowingly married to a prostitute, and that the other members of the board of directors had entertained this woman in their homes on numerous occasions. Knowing how the corporate grapevine worked, the news would have quickly spread to all their professional clients, and a lot of red faces and gossip would have forced him into resigning his position on the board. But getting even serves no purpose than to allow one a moment of power, then it is forgotten. I believed then, and still do, that the energy is better spent in a positive way improving oneself.

I did not let him get away with it totally, though. I phoned his office. 'You wanted to talk to me about something?' I said.

'Oh, it was nothing important. How are you?'

'You've been a naughty boy, haven't you, Barry?'

'I don't know what you mean?' he said defensively.

'I'm not stupid, Barry! Billi recognised you, she's been seeing you for months. If you wanted a word with me, wouldn't it be easier to pop around the corner to my apartment, rather than doing a massage parlour crawl hoping you'd come across someone you knew working there. Because no way could you have known Francy worked at Jezebel's.'

'Somebody told me, and I know nothing of any Billi. Now I must go, I'm running late for a meeting,' he said, and hung up. I got a lot of pleasure from his discomfort.

It was interesting to see the ever-increasing effects that the downturn in the economy was having within our industry. The fewer clients there were to go around, the more massage parlours sprouted up. There were now over seventy advertised. We had heard that at Fleure's the girls were now paying ten dollars a shift to work there, and any misdemeanour that would have had us struck off the roster was now a 'fineable offence'. At the end of a working day, the girls had to pay management from five to ten dollars for anything from being late out of the room to walking through the lounge without shoes on. These fees and fines varied from parlour to parlour, and we were very lucky that Ginny did not believe in them.

But as time went on, money was harder to come by and prices were starting to go down. Some establishments were advertising that a man could get the works for sixty dollars. I was not that desperate, so I decided to quit the industry. A visit to my bank manager fixed me up with a substantial loan, and I bought a busy hairdressing salon.

CHAPTER 20

I left the sex industry just at the right time. I kept in touch with Francy, and she told me stories of girls sitting around day after day doing nothing, sometimes only making a couple of hundred dollars over four shifts. Some of them were working six and seven shifts a week if they could get them, just to keep enough money coming in to pay for the basics. Workers like Francy, with a good clientèle, were faring okay, but were not bringing in what they were used to. To make matters a good deal worse, unemployment had reached record proportions, and an enormous influx of women wanted work in the sex industry because it had a reputation for fast and easy money.

Rumours spread from parlour to parlour about Fleure's and The Tokyo being extremely busy. Don had revamped the management, and they were doing between twenty and thirty massages per shift. What did not circulate with the rumours was that the shifts were 'stacked' (more girls working than there were rooms to work in), they had a very high proportion of straight massages, crippling shift fees and their staff weren't earning any more than the rest.

My income had gone down substantially before I left the sex industry, so I was not giving up the constant stream of cash we were used to back in the good old days. What I did find difficult to cope with was not working with my friends. I missed their humour, their straightforwardness and, above all, the comradeship. Life without them gave me a feeling of insecurity. My staff at the salon were no more than a bunch of dizzy, empty-minded kids. Even my family seemed shallow, with little understanding for anyone but themselves. I had heard over the years that this feeling of insecurity was quite common in women retiring from the industry, but did not realise how difficult it was until I actually went through it myself. My phone calls to Francy became more and more frequent, and once or twice I picked up in the conversation that perhaps I was being a nuisance calling so often, so I stopped.

However, my problem was taken care of when I received a phone call from a woman called Christine.

'Francy suggested I call you,' she said. 'Ginny has sold Jezebel's to a guy who is charging us enormous shift fees and fines, plus playing the old 'sex or you're fired' trick, so we've all walked out and rented a house in Newmarket to work in. It's very discreet and has a large carpark that can't be seen from the road or anywhere else. We are all set to start on Wednesday, working the daytime only, and have Pippa ready to do reception during the week, but are short of a weekend receptionist. We wondered if you would like the job? Saturday from ten to six, and Sunday midday to six, fifty dollars a shift in cash.

I liked the sound of Christine. She was well-spoken, friendly and obviously had the situation under control. So I said yes and promised to start on the coming weekend.

'I don't suppose it would be convenient for you to come in right now to look at the place? I'm here doing some cleaning. We could have a coffee while I explain the routine and such,' she said. That wasn't a problem for me, and within fifteen minutes Christine and I were sitting on the floor in the lounge drinking our coffee. She told me that she had been a working lady for quite a few years, and had actually owned a parlour in Queensland during the Fitzgerald Inquiry, where she was stripped of everything she owned by the tax department and had returned to New Zealand to start again. I was interested to learn that she had also raised a child on her earnings from prostitution, the one and only reason for starting in it. Her son knew from an early age what her profession was and, like Emma, accepted it without question. He was then in his mid-twenties and had an engineering degree, his own business and his own home. Christine was very proud of him.

The location was perfect, situated down a long driveway that ran off a small one-way street in an industrial area. The carpark had room for about six cars, and once your car was off the road, it could only be seen from a helicopter. The house had three bedrooms, a large bathroom and an open-plan lounge and kitchen. The whole set-up, though totally different from a parlour situation, was perfect for a brothel.

'Since you left the sex industry, Angie, massage parlours have changed dramatically,' said Christine. 'Because there are now seventy-odd establishments and more opening every day, compared with the twenty-odd operating fifteen years ago with the same number of clients to go around. And with the downturn in the economy, work is scarce. The guys just can't afford to pay what they used to. The parlour bosses are finding it tough as well, so to compensate they are charging the girls huge shift fees and fining them up to fifty dollars a throw for all sorts of minor offences. Sometimes, at the end of a day a girl can owe the boss more than she's made.

'Well, Francy, myself and a couple of other old hands decided enough was enough. We have all worked very hard over the years to get a good clientèle, and we're sure as hell not going to share our money with some low-down prick! So we got this place. The men will pay a door fee as before, which will be banked into an account and used only to pay the rent and sundries. If we fall short, we'll just have to dip into our pockets. There is only one way to make any real money for ourselves, and that is to cut out the parlour boss.'

Christine was petite, with warm friendly eyes, but her manner suggested she had good business sense and stood no nonsense. I knew instantly we would be good friends. She explained the credit-card system, day book and the general information I'd need to know.

'One thing I want to make quite clear to you, I do not want any of Don Springfield's tactics! Make sure the girls have time for lunch and coffee breaks throughout the day. If anyone is sick, send them home. A sick girl can lose a lot of clients for the house. I want this place a joy to work in for the girls, and a home away from home for the clients. I'm sure if we stick to this recipe we will succeed.'

I wholeheartedly agreed with her. Christine was like a breath of fresh air.

My first Saturday was a real eye opener. I arrived twenty minutes early, not wanting to keep the girls waiting outside for all the world to see. Not that the world could see much, because of the position of the place. I found two girls waiting to get in, plus two cars in the carpark, each containing a client. I made a mental note to be even earlier the next day.

The girls — Julie, a tall blonde lady in her mid-thirties with unruly hair that fell around her acne-marked face and the most unfortunate legs I'd seen for a long time, and Carly, a lady in her mid-forties who had long curly red hair which made her look much older than her years — bustled about making their rooms ready for the onslaught of the day. After a minute or two, the first client ambled through the door. He handed me a credit card.

'Is Julie here today?' he asked. I looked in the book to see if she had an appointment.

'Yes, she's here and she's free. An hour is it?'

'Oh no, I'm not free!' said a voice from behind. I turned to see Julie transformed into a vision of loveliness. Her hair was piled high on her head exposing a beautiful pair of cheekbones, and suddenly one was no longer aware of her scarring. She wore a long black slinky dress that covered her thick, ankleless legs and fell down over high stilettos, giving the impression of a tall, slender model's figure. What Julie lacked in legs she made up for with the most glorious bosom, which she took full advantage of. Tucked into a low-slung Wonder-bra, her magnificent cleavage thrust out from the front of the deeply cut neckline of her dress.

'I'm not free. I'm really quite expensive, aren't I, Bobbikins?' she whispered, and hugged him. Bobbikins was not a tall man, so when Julie hugged him to her, his face disappeared into her bosom. After a few seconds, gasping for air and grinning like the Cheshire Cat, Bob surfaced and followed her like a puppy to the massage room.

Bob was followed by a man in his late sixties who introduced himself as Peter. He handed me a fifty-dollar bill and asked for an hour with Julie. I explained that she was busy, but Carly was available, and he agreed to see her. After I had written his name and relevant data in the day book, I realised we didn't have any change to give him, and I had to raid my handbag for the ten dollars owing.

I called Carly from her room to take him through.

'Did you see if he had any money in his wallet?' she asked. 'I charge a hundred no matter what they want, and it makes me mad when they don't have enough money; it's a waste of my time.' I told her that I hadn't seen a wallet at all. Luckily Peter was out of earshot and didn't hear the conversation. While he was having his shower, Carly sat down and lit a cigarette.

'Oh, I hate working Saturdays. I told Christine I don't work weekends, but she still rostered me on. I'd leave, only it's a busy little place and they're hard to find these days.' Peter came out of the bathroom with a towel around him, and Carly reluctantly followed him into her room. Twenty minutes later he was out and back in the shower, and after another five minutes she was saying good-bye to him at the door.

When Carly had finished tidying her room, I said, 'Peter was booked in for an hour.'

'Yes, I know.'

'Was there a problem with him?'

'Oh, no,' she said. 'He had sex and paid me my hundred. He was quite happy. He's a lovely man, as easy as pie,' she beamed at me, obviously pleased with herself for getting him over and done with so quickly. Perhaps things had changed since I left the industry, I thought; maybe this was how the girls worked these days, getting the guys in and out as soon as they possibly could.

Julie came out of her room right on the hour and said good-bye to Bobbikins. 'Who's for a cuppa?' she asked.

'Oh, I will, coffee, milk and two sugars please,' said Carly, who had been sitting in the same chair since her client left, watching me do the cleaning, while telling me the story of her life. Everything that could go wrong had gone wrong in Carly's life. She'd had every disease and illness known to mankind, and others that had baffled medical science for years. She had been married three times, two husbands had run off with other women, and one with a man! She hadn't let any of them off lightly, and delighted in telling me how she had tipped brake fluid over their cars, made freaky phone calls to their new spouses at odd hours of the day and night, and reported one to the Inland Revenue for tax evasion. The poor man hadn't evaded any taxes, but it caused a good deal of aggro, and that pleased her no end. She was absolutely furious when husband number two had taken out a non-molestation order to stop the harassment, and had retaliated by paying someone to write some absolutely disgusting graffiti about him on a wall adjacent to his place of work, while she was in Brisbane. As much as I disliked Carly, I could not help but listen to her tales, wondering if they were all true.

Julie, on the other hand, was a barrel of laughs. She had been working in the sex industry for seven years, and had started at Jezebel's just after I left. Her home was in Wellington, where she'd run away from a disagreeable relationship to live in Auckland. Not long after her arrival she had been made redundant from her position as a personal assistant to the executive director of a large construction company, which had gone out of business. Then, to make ends meet, she got a job in an inner-city parlour. Like me, she loved the work, and turned out to be quite good at it, but found the shift fees and fines crippling. Someone from the Prostitutes' Collective mentioned that Ginny did not charge her girls, so she had joined Christine and Francy until the place was sold.

'The new guy is a prize bastard! He has a lovely wife, who does reception every so often, but as soon as her back is turned he's hitting on the girls for sex. It was after two were fired because they didn't oblige him, and also, of course, because of the amount of fees he wanted, we all walked out.'

By three o'clock in the afternoon we had taken in five clients. Because she got through hers quickly, Carly had done three to Julie's two. The phone had been ringing constantly, and I was kept very busy. Julie had a booking at three-thirty, and Carly's third lasted in her room for nearly three-quarters of an hour, which I found surprising. After she said good-bye to him, I noticed she was changing her bed linen and preparing to go home.

'Where do you think you're going?' I asked.

She pressed her temples between the forefinger of each hand and frowned. 'Oh! I have the most dreadful headache and must go home. The pain is absolutely astronomical, and you know how Christine hates us to work when we're sick.' She smiled at Julie over my shoulder. 'See you on Tuesday, Jules,' she said, and she left.

'She does that every day she works, unless Christine is here, but she never leaves until she's done three clients. It pisses me off, because we all have a regular clientèle and are kept quite busy, while she sits around leaching off our guys because she's the only one available. She charges them enormous amounts of money for even the smallest job. Then, as soon as she has three hundred dollars in her pocket, she buggers off home with some excuse of a headache. She's on a sickness benefit, so it's only pocket money for her. Christine is going to fire her as soon as she finds someone to take her place.'

By six o'clock Julie had taken care of two more of her regulars. She helped tidy up and we went home.

Sunday I arrived at eleven-thirty to an empty carpark and nobody waiting. Once inside the house, I checked the roster to find that Francy and a girl called Susan were on shift. I busied myself by putting the previous afternoon's towels into the washing machine and boiling the jug to make some coffee for when the girls arrived.

Francy was first in. She gave me a hug. 'So you couldn't keep away from us!' she said.

It was strange working with Francy as a receptionist, and I felt awkward for a while, but Francy was her usual jovial self and soon the difference in the working situation disappeared.

About five past twelve, Susan arrived. She was a woman in her mid-twenties, tall and willowy, with a gorgeous face and peaches and cream complexion. Her blonde hair was parted in the middle and fell like a flaxen sheaf of silk to her waist. If Susan had a flaw, it was the slight crookedness of her front teeth.

'Hello, I'm Susan,' she said, offering her hand. 'You're Diana, aren't you? I have heard so much about you from the clients. You're almost a legend in your own time. A bit like Francy.'

As the day wore on, I found out that Susan was married with three children. Her husband looked after them while she worked, and by the way she spoke, it seemed she and her husband were very happy together.

The first client that booked in asked for her, and when she had gone through I remarked to Francy what a lovely person she was.

'She is a lovely person,' Francy agreed, 'but we think she has a lot of problems. Quite often she comes to work covered in bruises.

She swears they're from some form of accident, but no one could be that accident prone, and they always appear the morning after she's had a slack day. And when she is having a slack day, she starts dirty hustling. One afternoon she charged a man only seventy dollars for two lots of sex and oral. Now that stinks of desperation if you ask me! We think her husband is beating her up if she doesn't bring home enough money for his liking. And between you and me, I've noticed on a couple of occasions she has arrived at work first thing in the morning stoned out of her brain. It's so sad for one so young; and she's a gun worker, really popular with the clients. She must earn very good money, but the car they drive is on its last legs, and the kids are far from well-dressed. The mind boggles at where the money goes.'

My talk with Francy was cut short when one of her clients turned up at the door, and that was the beginning of a constant stream that lasted to the end of the day.

Because the girls were busy for most of the afternoon I spent a lot of time on my own, but it was taken up with a multitude of phone calls from many recognisable voices.

'Good afternoon, can I help you?'

'Who do you have working today?'

'Today we have Francy and Susan.'

'Oh yes, and what would Francy look like?' I went into detail about her appearance.

'And what would she be wearing?' I told him what she was wearing.

'Oh yes, and what kind of underwear would she have on?' I said I didn't know.

'Is she dominant?' I said I thought not.

'And what would Susan look like?' By this time my patience was getting a bit thin, but I told him anyway.

'Oh yes, and what would she be wearing?' I described her attire.

'And what kind of underwear does she have on?' I told him through gritted teeth that I had no idea.

'Is she dominant?' I said I didn't think so.

'Do you have any dominant ladies working through the rest of the week?'

'No, John, I don't know if we have any dominant ladies working through the rest of the week, nor do I know what anyone will wear, or if they have underwear, neither do I bloody well care! Now, PISS OFF!' That man had been making the same calls to every parlour I'd ever worked in for ten years, and as far as I knew, he very rarely set foot in any of them. It made me feel really good to shout at him like that.

At six o'clock on the dot, Susan's husband arrived to take her home in an old beat-up Holden Kingswood. Three pale little faces peered from the back window up at the house, unsmiling and hollow-eyed. He came up the steps and knocked on the door, and from the minute I met him I disliked him. Susan's husband was a small, weedy man, his face swarthy and mean with dark eyes a bit too close together, and I got the impression you couldn't trust him as far as you could kick him. Susan introduced us and happily went off with him, chatting away as they disappeared down the steps.

'She's had a busy day, so she's got nothing to worry about,' said Francy, putting her jacket on. 'It's a different story when she hasn't, I can tell you.'

'Why does she stay with a man who abuses her? It never ceases to amaze me how a girl like that, obviously well-educated and well-brought up, can fall for an idiot like him. He's not even good looking! And she's heavier than him by quite a few kilos. If she put her mind to it, she could flatten him!'

Francy opened the door to go. 'It happens all the time, believe me,' she replied.

I found out later that Francy herself was once in a marriage where she was physically abused.

Christine telephoned that evening to find out how I'd got on.

'What did you think of Carly?' she asked.

'Well, if you want my opinion, she just hasn't got what it takes to be a good hooker!' I replied honestly. 'She wouldn't be any good if she looked like Marilyn Monroe. She has no warmth or understanding, and she doesn't have that inner sexual something that makes a good working lady, you know what I mean?'

Christine wholeheartedly agreed with me, and said she had a new girl starting next week and Carly was going to be fired.

*

The following Saturday morning I opened the doors at ten o'clock, and within a minute or two a woman arrived and introduced herself as Penny. She looked to be in her late-thirties, with short dark brown hair, lovely soft brown eyes, an hour-glass figure and the sauciest grin I'd seen for a long time. I showed her the rooms available, and she chose the one closest to the bathroom.

'I hope you don't mind, but I've given this phone number to a couple of friends so they can keep me informed of another friend who is seriously ill in hospital.' I said I was very sorry her friend was so ill, and of course it was all right.

The first call for Penny came about ten minutes later. It was a man, and she spoke quietly into the receiver with her back to us so no one could hear what was being said. When, after a short conversation, she hung up, I asked how her friend was. She threw me a big, broad smile. 'Oh, he's okay. Someone will phone again later if there is any change.'

The second call came almost immediately after the first, and once again she talked very quietly with her back to us. Penny had about eight to a dozen calls that day, all from men. Most of them she couldn't take, as she was kept pretty busy in her room.

The clients seemed to adore her, and she treated each one as if she were their lover, kissing them good-bye at the door as they left. I could tell that endearing smile worked wonders with them; even grumpy old Sid left grinning.

'I can see I shall have to keep my wits about me,' said Julie. 'I've lost two of my guys to her already. Still, a bit of competition doesn't do any harm, does it?'

I thought what a good-natured person Julie was. Back in the days of Fleure's, we would have been extremely worried about a situation like this, but she took it all in her stride.

Christine phoned to find out how the new girl was doing. 'I think you have a winner,' I said. 'She has everything a girl needs for the job.'

'Yes, I thought that when I met her. Almost too good to be true, don't you think?' I detected a negative note in Christine's voice, and asked her what she really thought. 'I don't know, just a hunch, I suppose. Something doesn't quite gel with that woman. Oh, perhaps I'm getting cynical in my old age. Time will tell.'

Time did tell. The following Saturday, Penny had as many phone calls as the week before, all from men. I put it down to her having a lot of boyfriends. After all, she was very attractive and very sexy, so why shouldn't she? I made a joke about it and she roared with laughter.

'Most of my friends are men,' she said. 'I don't get on with women all that well. And I'm a real social animal. I love entertaining, and my apartment is usually buzzing with people. It just so happens they are mostly men. It's not all sexual, you know.'

Then Saturdays started to become very quiet. Julie complained she hadn't seen a lot of her regulars for ages, and Penny said if it didn't get busier, she'd have to take on another shift to make up for the downturn in business. Christine gave her Wednesdays.

After a month or so, Pippa called me at home one evening.

'Christine suggested I call you,' she said. 'Business has done a dive on Wednesdays, and I think there is something fishy going on with Penny. She is very good at her job, and the guys all come back to see her, but only once. Francy suspects she's offering her services to them at her home for a lesser fee. What do you think? Christine doesn't want to fire her unless it's proven because she's such a good worker, and it could be coincidental.'

I told Pip about the many phone calls Penny received on Saturdays. 'She doesn't have any on Wednesdays,' said Pippa. 'I wonder what's going on? Look, if you notice anything suspicious, let Christine know immediately. We have to get to the bottom of this before we all go broke.'

The following Saturday a new girl arrived.

'Hi, I'm Paula,' she said and handed me a sheet of paper. 'I specialise in bondage and caning, and I have an ad running in *Truth* this week letting my clients know where I am. I've written all my particulars down, so if anyone phones asking about my services, you will know what to say. Now, where would you like me to work?'

I suggested she take the farthest room from the lounge, and she disappeared into it, carrying a large bag with two canes and a leather strap sticking out of the top.

Before long Julie came bustling through the door, bursting with gossip.

'You'll never guess. Penny's been fired for pirating our clients for her own establishment! She has an apartment in Parnell, where she works privately with two other girls. They've been undercutting our prices by half in some cases. Pippa went through the adult entertainment pages of *Truth* and found an ad for someone called Lexie, and it was the same phone number she gave us for her personal phone. Anyway, Christine got her brother to call the number and ask some questions, while she listened on the extension. It was Penny's voice that did all the talking, and when she had finished, Christine told her she was fired. Apparently, on Saturdays Penny had all the calls from her *Truth* advertisement transferred to this number so she wouldn't miss out. Business has gone down by a quarter since she started. What a bitch!'

The first call of the day was a regular of Mistress Paula's, who wanted to see her at eleven-thirty. I jotted it down in the appointment book. Then Sid came through the door.

'Hello, Sid, this is a pleasant surprise. We haven't seen you for ages.'

Sid looked at me sheepishly. 'Oh, I went to see that Penny at her place,' he said, 'but I only went the once, because there were all these hippies hanging around smoking "wacky backy". I didn't like it at all. She's a bad'n, that one. She even had her kids there smoking the stuff. She was cheap though. But I just couldn't put up with all those hippies, so I came back here to see Julie. Is she available?'

Suddenly, Sid stared over my shoulder and a look of horror enveloped his face. 'Shit oh Lord! Who's that?'

I quickly turned to see Paula coming out of her room, flexing a long whippy-looking cane. She was wearing a leather G-string teddy over fishnet pantyhose, and long thigh-length boots.

'That's Mistress Paula,' I said. 'She punishes naughty boys, especially ones like you who go wandering off to marijuana dens with loose women!'

Sid's old boot-like face folded itself into a smile, exposing a top set of perfectly white dentures and a row of yellow teeth that sat like tombstones on the bottom. 'No blooming fear! I'm not into all that torture stuff. I like my women soft and cuddly. I like tits big enough to bury your face in.' He licked his lips, chuckled, and staggered sideways, and· I had to find him a chair because I was fearful he'd fall over with the excitement of it all. Sid must have been well into his seventies.

After Julie took Sid through to her room, Paula's client booked in. He was smartly dressed and in his early forties, a tall man, quite slender, with short corporate hair and a moustache. Paula took him through to her room, and after a good ten minutes she came out again.

'He's just getting dressed. Now, when he's had his session, he likes to sit in the lounge and have a cup of tea with the girls in his outfit. Do you have a problem with that?'

'No, I don't think so. What outfit?'

'He cross-dresses. Very smart clothes, they must be worth a fortune. All his underwear is made from pure silk. He likes me to call him Michelle during the session. He is very quiet; just drinks his tea, gets changed and buggers off. He won't be any trouble.'

Twenty minutes later 'Michelle' came striding into the lounge. He wore a straight black skirt, black stockings and high-heeled court shoes. A beautiful white silk blouse topped the skirt and his white lace bra was visible underneath. Firm, pert breasts filled the front of the blouse and a thick black mat of hair filled in the V-neckline up to the base of his neck, a stark contrast against the white silk. I handed him his tea, and he sat sipping it delicately, little finger extended exposing hairy knuckles. The dark moustache gave the finishing touch to a very odd picture.

'Mm, awful weather, don't you think?' I asked, trying to sound casual. A huge burble of laughter was lurking in my throat and threatening to make itself heard, but I knew from previous experience that even uttering the smallest titter could lose this man as a client forever.

'When I left Hamilton this morning it was warm and sunny,' he replied in a very deep voice. 'The Met Office promised some rain, and the gardens certainly need it so I suppose we can't complain.'

I was extremely pleased when Paula had finished tidying her room and joined us.

'How's the wife and kids, Michelle?' she asked.

'Oh, they're well, Elizabeth starts college in the new year, and Daniel's doing very well at school.' He crossed one hairy stocking-covered leg over the other. 'Marie is going back to varsity next year as an adult student.'

'I expect she has more time now the children are old enough to look after themselves a bit,' said Paula, kicking off one of her thigh boots and wiggling her toes about. She shook her breasts deeper into the boned cups of her leather teddy. 'I want to do psychology at Uni as soon as my kids are old enough to do for themselves. Another three or four years I reckon.'

Michelle nodded with approval and said, 'Well, Paula, I must fly. I have an important meeting at one o'clock.' He put his teacup and saucer on the coffee table, stood up, smoothed his skirt over his bottom and strode back into Paula's room.

I had been in situations similar to this in the past but, looking at it from a receptionist's point of view, it had an Alice in Wonderland sense of the ridiculous about it.

When he'd gone, Paula said, 'I have to act out the jealous big sister and punish him for being more beautiful than me. It's much easier than normal sessions. I don't even have to take my clothes off, and there is very little sex involved. It's a piece of cake!'

'What does he have in his bra? He hasn't had . . .?'

'Oh, no, nothing like that,' said Paula. 'He cuts a polystyrene ball in half and pops one in each side. They look authentic, don't they?'

For the rest of the day, our cosy little house rang with the sound of slapping, whipping, and smacking. Julie said nothing could be heard in her room, which was just as well because Sid didn't believe in 'that sort of thing', labelling it 'the work of the devil'. We agreed it was lucky Sid hadn't arrived while Michelle was having his cup of tea!

Francy announced that this Sunday was going to be a quiet one, because there was live coverage of a test match and everyone would be watching cricket on television.

'It's a total waste of our time being here today,' she said, settling down with her knitting. 'They're showing an old Humphrey Bogart movie this afternoon on Sky. We can watch that.'

'Not everyone will be watching cricket, surely?' said Susan, looking agitated. 'I can't afford a slack day. The rent is due on Tuesday.' She scurried into the kitchen to put the jug on.

'You watch this,' murmured Francy under her breath. 'She's

shit scared that she'll have to face that bastard tonight without making enough money, and I can guarantee she'll be in on Tuesday covered in bruises. I'd stake my life on it!'

The day was as slow as Francy predicted. By three in the afternoon not a single person had come through the door, the phone was as quiet as the grave, and Susan was a nervous wreck. One of Francy's clients checked in around four, and as soon as he set foot in the door, Susan leapt to her feet and started hustling the guy. She stood so close to him that her breasts were stroking his bare arm, and was blowing in his ear. But Arthur only had eyes for Francy, and seemed not to notice Susan's advances. I found it all very embarrassing, and when Francy and her client had gone through to the room, I told Susan what I felt. She lit a cigarette, having just put one out, and sat in the corner with her arm folded across her chest.

'I hate not having enough money to pay the rent,' she said.

A young Indian man came to the door and asked the prices. I told him the door prices, and explained I could not go into detail about the room prices.

'I'll tell him!' said Susan, dragging him into her room. A couple of minutes later the young man left, and she went back to her seat and cigarette. I could almost feel the anger radiating from her.

At around five o'clock, Susan's mood changed from one of anger to one of fear. 'Is there any wine in the fridge?' she asked with a nervous chuckle. 'Do you want one?'

As I was about to drive home, I said no. She poured herself one and sculled it, then poured another and sculled that. By six o'clock she was blotto. She had drunk glass after glass of wine, and when her husband arrived she staggered down the steps before he had a chance to come up. With a roar of motor and a squeal of tyres, the car took off up the drive. She must have told him she'd made no money that day.

'See what I mean? The poor girl's terrified of him, and you'll see, she'll have had an accident by Tuesday!' said Francy.

Susan did not come into work on Tuesday. She had fallen down a flight of stairs at home that had blackened her left eye, and her arm was so badly bruised she was unable to use it for two weeks.

*

212

Christine announced she was going to look for bigger and better premises because she suspected the landlady had guessed what we were up to. An advertisement ran in the *Herald* on Wednesday and Saturday, and I was asked to take a note of any calls that came in. There were several, but one sounded promising. I phoned Christine, who said she'd come in and perhaps we could look at it together. She arrived about twenty minutes later, and off we went to Grafton, where an old villa, currently used as a parlour, was up for lease. The owner, a short stocky man in his mid-forties, welcomed us in. Four young, scantily clad girls no more than eighteen years old sat in the lounge watching television.

'Gilly, can you get us some coffee please, love. We'll have it in the office.'

'Fuck off!' she replied. 'If you want coffee, get it your fucking self,' and they all hooted with laughter.

Dave, the owner, smiled sheepishly at us and asked, 'Coffee?' Both Christine and I accepted. He settled us in his extremely untidy office. 'I'm sorry it's such a mess, but I can't get any of them to clean it. They won't lift a finger to do any cleaning at all. I have to do it all.' Off he went to get the coffee. When he came back he said, 'I don't want any money for the place, just someone to take over the lease. I have spent megabucks on it, and I'm quite willing to walk away from it as long as I don't have to go on paying the lease.' He slurped his coffee loudly. 'I thought it would be the perfect situation, to own a massage parlour. Plenty of cash coming in every day, and a good bonk when I wanted one. But it turned out to be a nightmare. Those bitches in there,' he pointed in the general direction of the lounge, 'they steal everything that isn't nailed down. If I wasn't here to do reception, there wouldn't be a cent in the till when I came to do the banking. And of course, they all swear they don't know who's nicking the takings. So I'm obliged to be here from ten-thirty in the morning until two the following morning, seven days a week, and I'm absolutely exhausted. I haven't had a day off for over a year. And none of them will give me a bonk unless I pay full rates. I don't even get a discount! Then last month one of the girls told my wife I'd asked her for sex, and she left me. And, of course, I have to pay maintenance for the kids. But now I'm broke, and my wife is going to sue me for half of everything I put into this place, because she was against it in the first place. And you know how much lawyers charge. No, I'm quite happy to walk away from the place as long as someone takes the lease. Come along, I'll show you around.'

The old villa was very roomy, with four large double bedrooms, a good-sized lounge, modern kitchen, wash-house and two showers that needed a good clean, and the office. There was public parking close by, but the doorway in was very exposed. What put us off altogether was that it was within spitting distance of a primary school.

Back in Dave's office, he started pleading with us. 'Look, I'll throw in all the furniture, television and sound system. How's that?'

Christine explained that she definitely did not want an establishment anywhere near a school.

'Well, I have a mate who could erect a tall fence so you won't see it. He'll do it for mate's rates.'

When we finally got outside, Christine said, 'I don't believe anyone could be so gullible, and did you see those girls of his? They looked like a troop of blow-up Suzies. Men like that deserve all they get. "Plenty of cash and bonks," that's all they can think of. What a Wally!'

The landlady gave us notice to quit as soon as the six-month lease was up. She said it was all right by her us running a brothel from the house, but her husband was worried the place could be burned down and he wouldn't be able to claim insurance. No amount of talking could change his mind, so suddenly it was extremely important to find somewhere new. By the time our move-out date was upon us, Christine had some premises organised in the city, in a massage parlour above a shop just off Karangahape Road. The previous owner had gone broke trying to run the place, and had just cut his losses and walked out, so it was filthy. It smelled of a mixture of nicotine and mould. The pink carpet looked quite new, but was heavily stained with coffee, cigarette burns and general grime. Cigarette packets, cigarette butts, dead matches, old tissues and condom packets littered the floor throughout. In the bathroom, a blow-up doll reclined in the bath, her head hanging at an unnatural angle due to lack of air. The two showers were absolutely black with mould from floor to ceiling, with tiny little dried up pieces of soap scattered across the stainless steel base.

But once the place had been cleaned up, it looked really good. We changed the light bulbs to tone down the harsh white light, and when the furniture was arranged it started to feel like home. Christine said it would suffice until something better came up.

But it seemed our clients did not like the new premises, and business dropped off very quickly. Even men who'd been regulars for ten years or more just seemed to disappear, and the girls started to get fed up with sitting around most of the day doing nothing. A couple of them left to look for greener pastures, but the message that came from their replacements made it clear that daytime work in a parlour was pretty non-existent, and only Fleure's and The Tokyo were busy. The only money to be made was by working nights.

It seemed a gradual change had been taking place in the sex industry right under our noses. A new trend of working privately from an apartment in the city area was becoming very popular. Girls were now using cell-phones rather than receptionists, which gave them the freedom of talking to clients anywhere, from the bathroom to the supermarket, to make appointments. Several workers could share an apartment to lessen expenses, and it seemed the men loved the idea.

Christine called a staff meeting.

'This place is not working for us,' she said. 'We are being wiped out by the private ladies. So I think, if we can't beat them, we must join them.' Everyone nodded in agreement. She went on, 'My only concern is Pippa and Angie, because we will not be needing receptionists.' She looked kindly at Pip and me. 'Sorry, guys! I'm afraid your employment is terminated as from now. We just can't afford to pay you any longer.'

Pippa looked a bit concerned, but said she was half expecting it. 'Business was that bad I felt guilty taking my wages,' she said.

On the other hand, I was quite pleased. I had been working seven days a week, five in the salon and two in the parlour, for eighteen months and was tired of the long hours. The salon was doing well. I'd taken on two stylists and rented two work stations to self-employed stylists and one to a nail technician. Business was booming. I think the reason I'd hung on so long to the parlour job was for the company. I hadn't taken a wage for months, due to the lack of funds.

Emma had a career, a house of her own, and worked extremely hard. We had dinner together quite frequently, and we talked on the telephone a lot, but I missed her at home.

Now it was time for me to 'get a life' and have some fun, I thought, and on the way home I stopped in at a travel agent and picked up some brochures for the Greek Islands.

EPILOGUE

It is a little over three years since my return from the Greek Islands, and my life has changed immensely. I have now remarried, and my husband is a wonderful, warm, kind and loving man, who only drinks the occasional wine with his dinner. I can honestly say I have never been so happy.

I look back on my years in the sex industry with affection, and not once have I regretted a moment of it. It provided Emma and me with a comfortable lifestyle that I could not have dreamed of as a hair technician. I have never had to ask the government for handouts and was always able to pay my rates and taxes. I feel that my experiences in the industry have made me a better person. I am more understanding of other people's ways and cultures, and far more understanding of men — I almost see myself as an expert when it comes to their sexual problems. I recently read that one in four New Zealand men has a problem with sex, and I can well believe this.

I still keep in touch with Christine. She has a beautiful upmarket apartment in the city, which is a hive of activity, with clients coming and going constantly. Her present staff is made up of a small number of extremely good and experienced women, and they are always busy.

Chrissy seems to have retired from the industry, as nobody has heard from her for years. I think being busted as she was had something to do with that.

Francy works privately, and although now in her mid-fifties, is as beautiful as ever and has a full book of regular clients, which goes to prove that age has nothing to do with being a successful prostitute.

The industry itself is going through yet more changes. The Inland Revenue Department has made it very plain that all working men and women must pay tax. (They should have thought about this in the early eighties when big money was being made; they could have cleared the national debt with the revenue!) Nobody really disputes this, but the popular consensus is that they will pay tax once the law is changed and soliciting becomes decriminalised. Some people see it as unfair that sex workers pay tax to the government for something the government can arrest them for later. Meetings have taken place between Inland Revenue, the NZPC (the Prostitutes' Collective) and any sex worker or parlour boss wanting to attend. The outcome was one of stagnation. The NZPC asked for a period of amnesty, where workers could start paying tax and not have to put in returns for years gone by. So far this has not come to pass, and there is a stalemate, as the IRD are dreadfully slow when it comes to making decisions. They can be relentless in their search for tax dodgers though, and I know of one worker who was hounded by them for weeks, and nearly took her own life because of it. She started working in the industry because she was a single parent with two mouths to feed. I honestly feel that anyone starting in the sex industry now should pay tax from day one.

In 1996 a rumour circulated the sex industry that certain city councillors who blessed us all with their piety and Christian ethics, their abhorrence of bare buttocks and bosoms, wanted to rid Auckland of massage parlours, rap parlours, brothels, private workers, street workers or, indeed, anyone who even remotely looked as though they were capable of giving a man (or a woman) a good time for a fee! As these councillors were not stupid enough to think they can achieve this goal, we heard they were planning to take over the organisation of the sex industry by rounding up all the prostitutes in Auckland and settling them into one area, somewhere out of the central city. As you can imagine, all the people involved were extremely worried about this situation, especially people like Christine and the private workers. Their clients would not be seen walking into a designated red-light area for their pleasures. In fact, in my opinion, the only men who would brave a red-light area would be tourists and drunk stag-party goers, and earnings would have been very lean indeed. It would have resulted in hundreds of girls working 'underground'. And in turn would have caused problems with health, organised crime and many other nasties that crop up when something popular is made illegal, as has been proven in the past with the prohibition of alcohol and marijuana. Gangs and pimps would suddenly appear to feast on the earnings of unsuspecting girls.

The Auckland office of the New Zealand Prostitutes' Collective was especially worried about the health issue. At the moment they are free to visit sex workers and advise them of the latest news about the HIV and AIDS epidemic overseas, hand out free condoms, and give advice on all sorts of questions the average working girl or boy would want to know. Their office in Karangahape Road is always a hive of activity, with Michelle and her helpers kept busy at all hours of the day and night. If it is all pushed underground, and workers live in fear of being busted for not working in the right area, their efforts would all have been wasted, and maybe we would have ended up with the full-blown epidemic of HIV and AIDS that the rest of the world has been burdened with.

However, prostitution has been rampant since the beginning of time. Women have been entertaining men for a fee well before religion became known to us and enjoying oneself sexually became a sin. It would take more than a mayor and a city council to keep it down.

And as an afterthought, I wonder if the councillors ever realised that if the likes of Christine, Francy and the many other sex workers who have all been paying their rates for decades moved into a designated red-light area, it would make the Auckland City Council the biggest organiser of the sex industry in New Zealand, and living off immoral earnings to boot.